William Howe Tolman

History of Higher Education in Rhode Island

William Howe Tolman

History of Higher Education in Rhode Island

ISBN/EAN: 9783743320314

Manufactured in Europe, USA, Canada, Australia, Japa

Cover: Foto ©ninafisch / pixelio.de

Manufactured and distributed by brebook publishing software (www.brebook.com)

William Howe Tolman

History of Higher Education in Rhode Island

THE

A.D

TABLE OF CONTENTS.

	Page.
Letter of transmittal	9
Introduction	11

PART I.

COLONIAL AND LATER EDUCATION	13
Sketch of the colony	13
Colonial traits	13
Roger Williams	14
Contributory sources of education	16
Sunday schools	16
Stephen Hopkins, a type	17
Libraries	18
Colonial education	19
Variety of schools	19
Support of schools	20
Schoolhouses and rooms	21
Slow educational development	23
Separation of church and State	23
Disputes regarding the boundary	24
Isolation of the planter life	25
Free public school system	25
Early methods	25
Efforts of the proprietors	25
John Howland	27
Petition of the Mechanics' Association	29
Providence schools	29
Revival of public schools	30
Henry Barnard	30

PART II.

ACADEMIES AND PREPARATORY SCHOOLS	33
Introductory	33
University Grammar School	34
Kingston Academy	39
Friends' School	41
Washington Academy	52
Kent and East Greenwich Academy	57
Smithfield Seminary and Lapham Institute	66
Smithfield Academy	71

PART III.

EDUCATION OF WOMEN	77
Young Ladies' High School	77
Young Ladies' School, Prof. Lincoln	83
Warren Ladies' Seminary	84
Normal School	88

PART IV.

	Page.
BROWN UNIVERSITY	93
Introductory	93
JAMES MANNING, 1764–1791	94
Design of the college	94
Biography of Manning	95
Correspondence	96
Funds	97
Location	97
First commencement	101
Course of study	103
Management	104
Prominent men	104
Discipline	105
Land and buildings	107
Revolutionary period	108
Closing years of Manning	111
JONATHAN MAXCY, 1791–1802	111
Policy of the college	112
Sketch of President Maxcy	112
ASA MESSER, 1802–1826	114
Introduction	114
Foundation of professorship of oratory	114
Change of name	115
University Grammar School	116
Hope College	116
Biographical sketch of Messer	117
His policy	118
Reminiscences	119
FRANCIS WAYLAND, 1826–1855	120
Biography	120
Characteristics	121
Class-room manner	122
Discipline	124
What he did for the college	125
Public services	127
New system	128
Manning Hall	131
Rhode Island Hall	132
University extension	133
BARNAS SEARS, 1855–1867	133
Early days	134
Public services	136
Peabody trust fund	136
Scholarships	139
Exemption from taxation of college property	142
Agricultural lands	144
Professor Dunn	145
ALEXIS CASWELL, 1868–1872	148
Biography	148
The man and teacher	149
Professional services	150
Closing days	151

	Page.
E. G. ROBINSON, 1872–1889	152
Slater Hall	153
Sayles Memorial Hall	153
Library	156
Professor Diman	158
Professor Chace	162
Professor Greene	165
ELISHA B. ANDREWS, 1889	167
Course of study	168
Wilson Hall	182
Present policy	183
Professor Gammell	188
The library	190
Brown in '61	194
Societies	196
Athletics	199
Professor Lincoln	199

PART V.

THE RHODE ISLAND COLLEGE OF AGRICULTURE AND MECHANIC ARTS	201
Courses of instruction	202
Bibliography	209

ILLUSTRATIONS.

	Page
First Baptist Church, Providence	Frontispiece.
East Greenwich Academy	60
BROWN UNIVERSITY—Front campus	96
University Hall	108
Hope College	116
Manning Hall	130
Rhode Island Hall	134
Slater Hall	152
Sayles Memorial Hall	156
Library	158
Middle campus—Slater, Manning and University Halls	168
Chemical laboratory	178
President's house	184
Interior of library	190
Gymnasium	198
RHODE ISLAND AGRICULTURAL COLLEGE:	
Chemical Laboratory, College Hall, Dining Hall	202
College farm house and barns	204
A corner in the mechanical laboratory	206
Woodwork done by students	206
A part of the art hall	208
Horticultural department vineyard	208

LETTER OF TRANSMITTAL.

DEPARTMENT OF THE INTERIOR,
BUREAU OF EDUCATION,
Washington, D. C., July 31, 1894.

SIR: I have the honor to transmit herewith for publication the monograph entitled "History of Higher Education in Rhode Island," by Dr. William Howe Tolman. This monograph is No. 18 in the series of "Contributions to American Educational History," edited by Prof. Herbert B. Adams. The present circular, relating to the history of one of the original thirteen States, whose colonial history goes back to 1636, is of interest to the student and reader because it raises the question whether religious freedom reacted favorably on the establishment of a system of education in the early colonial days of the New England colonies. It is claimed that union of Church and State existed among the Puritans, and the educational system became the care of the Government through the clergy, who were in civil authority and gave their attention to education and educational systems. In Rhode Island no person was molested, punished, disquieted, or called in question for any matters in religion that did not actually disturb the civil peace of the colony. By reason of this emphasis placed on the separation of Church and State, and the consequent feeble efforts toward united action in founding schools, a large number of the clergy were found to be without any special training, and this led to the agitation which resulted in the establishment of Rhode Island College (now Brown University) in 1764, in order that members of the Baptist denomination might have an institution where a liberal education could be acquired.

The first part gives an account of colonial and later education. The personal influence of Samuel Slater, who opened his house as the meeting place of the first Sunday-school in the colonies, September, 1799, and Stephen Hopkins, of whom President Manning said: "Few men in public life at that time had so thoroughly applied themselves to the study of books and men," furnish interesting studies for the historian of education. The name of Dean Berkeley (George Berkeley, Dean of Derry, and afterwards bishop at Cloyne) is prominent in the origin of the first public library in the colony, 1730.

The variety of schools, the slow educational development, and the free public school system (first developed in Newport in 1640 and in

Providence in 1663), with the efforts of John Howland and Henry Barnard in education, are briefly but intelligently discussed.

The second part is devoted to the study of academics and preparatory schools. The University Grammar School, whose principal, James Manning, was the first president of Rhode Island College, Greenwich Academy, and the Friends' School are perhaps the three most important. The third part is devoted to the education of women.

The fourth part is a history of Brown University. The history of higher education in Rhode Island is properly said to be a history of Rhode Island College and Brown University, and accordingly the history of this institution occupies the greater part of this monograph. Under such presidents as Manning, Wayland, Sears, Robinson, and Andrews, the labors of such professors as Lincoln, Harkness, Dunn, Diman, Gammell, and others were and are of that efficient because personal character that imparts the highest intellectual instruction to the student.

The Rhode Island College of Agriculture and Mechanic Arts was organized and chartered subsequent to the date of preparation of original manuscript of this circular.

To the foresight and wise discrimination of my predecessor in the office of Commissioner of Education, Hon. N. H. R. Dawson, the credit is due for the development and inauguration of the plan to publish this valuable series of monographs.

Very respectfully, your obedient servant,

WM. T. HARRIS,
Commissioner.

Hon. HOKE SMITH,
Secretary of the Interior, Washington, D. C.

HISTORY OF HIGHER EDUCATION IN RHODE ISLAND.

INTRODUCTION.

The history of higher education in Rhode Island is the history of Brown University, because that is the only university in the State. But the term "higher education" has been interpreted generously, in order to include academies and schools of a similar nature. Many of these were preparatory for college and others furnished a practical education in navigation, surveying, or other special branches. In some cases the academy or school was established in response to a feeling of special need on the part of a particular community. There were no graded schools nor was there a general system of education. It is, therefore, difficult to determine which were the institutions for higher education. Some with no more pretentious title than "school," "academy," or "seminary" gave instruction in their advanced classes in some of the studies pursued in the freshman class in college. It seemed fitting that such institutions should have a place in the history of higher education, and a portion of this monograph has been devoted to academies. A sketch of common-school education has been given in order to connect colonial with the more recent phases of educational development.

In comparison with her sister colonies Rhode Island was slow in establishing a general system of education and the University was not founded till 1764. Accordingly, a sketch of the colony has been given stating the condition of education at that time; noting the contributory sources to education, and showing why the general educational development was so tardy. In colonial days Newport was the second city in the country, ranking next to New York. The superiority of Newport was gained through her commercial relations, for a prosperous commercial center is progressive. The relations between commerce and education are of interest in the earlier history of the State.

Nearly all of the academies were founded under denominational influences, but their advantages were extended to all. They were all of a high grade, and formed educational centers, where a student obtained preparation for Brown University, or received a general education. The majority of the academies offered instruction to both sexes. Some were entirely for female instruction, and have been described in the chapter on education for women.

The history of Brown University occupies the greater part of the monograph; the natural divisions of the subject are the periods of the various administrations. There have been seven presidents previous to Dr. Elisha B. Andrews. The treatment of the earlier administrations has been largely biographical. "An institution is the lengthened shadow of one man." Hence the life purpose, the striving for its accomplishment, the character of the founders and the early administrators of the University are of interest to the students of institutional history. As the University became firmly established, and as it increased in material equipment, attention has been directed to those phases of its history, yet even here the personality of the leaders must be noted. The growth of the University has been steady and peaceful; high standards of instruction have been maintained; and the relations between the institution and the community have been cordial. When the State or municipality has needed the aid of educated men for special services of a public character, cheerful responses have been accorded by the academic staff. Some of the presidents gave the University the benefits of the best years of their experience, and withdrew from its councils while still in their maturity to engage in pursuits of a public nature. The charter of the University is most liberal, and the same characteristic is true of its policy. While the administrators of the University have been conservative, they have ever shown themselves willing to adopt methods that would advance the best interests of Brown. Under the presidency of Dr. Andrews the present departments have been strengthened, University extension has been successfully organized in neighboring cities, and plans are being formulated to found a school of applied sciences. There is every indication that Brown is fulfilling all the hopes of her best friends, in becoming a center for higher education.

PART I.

COLONIAL AND LATER EDUCATION.

SKETCH OF THE COLONY.

In writing the history of education in Rhode Island, it is necessary to sketch in outline the early history of the colony, in order to learn its personnel and its relation to the other colonies. In treating of the early history of the colonies, it must be remembered that underneath all the variety of local developments, was the broad foundation of Anglo-Saxon self-sufficiency. Each colony had the roots of its early life far back in the past, and did not gain its more rounded development at a leap. It was a plant of slow growth. These men, the founders of our constitution, practical politicians who knew how infinitely difficult a business government is, desired no bold experiments. They preferred, so far as circumstances permitted, to walk in the old paths, to follow methods which experience had tested.

The early life of the colonies was varied. In Massachusetts the close union of church and State gave rise to a system which early fostered educational movements, although it can not be admired for that amount of toleration which characterized some of her sister colonies. The educational movements in the different colonies varied according to their physical characteristics, personnel and religious rule. In any account of the history of education in Rhode Island, the unity of the work would be incomplete were there no reference to the early colonial period. Were the founders and settlers of this State men to demand and appreciate the advantages of education? Was the environment such that when an educational movement was started it could grow under the stimulus of a broad and catholic public opinion?

COLONIAL TRAITS.

To answer these questions and to get an idea of those times, in order that the animus of the colonists may be seen, it will be imperative by way of introduction to the educational history to glance at the early history of the colony. This is all the more necessary because events of the past are so liable to be viewed with the eyes of the present.

Some idea of the manners and customs may be gathered from the reminiscences of Samuel Thurber.

As respects schools previous to the year 1770, they were but little thought of; there were in my neighborhood 3 small schools, perhaps about a dozen scholars in each. Their books were the Bible, spelling book, and primer. Besides these there were 2 or 3 women schools. When one had learned to read, write, and do a sum in the rule of three, he was fit for business.

Manners and fashions were very plain. The dress in general was meant to be durable. Men mostly with wash-leather breeches; cloth for most purposes generally manufactured in their families; laborers of almost every description with leather aprons; the best dress of the most opulent was of English manufacture, in a plain style. The mail was carried by a Mr. Mumford on horseback, once a week, between Providence and New London, and so back. May, 1776, I went to Pomfret, 36 miles, in a chaise. The road was so stony and rough that I could not ride out of a slow walk but very little of the way. I was near two days in going, such was the general state of our roads at that time.

Business and occupation was similar to what it now is, except machine manufacturing. Furniture in general was very plain, mahogany was little known. Almost every article of wood was straight, without much paint or polish. But little crockery and that of a coarse kind. Pewter and wood were the principal table furniture. Two would often be eating out of the same dish, and perhaps a dozen drinking out of the same pewter quart pot or earthen mug. In my youngest days there were few carriages besides carts, consequently when women wanted to go abroad it was very common for them to go on horseback, sitting on a pillion behind a man. The rising generation will not have so good times as the latter have had. What wars and troubles we have had, have been but a trifle to what are to be.

Such was the statement of a man writing of the early part of the eighteenth century.[1]

ROGER WILLIAMS.

The early settlers of our colonies need no eulogy. What they wrought speaks for itself, and we of to-day have entered into the inheritance, and are reaping the benefits of their labors. The colonists were determined and firm adherents to what they believed was right. Principle guided those who were in rule. It is easy to bring against these men the charge of intolerance and uncharitableness; but they had left their homes and had severed nearly all the ties which bound them to their fatherland, and here they were to conduct themselves in accord with those principles which they could not enjoy in England. All the colonists who left England were of the same nation. They were all Englishmen, holding firmly to their religious belief, stubborn if you will, but none the less inflexible. When, therefore, men came who indulged in views and opinions counter to their own, they were not tolerated. Too much hardship and risk had been undergone by those who came first, to have their colony subverted by those who thought differently. The reformation had wrought a mighty work, and made a great upheaval in established notions, but what it accomplished was rather as a grand whole than in detail. When men came to the colony of Massachusetts and expressed opinions counter to those prevalent, objection was made and measures taken to put a stop to such conduct. Those who incurred censure were men from the same stock as those who sat in judgment, and felt firmly that they too were in the right; hence, they would not yield. Among such was Roger Williams, who had spent some time at Plymouth and at Salem. Several times he had

---

[1] Staples' Annals of Providence, pp. 600–607.

been summoned before the court to answer to charges preferred against him. The ground of these charges can best be gathered from the decree of banishment pronounced against him in 1635.

> Whereas Mr. Roger Williams, one of the elders of the church of Salem, both broached and divulged divers new and dangerous opinions against the authority of magistrates; as also writ letters of defamation both of the magistrates and churches here, and that before any conviction, and yet maintaineth the same without any retraction; it is therefore ordered that the said Mr. Williams shall depart out of this jurisdiction within six weeks now next ensuing, which, if he neglect to perform, it shall be lawful for the governor and two of the magistrates to send him to some place out of this jurisdiction, not to return any more without license from the court.[1]

He was allowed to remain till spring, provided he would not disseminate his views. This he refused to do. Because of his refusal and his thought of founding a settlement in Narragansett Bay, it was decided to send him to England. He fled to the Indians, and was received by one with whom he had been friendly in Plymouth.

> In reviewing the measures which led to the banishment of Roger Williams we find that they all proceeded from the firmness with which on every occasion he maintained the doctrine that the civil power has no control over the religious opinions of men. To adopt this new theory to practical life was to effect a revolution in the existing systems of government; to sever the chain which, since the days of Constantine, had linked theology to the throne; to restore to the free mind the distinctive but long-fettered gift of Deity—free agency; and, in fine, to embody in civil polity that principle, but dimly understood by the reformers, which, from Wittenberg to Rome, in the cloister and camp, had aroused the spirit of all Europe—the right of private judgment.[2]

The early history of Rhode Island seems to shadow the realization of the idea of a nation which was secured by the adoption of the Constitution. When the charter was suspended during the administration of Andros, in 1686, the government was simply taken up by each town and these local units continued. In 1642 there were three colonies in Rhode Island, and they were independent. A strong need was felt for cooperation. The neighboring colonies were claiming their territory; the Indians were an uncertain element, threatening the people, and strongest of all reasons was that which demanded every exertion to keep the colony secure in the principle of its foundation—civil and religious liberty. Roger Williams was the agent selected to go to England to secure the charter, and he was successful.

> He reached Providence by the same route that eight years before he had pursued, a homeless wanderer, dependent on the kindness of the red man. His entry was like a triumphant march. Fourteen canoes, filled with the exulting population of Providence, met him at Seekonk and escorted him across the river, while the air was rent with shouts of welcome. How the contrast, which a few short years had wrought in all around him, must have pressed upon his mind, and more than all the feeling that the five companions of his exile, and those who had followed them were now raised, by the charter he had brought, from the condition of despised and persecuted outcasts to the rank of an independent state.[3]

---

[1] Arnold, History of Rhode Island, vol. 1.
[2] *Ibid*, p. 41.
[3] *Ibid*, p. 115.

The charter was signed Thursday, March 14, 1643-'44, and the colonies were united as "The Incorporation of Providence Plantations in the Narragansett Bay in New England." During the interval between the establishment of the government in 1647 and the restoration there were the usual occurrences incident to colonial life. It was a long time before the colony could secure that amount of repose which was necessary in order to carry out a general policy of education.

CONTRIBUTORY SOURCES OF EDUCATION.

Although a system of education was slow, yet there were many influences at work to continue the life of movements in this direction. It will be shown why this development was so slow. Among the contributory sources were the personal influence of men of whom Stephen Hopkins was a type, the conservative force of libraries, and the impulse of Sunday schools, and private schools of all kinds.

SUNDAY SCHOOLS.

Among the earlier contributory sources to education was the Sunday school. These schools were founded by Robert Raikes in England in 1781, and were designed at first to give secular instruction. They were chiefly for the children employed in manufacturing establishments, who had no opportunity during the week for attending school. The first Sunday schools in the colonies were in Rhode Island.

Sunday schools were started in Pawtucket at an early date and under peculiar circumstances. Although the attempt to rear a meetinghouse was begun in 1793, it was years before the edifice was so far completed as to be fit for a congregation, and still longer before a regular preacher was settled. The Sabbath was, therefore, a day of recreation and amusement rather than of religious rest. Mr. Slater was compelled to see that moral agencies could not safely be neglected in the community. Among the boys who came to work in his mill was one 11 years of age. He found an irreverence towards the Sabbath which shocked his sensibilities. Not knowing what to do on that day he was subjected to peculiar temptations. It so happened that some of the lads who worked with him in the mill were conferring together one Sunday morning as to where they should go. Said one of them, "Let's go up to Smithfield and rob Mr. Arnold's orchard; that will be fine sport." But the youth first named demurred. "I don't believe it is right to go off Sunday to rob people's orchards," said he. Mr. Slater happened to be passing at that moment and caught a part of the reply. He stopped and asked, "Boys what are you talking about?" He was told of what had been proposed, and one of the boys added, "Nat doesn't think it is right to go off so on Sunday." "No, nor I neither," responded Mr. Slater, and he doubtless felt, if he had never realized the matter before, that he owed a duty to those youth, whom God had placed for a time under his charge. He resolved to remove from them one form of temptation and promptly said, "Boys, go into my house and I will give you as many apples as you want and I will keep a Sunday school."[1]

Eleven boys from his cotton mill composed this school first opened in September, 1799. The school was founded on the Raikes model for secular instruction. Its library consisted of two testaments and three Webster's spelling books.

---

[1] Historical sketch of Pawtucket, Rev. Massena Goodrich, p. 9.

STEPHEN HOPKINS.

Although the educational activity of the other New England colonies was in advance of the colony of Rhode Island and Providence Plantations, yet it must not be inferred that there was no life. All movements for advance and reform are slow; often the work seems to stand still, yet, to him who views the period from a distance, movements that appear feeble and isolated are those which have guarded and advanced the life. Education is not merely the result of knowledge obtained from books. Said Prof. Conrad, of Halle: "I have learned more from life than from books." President Manning, referring to Stephen Hopkins, said:

> Few men in public life at that time had so thoroughly applied themselves to the study of books and men.

Hence in colonial days, everything which tended to bring the people into relation with their fellows, either by individual or associated effort; all work of a public nature, like the establishment of customhouses, the improvement of the roads, provision for a postal service, all such efforts lessened their isolation and rendered possible the contact of mind with mind. Then arose the need for such training as the school, the academy, and the university would supply. As confirming this view, that the education afforded by the school is not self-sufficient, Arnold says:

> Thus freedom and education went hand in hand with industry and economy in the minds of the fathers of the Constitution.

Among the contributory sources to education in the colonies was the personal influence of the colonists. Stephen Hopkins may be taken as an illustration. In early life he had felt the need of an education, and when in after life by his own efforts he had realized the attainment of a liberal education, he determined to do all in his power to aid others in securing the means of obtaining an education. He was one of the founders of a public library in 1750. He had a library of his own which, for that day, was a good one. It was said of him:

> He attached himself in early youth to the study of books and men, and continued to be a constant and improving reader, a close and careful observer, until the period of his death.

He was fond of history and poetry. Pope, Thomson, and Milton were his favorites. When he had removed to Providence, he, with several other citizens, sent to England for some books, which laid the foundation for the Providence library. He said:

> Nothing tends so much to the good of the commonwealth as a proper culture of the minds of its youth.

For several years he served as governor of the State, and was one of the delegates to the Albany congress.

> To a young man of his marked capabilities, his quick instincts, his lively appreciation of all phases of human life, there can be no doubt but t the two or three occasions in every year when his duties called him to Newport were opportunities

which he would by no means allow to pass him unimproved. This, it must be remembered, was the Newport of Dean Berkeley and of the genial divines, Rev. Mr. Honyman and Rev. Dr. MacSparran; of Smibert, the painter, and, a little later, of the youthful Gilbert Stuart; of such merchant princes as the Wantons, the Malbones, Abraham Redwood, and Whipple; of such accomplished historical scholars as Dr. Stiles and John Callender, and of scientific men like Joseph and Peter Harrison and Dr. William Hunter. It was the period when such families as those of Wanton, Brenton, and Vernon, Bull, Coddington, Brinley, and Robinson furnished the cultivated society for which the town became eminent, and when the distinguished literary club which was founded by Berkeley, and which numbered among its members such men as Callender, Ellery, Ward, Honyman, Checkley, Updike, and Johnston, was a most potent influence in fixing upon the society of Newport that character for refined and dignified culture which it has since borne. "A similar auspicious influence," says Dr. King, "on the character, intelligence, and public spirit of the town, on her rising statesmen, her liberal merchants, her cultured scholars, and her able lawyers, must be attributed to the Redwood Library."[1]

From the brief sketch of Hopkins, who may be taken as a type, it may be seen how the influence of a man like him would be exerted in favor of all that concerned education.

LIBRARIES.

Another contributory source to education, although closely allied to personal influence, is that exerted through the libraries of the day, more or less extensive. A name prominent in the origin of the first library in the colony, is that of Dean Berkeley.

The arrival of George Berkeley, Dean of Derry, and afterward bishop at Cloyne, was a joyful event in the history of Newport, and important in its results to the other colonies. A corps of literary men and artists accompanied him, among whom was Smibert, to whose advent is due the earliest impulses to American art. From the collection of pictures that he brought, Copley first drew his inspiration, and West was taught to breathe his spirit upon the undying canvas. The benevolent design of Berkeley, to found a college in the Bermudas, was abandoned from necessity; but his liberal benefactions to Harvard and Yale still exist, as proofs of his zeal in the cause of classical learning.[2]

Dean Berkeley had the opportunity to lead just the life of retirement that he wished, and selected for his residence the town of Newport. Here he wrote his philosophical tractates. He came in contact with the scholars of the day in his adopted city. Berkeley did not live to himself alone; he established a literary and philosophical society. Among the objects of this society was the collecting of books. From the fact that this society was in all probability among the oldest of a similar nature in the country, some of its rules are of interest.

Whereas, A. D. 1730, Messrs. Daniel Updike, Peter Bours, James Searing, Edward Scott, Henry Collins, Nathan Townsend, Jeremiah Condy, and James Honyman, jr., did form a society for the promotion of knowledge and virtue, by a free conversation according to several regulations by them agreed.

We, the present members of the said society, finding it necessary on many accounts for the more effectual answering the end of our institution, do agree to enter into a

---

[1] Foster's Stephen Hopkins, vol. i, pp. 74, 75.   [2] Arnold, vol. ii, p. 99.

more strict engagement and establish the following as the laws and orders to be observed in this society:

(1) The members of the society shall meet every Monday evening at the house of one of the members, seriatim, and converse about and debate some useful question in divinity, morality, philosophy, history, etc.

(2) The member who proposed the question shall be moderator (*pro hac vice*) and see that order and decency be maintained in all the debates and conversation.

(3) Every member in order shall freely give his opinion, with his reasons, having liberty to explain the sense of the question or his own expressions, and to retract or alter his opinion as to him shall seem right.

(4) The member at whose house we meet shall propose a question for the next evening's conversation, the society to judge of its propriety and usefulness, only nothing shall ever be proposed or debated which is a distinguishing religious tenet of any one member.

The remainder of the 13 rules concern the election of members, fines and dues, and the general government. The plan for collecting books was aided by Abraham Redwood, who gave the society £500 on condition that the society would erect a suitable building. This was done, so that the money was forthcoming. The fact that this library was in Newport was one reason which induced Dr. Ezra Stiles, afterward president of Yale College, to settle there. "At length," to use his own language, "partly an agreeable town and the Redwood library * * * induced me to yield, and I gave an affirmative answer to the church and society." The condition of the library at that date may be seen from the sketch given by Holmes, the biographer of Stiles:

The Redwood library, at Newport, consisting of about 1,500 volumes at the time of his settlement there, and augmented afterwards by books imported from Europe, intrusted to his selection, was highly propitious to his wishes and to his literary improvement. To the accomplishment of an end, Providence always furnishes adequate means. This library, the benefit of which Mr. Stiles enjoyed above twenty years, and to which, being librarian, he could always have access, was eminently subservient to his preparation for the presidential chair, to which he was in due time to be called.[1]

COLONIAL EDUCATION.

VARIETY OF SCHOOLS.

As preparatory to the period of educational activity, and as affording a connecting link, a brief account of colonial education must be given. There seems to be no justification for the use of the term "science of education" till well into the present century, but there were many and varied educational movements. The need and advantage of education were appreciated. A glance at the colonial records will confirm this. The ways and means may cause a smile to-day, but they were the best which could be then devised, and they accomplished in very many cases their object. If fewer branches were taught, great

---

[1] The Life of President Stiles, by Abiel Holmes, pp. 68.

thoroughness was gained. One extract from the records will show the sentiment regarding higher education:

In 1696 a tract of land in the town of Kingston was conveyed to Harvard College for and towards the support and education at the said college of those youths whose parents were not of sufficient ability to maintain them. In 1716 a gift of £50 for the college in Connecticut was made by Jahliel Brenton, of Newport. In spite of what Rhode Island had to contend against in her settlement and government, there were schools of all kinds, although no uniform organized system.

The early schools were select or private schools, although movements for free schools were very early made, but the time had not come for them. An advertisement from the Newport Mercury of May 22, 1759, will show the character of one of them:

John Sims, schoolmaster in the town school, teacheth reading and writing, arithmetic, both vulgar and decimal, geometry, trigonometry, and navigation, with several other branches of mathematics. He proposes to open a separate school on the first Wednesday of June next, to continue the summer season, beginning at half after six o'clock and concluding at eight, and in the afternoon (each day except Thursday and Saturday) from five till half after six, for the instruction of young ladies in writing and arithmetic. As he endeavours to study the genius of his scholars, whether of exalted or inferior capacities, and conducts himself accordingly, he hopes to receive the greater encouragement.

Another notice from the same paper, under the date of December 19, 1758, states:

Sarah Osborne, schoolmistress in Newport, proposes to keep a boarding school. Any person desirous of sending children may be accommodated and have them instructed in reading, writing, plain work, embroidering, tent stitch, samplers, etc., on reasonable terms.

Another school appears to have given more attention to a commercial training:

Thomas Greene, in Barrister's row, hereby informs the public that he proposes to open a school the first Monday in May, to teach reading, writing, arithmetic, and merchants' accounts—the Italian method—and as he don't incline to undertake for more than twenty (besides a very few small readers), they that favor him scholars may depend on their being taught with the greatest alacrity. He has, as usual, an assortment of English goods, &c., at a reasonable rate.

NEWPORT, *April 14, 1766.*

The notices of these schools were taken from advertisements in the papers of that time. There were in addition other kinds of schools—for vocal and instrumental music and for dancing. French was generally taught by the masters of dancing schools.

SUPPORT OF SCHOOLS.

The schools were supported in various ways. A favorite method of raising money for nearly everything was by lottery, the public sentiment then being different from what it is now. The following notice in the Mercury for October 5, 1767, will illustrate this method:

Scheme of a lottery granted by the general assembly of the colony of Rhode Island, &c., for raising £150 lawful money, to be applied towards finishing the parsonage house belonging to the Baptist Church in Warren and rendering it commodious for the reception of the pupils who are or who shall be placed there for a liberal education. * * * It is hoped that the extraordinary expense of that infant society in building a new meetinghouse and parsonage house, as far as the building is advanced, together with the immediate necessity of room for the pupils under the care of the Rev. Mr. Manning, and the great encouragement for the adventurers, there being but little better than two blanks to a prize, will induce those who wish well to the design speedily to purchase the tickets.

Another means of support for the schools was the income from the school lands.

QUARTER MEETING, *April 17, 1709.*

Mr. William Gilbert being chosen schoolmaster for ye town of Newport, and proposing that upon conditions the quarter meeting grant him the benefit of the school land, viz., the chamber and sellar and the profit arising from ye school land in this part of the town, and some conveniency for keeping of fire in the winter season, he is willing to teach school for the year ensuing, and to begin the second Monday in May next, voated and allowed an act of the quarter meeting.

Tuition also defrayed some of the charges. At the fourth meeting held in Bristol, September 7, 1682, it was voted "that each person that hath children in town ready to go to school shall pay 3d., the week for each child's schooling to a schoolmaster, and the town by rate, according to each rateable estate, shall make the wages amount to twenty-four pounds the year." In the same town a source of revenue was acquired from allowing certain persons to keep houses of entertainment, on condition of their paying sums of money for the benefit of the school. The licenses varied from 21s. to £4.

Yet again in 1729 the schoolmaster was instructed to receive from each scholar 4s., or in default of the money, which was not always easily obtained, its value in firewood. The money thus raised was called "wood money." Payments in kind were often received, the latter being one of the various commutations.

SCHOOLHOUSES AND ROOMS.

From various places descriptions of the school buildings and rooms have been gathered.

Rooms occupied for school purposes for the common grades were some vacant carpenter's shop, some spare room in an old dwelling house, or, if you will indulge credulity, some unoccupied barn with a stove pipe chimney.

Schoolrooms in those days were unique and curious to the refined taste. The old stone chimney, with a fireplace 6 or 8 feet wide and stone andirons, with a glowing fire made of oak or walnut wood, the cross-legged table and the long writing desks on two or three sides of the room, the benches of sawmill slabs and round legs with the bark on, are true emblems of "ye olden time."

Round the walls of the room, on three sides, wide boards were fastened at a suitable height and inclination for writing desks, in front of which seats, usually made of slabs or plank, were placed. The rooms were sometimes ceiled, but rarely, if ever, plastered. The huge fireplace and numerous cracks served for ventilation.

At first private schools were kept in unoccupied rooms of dwelling houses, accommodated with rude fixtures not the most convenient. Within the bare walls of those cold but well-ventilated schoolrooms were gathered the children, the youth, and the full-grown young men and women with their Testaments, Dillworth's Spelling Book and Arithmetic, Murray's Third Part, slate and pencil, and two sheets of foolscap, goose quill, and ink blotter.

The schools were often very crowded and very uncomfortably seated. Stoves were unknown, and, as a consequence, the huge chimney, with its broad fireplace, insured the best of ventilation, thus furnishing the sturdy boys of the olden time an abundance of pure air.

With reference to books, with which the schoolroom of the day is so well furnished:

But few books were to be obtained. Indeed, the spelling book was nearly the only kind of printed book known to the schoolroom in early times. This contained, in addition to the lessons in spelling, lessons in reading. Usually no printed text-book on the science of arithmetic was used. The master had what was called his "ciphering book." This was in manuscript—a copy of some other master's book. Probably originally it was a copy of a printed text-book on the subject, with the addition of the solutions of the problems. The scholars copied the definitions and rules. Usually the master wrote the problems in the books and then the learners solved them, if able, and copied the solutions into their books. Fractions were omitted as being useless. Much stress was placed on the "rule of three," especially what was called the "double rule of three." For writing the scholars used loose sheets of paper or a number of sheets stitched together. Copies were written by the masters, some of whom have left proof in this form of wonderful caligraphy.

Channing, in his Early Recollections of Newport, relates the following incident regarding Webster's Spelling Book:

William Cobbett, a renowned satirist of the day, published in one of his political essays a last will and testament, which contains the following item:

I give and bequeathe to Noah Webster the sum of fifteen Spanish milled dollars, to enable him, the said Noah, to procure a new engraved likeness of himself for his spelling book, that children may no longer be frightened from their studies; with this special proviso, that he omits the usual addendum of esq. from his name.

To the educator of the present day the old ideas of discipline seem strange, yet they were effective in cultivating a spirit of reverence for authority, and the youth of those days were not very deficient in courtesy and politeness. Regarding the discipline of the schools G. G. Channing says:

On the rostrum were two or three chairs for distinguished visitors and a small desk for the master, on which reposed, not often, a punctured ferule, surmounted by an unpleasant-looking cow skin. So exceedingly disagreeable were the daily ministrations of these instruments of instruction that every method was adopted for their destruction. But the master was more than a match for our organ of destructiveness. It certainly was not the prototype of the school at Rugby, where Dr. Arnold ruled successfully without making any of the distinguishing marks which characterized my pupilage. Exhibitions of authority constituted day by day a series of domestic tableaux. The discipline of the school was in accordance with the government of the home. It was arbitrary, with rare exceptions, in the extreme. The ferule and cow skin were almost deified. Apologies increased rather than abated the swellings of the hand and the wales upon the back. An appeal to parents was of no more avail than beating the air. The severe discipline was not interfered with by the clergy, for in their day they had to run the gauntlet; and as the men, and even the boys, of that age were notoriously addicted to swearing, drinking, gambling, and other vices, it was deemed necessary to subdue these evils by blows. No faith existed, then, in moral suasion.[1]

---

[1] Early Recollections of Newport, R. I., by Rev. George G. Channing.

SLOW EDUCATIONAL DEVELOPMENT.

CHURCH AND STATE.

In the colony of Rhode Island the attention that was given to education was not so definite nor so early as in the sister colonies. Harvard was founded in 1638, Yale in 1702, while Rhode Island College, later Brown University, was established in 1764. But while this fact may be regretted on some accounts, that early period was schooling the colonists in independency and in true fraternity. Although the colonists were not skilled in the text-books of the schools, the Bible, spelling book, and primer, and an ability to use "the rule of three"—a training then sufficient for a business man—yet they firmly maintained their rights against royal and colonial encroachments.

It might seem that religious freedom would be advantageous to a system of education, but it was not. Among the Puritans there was the close union of church and state. When their religion was established the clergy who were in civic power gave their attention to education, and the educational system became the care of the authorities. In the colony of Rhode Island, with her aversion to anything like an establishment, the need of a system of education was not felt so keenly. The entire religious freedom which prevailed in this colony brought in many settlers, because freedom in matters of conscience was extended not only to Christians but to all others of whatever belief.

The liberal Baptist, denying any mortal power over the immortal mind; the benign Quaker, seeking only to be guided by "the inner light;" the mystical Gortonist, merging his humanity in the divine essence—these had framed and founded the institutions of a State upon principles broad enough to embrace the whole human family as the children of one common Father. The polished Episcopalian and the zealous Puritan, each claiming in his dispatches to be "the true Church," speedily followed to occupy a field at once so novel and so inviting. Each learned something he had never known before, and all were improved by the mutual contact; so that even Mather, a quarter of a century later than his previous denuniciation, after having himself assisted at the ordination of a Baptist clergyman in Boston, writes in a letter to Lord Barrington, describing, although not acknowledging, the progress of Rhode Island principles, that "Calvinists with Lutherans, Presbyterians with Episcopalians, Pedobaptists with Anabaptists, beholding one another to fear God and work righteousness, do with delight sit down together at the same table of the Lord.[1]

Church and state were separated. In other colonies appropriations were made for schools and churches. In the year 1650 public education was compulsory in every other colony in New England. On account of the doctrine of separation in Rhode Island, large numbers of the ministers were without any special training; in fact, the foundation of the college was in order that members of the Baptist denomination might have an institution where a liberal education could be acquired. Children grew up without the opportunities of securing an

---

[1] Arnold, vol. ii, p. 88.

education, even if their parents had sufficient means to furnish it to them. Neither the town nor colony made any provision for public schools. This situation was but the logical outcome of the doctrine of the settlers of the State, who believed in the rigid separation of the civil and religious functions in administration. The experiment which was here tried was of benefit to the country, but of injury to the early life of the colony. How great was the religious freedom the following extract from the charter will show:

> Our royal will and pleasure is that no person within the said colony at any time hereafter shall be any wise molested, punished, disquieted, or called in question for any differences in opinion in matters of religion, and do not actually disturb the civil peace of the said colony; but that all and every person and persons may, from time to time and at all times hereafter, freely and fully have and enjoy his and their own judgments and consciences in matters of religious concernments throughout the tract of land hereafter mentioned, they behaving themselves peaceably and quietly, and not using this liberty to licentiousness and profaneness, nor to the civil injury or outward disturbance of others; any law, statute, or clause therein contained, or to be contained, usage or custom of this realm to the contrary hereof in any wise notwithstanding.

BOUNDARY DISPUTES.

A second reason for the non-establishment of a public-school system was the dispute concerning the boundary between Rhode Island and the neighboring colonies. The principles and ideas of the colony in Rhode Island were new to the others, and the hostility of her neighbors was aroused. Before education could receive the necessary attention, colonial life was to be maintained and the encroachments of her neighbors warded off. Not till 1746 was the grant made by the royal charter settled. The geographical knowledge of the day was crude. The location of this colony was described as in the "West Indies in America."

Disputes concerning the boundary were of frequent occurrence in the colonies. These arose from conflicting patents granted by the sovereign and various boundaries as prescribed in successive charters. The ignorance of the geography of the colonies will account for the mistakes in defining boundaries. Another fruitful source of dispute was the ambiguity and vagueness of the grants received from the natives. In some cases the uncertainty arose from the difficulty of communication between the parties and in others from design. In either case the jealousy and distrust of the natives were aroused and the colonists were kept in constant alarm. In addition to the quarrels with the natives, bickerings and disputes as to title arose with the adjoining colonies, and disturbed the peace of the settlements. Disputes with the natives could generally be settled by appeal to the sovereign from whom the grants were made, because they were questions of jurisdiction, but disputes between the colonists, involving individual interest and private feeling, were more bitter and continuous.

PLANTER LIFE.

Another reason why the development of education was slow was the character of the settlements in the southern part of the State. The section of land adjoining the west shore of the bay was productive, and was owned in large plantations by wealthy proprietors. They were gentlemen of leisure and were the most cultivated and educated among the colonists. Many of them had, for that day, large and extensive private libraries. These planters had the pleasure and profit of intercourse with each other. But the people in the interior and more western part of the State were scattered, the means of communication were poor, and they enjoyed but few of the comforts and luxuries of life. The centers of communication and information were the villages, for there were no towns. The opportunities for the inhabitants to add to their knowledge were those which came from the religious and town meetings and the county courts. Even the villages were few in number in the western part of the State at that time, and nearly all of the present day are of recent growth and the result of manufacturing interests.[1]

The religious freedom, disputes concerning the boundary, and the planter life in the western part of the State were the chief reasons for the slow growth of a system of education.

PUBLIC-SCHOOL SYSTEM.

EARLY METHODS.

The adoption of a free public-school system by the State was late, but provisions for education by the towns were early. There were a few private schools of high grade, but the characteristics of the greater part of these schools have been described in the section on colonial education. The reasons have been given why the educational development of the State was so slow. The first provision for education was made by the colony August 20, 1640, in Newport. It was voted "that one hundred acres should be laid forth and appropriated for a school, for encouragement of the poorer sort, to train up their youth in learning."

Public education in Newport continued till 1774, when from that time till about half a century later no school was supported by the income from the school land.

EFFORTS OF THE PROPRIETORS.

In Providence, May, 1663, the proprietors passed this order with reference to public education:

It is agreed by this present assembly that one hundred acres upland and six acres of meadow (or lowland to the quantity of eight acres in lieu of meadow) shall be laid out within the bounds of this town of Providence; the which land shall be reserved for the maintenance of a school in this town and shall be called by the name of the school lands of Providence.

---

[1] An address by E. R. Potter before the Rhode Island Historical Society, February 19, 1851.

There were also smaller schools supported by private charity. A school in Newport was established by Nathaniel Kay, to "teach ten poor boys their grammar and the mathematics gratis."

Mr. E. Trevett announced in the Newport Mercury in 1807 that he "will gratuitously teach as many poor children as he can attend in the State House a few hours in the morning." The "Female Benevolent Society" announced that a few children could be admitted into their school. In 1808 the "African Benevolent Society" opened a school, the object of which was the "free instruction of all the colored people of this town who are inclined to attend."

The Sunday school, in its early days, was an element in secular instruction. These efforts for education outside of what was done by the State kept the matter of State action for public schools before the community.

We retrace our steps to the year 1767 in Providence. At that time the town made a vigorous effort for free public schools. A proposition was made to build four schoolhouses and place the control of the schools in the hands of a committee. Accordingly two committees were chosen, one to supervise the construction of the buildings and the other to provide for the government of the schools. The reports on this matter were both rejected, but the report of the second committee was in writing and shows the design of those who were interested in the free public schools. At the beginning of the report it was stated:

> The education of youth, being a thing of the first importance to every society, as thereby the minds of the rising generation are formed to virtue, knowledge, and useful literature, and a succession of able and useful men are produced with suitable qualification for serving their country with ability and faithfulness; and institutions of this nature are the more useful by how much the more liberal and free the enjoyment of them is, etc.

Good and sufficient masters were to be supplied to the schools by the town; firewood also was to be provided at the expense of the town. Every inhabitant of the town was to enjoy the equal right and privilege of sending his children to the school. The scholars must have learned their letters and have acquired some knowledge of spelling before they were to be admitted to the smaller schools. For admission to the larger school they must have gained considerable knowledge in reading and writing. The rest of the report concerned the duties of the teachers and the government of the schools. Accompanying this report, which had been drawn up by Governor Bowen, was a memorandum made by Moses Brown:

> 1768. Laid before the town by the committee, but a number of the inhabitants (what is most surprising and remarkable, the plan of a free school, supported by a tax, was rejected by the poorer sort of the people), being strangely led away not to see their own as well as the public interests therein (by a few objectors at first), either because they were not the projectors or had not public spirit to execute so laudable a design, and which was first voted by the town with great freedom. M. B.

COLONIAL AND LATER EDUCATION. 27

At this time in Providence there were 102 houses, and 911 inhabitants (including 189 children between the ages of 5 and 14) on the west side of the river.

By the rejection of the report of the committee the action of the meeting was repealed. However, one schoolhouse was built by the town and by individuals, the town having the control of the lower story. This state of affairs continued till 1785, when a committee, chosen to draw up a plan of education, reported:

They have endeavored to suggest some general outlines for the regulation of schools as they are now supported by individuals, but are of opinion that no effectual method can be devised for the encouragement of learning and the general diffusion of knowledge and virtue among all classes of children and youth until the town shall think proper to take a matter of so much importance into their own hands and provide and support a sufficient number of judicious persons for that purpose.

The town took no action at all upon this suggestion, but accepted Whipple Hall, known as the "First District School House." The town was to pay rent for it and keep it in repair. It also set apart certain sums of money for its support, but the outcome of the arrangement was that those attended who could pay the tuition asked by the instructors. In 1791 a petition was made for the establishment of free public schools.

In 1795 a resolve was passed to establish "schools for the free education of the inhabitants of the town, and that the expense of the same be defrayed out of the town treasury." Till the year 1800 the resolutions that were passed were excellent, but their provisions were not carried into effect.

JOHN HOWLAND.

The public school system of the State is indebted as much to John Howland as to any other man. He was not wealthy or highly educated; nor did he occupy an influential position in the community. He was born in Newport in 1757, and at an early age was sent to Providence to be apprenticed to a hair-dresser. He served eighteen months in the Revolutionary army. A short while after his return to Providence he had a barber shop of his own, and it was a favorite resort of the townspeople. Judge Thatcher recorded in his diary that he was recommended to go and be shaved by Mr. Howland as the best preliminary to any important information on subjects of local history.

Later he became treasurer of the first savings bank in Providence. He was also at one time president of the Rhode Island Historical Society, and assisted in the formation of a peace society, of which he was president. He was a member of the Mechanics' Association, and in connection with this organization he began to work for a system of free public schools.[1]

---

[1] History of Public Education in Rhode Island. T. B. Stockwell.

The record of this movement is best presented in the words of Howland himself:

In 1789 the Mechanics' Association was formed, and in this body begun the agitation that led to the establishment of public schools. When we came together in our association we made the discovery of our deficiencies. There were papers to be drawn, and various kinds of writing to be done, that few of us were competent to execute. Then we began to talk. The question was asked: "Ought not our children to have better advantages of education than we have enjoyed?" And the answer was "yes." Then it was asked: "How shall these advantages be secured?" The reply was: "We must have better schools." So when we had talked the matter over pretty thoroughly among ourselves we began to agitate. As I was something of a talker and had practiced writing more than most of my associates, a good deal of this work fell to my lot, and I was very willing to do it, because I felt and saw its importance. So I wrote a number of pieces for the newspaper and induced others to do the same. I prevailed, however, with only one, Grinall Reynolds. He felt as I did about the matter, and wrote a piece for the Gazette in favor of schools. We had, indeed, the good will of many educated men. We met no opposition from the wealthy, but they, having the advantages for their sons and daughters that wealth can always procure, did not feel as we poor mechanics did. They were not active. In this beginning of the movement they seemed willing to follow, but were unwilling to lead the way. It is a curious fact that throughout the whole work it was the most unpopular with the common people and met with the most opposition from the class it was designed to benefit. I suppose this was one reason why the most influential citizens did not take hold of it heartily in the beginning. They thought its success doubtful and did not wish, in a public way, to commit themselves to an enterprise that would curtail their popularity and influence. This was not the case with all, but it was so with many.

The more we discussed the subject the greater became its importance in our eyes. After a good deal of consultation and discussion we got the Mechanics' Association to move in the matter. This was an important point gained, and an encouragement to persevere. A committee was chosen to take up the subject. Of this committee I was a member. They met at my house, and after mature deliberation it was resolved to address the general assembly. I told them that as neither of us were qualified to draw up a paper suitable to go before that body, we had better write a petition embodying our individual views and bring it to the next meeting. Out of these mutual contributions we could prepare a petition that would do. This was agreed to, and the committee separated. When we next met it was found that but two had written according to previous recommendation. These were by William Richmond and myself. Richmond then read his. It was in the usual petition style, ending "as in duty bound we will ever pray." I told the committee I did not like the doctrine of that paper. It was too humble in tone. I did not believe in petitioning legislators to do their duty. We ought, on the contrary, in addressing that body, to assume a tone of confidence; that with the case fairly stated they would decide wisely and justly for the rising generation. I then took out my memorial and read it. It was not in the shape of an humble petition. It expressed briefly our destitution and the great importance of establishing free schools to supply it. It received the approbation of the committee and was adopted. This memorial was presented to the general assembly in the name of our association. It was there warmly debated, and after pretty severe opposition the assembly referred the whole subject to a committee, with directions to report by bill. This bill, embodying a general school system, was drawn up by James Burrill, jr., attorney-general of Rhode Island. I was with him all the while, and he readily complied with my suggestions.[1]

---

[1] Life and Recollections of John Howland, late president of the Rhode Island Historical Society, by Edwin M. Stone, pp. 138 et seq.

COLONIAL AND LATER EDUCATION.

PETITION OF THE MECHANICS' ASSOCIATION.

This memorial stated that at present the means of education were very inadequate and what should be provided by the State was left to the exertions of individuals. The supply fell far short of the demand. Appreciation on the part of the association was expressed for the chartered privileges of their own corporation, and they petitioned the assembly that provision might be made for the establishment of a system of free public schools. This they urged in order that the youth who were pressing forward to take their places as active citizens might have the means of gaining an education. The petitioners hoped that their occupation as mechanics and manufacturers would not prevent them from adding to these reasons the fact that liberty and security under a republican form of government depend on a general diffusion of knowledge among the people. This petition was signed by a committee of eight.

This subject was referred by the assembly to a committee, and in 1800 an act establishing free schools became a law. This act provided that each town in the State should establish annually, at the expense of the town, one or more free schools for the instruction of all the white inhabitants of the town between the ages of 6 and 20. Reading, writing, and common arithmetic were to be taught to all who "may stand in need of such instruction and apply therefor." The remaining sections, eleven in number, provide for the maintenance and the government of the schools that may be established.

The law met with great opposition and was repealed in a few years. From the newspapers, there seems to have been no hint of the special influences which brought about the repeal. In 1801 instructions from several towns were read against the school bill and occasioned a motion for its repeal. It was referred to a committee, who were to report an amended bill at the next session. No such bill appears to have been passed; the whole measure was defeated by simple non-enforcement, and the law was repealed at the February session, 1803.

PROVIDENCE SCHOOLS.

Providence was the only town which had ever carried it into effect. But as the Providence schools have been sustained ever since under the organization thus begun, and as the whole State was afterwards brought under a system essentially identical with that proposed by Mr. Howland, he may justly be called the founder of the public-school system of the State.

Four schools were opened in Providence on the last Monday in October, 1800. The number of scholars was beyond anticipation, and a fifth school was soon opened. For twelve years, however, the whole attendance rarely exceeded 800. The four original schools had each a master, with a salary of $500, and an usher, who was paid $200.

REVIVAL OF PUBLIC SCHOOLS.

The second movement for a State system of public schools began by the passage of a resolution in 1820 by the assembly, "calling on the several towns for information on the subject of public schools." Scarcely any town had any information to give. This same year the importance of public education was urged by the press of Providence and Newport. Another committee was appointed "to prepare and report a bill establishing free schools." No report was made and the impulse died away. Later there was a local movement in Newport, and various schemes were suggested to make the education a State matter. In 1827 Mr. Joseph L. Tillinghast, of Providence, was the leader in urging free schools upon the assembly. The subject was first introduced by memorials from Smithfield, Cumberland, Johnson, East Greenwich, and other towns. The bill of this year was passed in 1828, nearly unanimously.

This act of 1828 is the foundation of the present school system of the State. When this law went into operation the schools had been detached and isolated, dependent wholly on the degree of enlightenment or energy prevailing in a particular town. Now they were to be part of a State system. There were various modifications of the school laws till they were codified in 1839.

HENRY BARNARD.

In 1843 Henry Barnard was appointed to take charge of the public-school system, and this was considered as the most important step yet taken in the history of the schools. So great was the confidence felt in Mr. Barnard, that the school legislation of the State was virtually placed in his hands, and he was instructed by the assembly to prepare and present the draft of a school law which should cover the whole ground of existing statutes. This law was passed June 27, 1845. He was very efficient in inspecting and reorganizing the whole school system. He remained in office five years, retiring in 1849 on account of failing health. The testimonial presented him by the teachers of the State, on his retirement, gives the best summary of what he did for the State in his system of public schools:

Of the extent of your labors in preparing the way for a thorough reorganization of our system of public schools, and in encountering successfully the many difficulties incident to the working of a new system, few of us can probably be aware. But we can speak from a personal knowledge of the value of the teachers' institutes which have, from time to time, been held by your appointment, and provided (too often, we fear, at your expense) with skillful and experienced instructors and practical lecturers; and of the many books and pamphlets on education and teaching which you have scattered broadcast over the State. We can speak, too, of what the teachers of the State know from daily observation—many of them from happy experience—of the great change, nay, revolution, which you have wrought in our school architecture, by which old, dilapidated, and unsightly district schoolhouses have given way for the many new, attractive, commodious, and healthy edifices which

COLONIAL AND LATER EDUCATION.

now adorn our hills and valleys. We have seen, too, and felt the benefits of the more numerous and regular attendance of scholars, of the uniformity of text-books, the more vigilant supervision of school committees, and the more lively and intelligent interest and cooperation of parents in our labors, which have been brought about mainly by your efforts. The fruits of your labors may also be seen in the courses of popular lectures, which are now being held, and in the well-selected town, village, and district libraries, which you have assisted in establishing, and which are already scattering their life-giving influence through our beloved State.

Mr. Barnard was succeeded by Hon. Elisha R. Potter, who ranks second to his predecessor only in the quantity of his labors, not their quality. His legal experience was of the greatest value in codifying the school laws of the State; laws which he, on the bench, was afterwards able to expound and apply with authority. In 1850 he recommended a board of education, and was a persistent advocate of a normal school, which was established in that same year. Another service rendered by him was the discussion and elucidation of the religious question in public schools. Succeeding him were Rev. Robert Allyn, from 1854 to 1857; John Kingsbury, 1857-1859; Dr. Joshua B. Chapin, 1859-1861 and from 1863-1869; Henry Rousmaniere, 1861-1863; Hon. T. W. Bicknell, 1869-1875; Hon. T. B. Stockwell, 1875 till the present time.

PART II.

ACADEMIES AND PREPARATORY SCHOOLS.

INTRODUCTORY.

The educational phases of the academy in New England within the last century and a half are varied. There are nearly as many grades as there are academies. The lowest in grade are merely district schools, teaching the "three R's," while the highest are preparatory schools for the colleges of New England, and in some cases take their students as far as the studies of the freshman year. Yet academies of the lowest grade were by no means a small factor in the educational growth. Scattered throughout the sparse and rugged settlements, they offered the only means for instruction that could be then obtained. They were powerful in character building and in furnishing many a man for the struggle of daily toil, so that when he had gained a position where he could look back, it was the old academy that he thanked for his start. These institutions were as altars, small and with few attendants, yet with the fire from the prytanæum jealously guarded, till by constancy and devotion schools became shrines to which came boys from distant homes. In more than one instance an academy which to-day is doing preparatory work for college, at first was very unpretending. Then, too, in those days, when the helps to knowledge were few, when the student retained what he mastered because he had to work for it, what little was offered was thorough, and a desire was created for something more. The lives of many of the self-taught men of the early decades of this century will demonstrate this. The early days of academies were not days of wealth. The erection of these buildings represented self-sacrifice and a firm belief in the advantages of education. This fact finds repetition in the preamble to many of the charters, in which there is recognition of the blessings of education, not only to the immediate vicinity, but also to the Government. As contributory rills to the great stream of collegiate instruction all these smaller institutions are important. In education nothing is small, for often an idea or an impulse is implanted in the mind of some one so that he is the means of placing within the grasp of others those advantages from which he himself was debarred.

Between the years 1790 and 1865 as many as 19 institutions of learning received charters from the assembly. Charters were granted to an academy, a seminary, an academy company, an institute, a school society, a collegiate institute, and a school association. Such were some of the institutions which made application for charters, as they appear on the records of the assembly. Some advanced no farther than the charter; others made a creditable beginning; while a few existed for such a period that a more detailed account is fitting. There was only one college in the State—Rhode Island College. While there were all grades in the schools and academies, yet each was a center of education which fulfilled the demands of that locality. At Wickford in the days of commercial activity there was a demand for instruction in navigation, and that was taught at the academy. If it appears that their teaching was very rudimentary, these academies should not be despised. Their existence showed that the community felt the need of educational advantages, and some of them developed into institutions affording opportunity for the student to pursue studies taught in the freshman class of our colleges. A great amount of good was accomplished by the moral influence of these schools through the strong personality exerted by the teachers. There were not many aids to the student and the text-books were limited in variety, so that an education was attained only by hard work. The teacher had an intimate knowledge of his subject and could exert his influence for the best interests of the scholar.

In a history of education every institution of learning has its value, but the institutions of higher education will be especially described in this monograph.

UNIVERSITY GRAMMAR SCHOOL.

The University Grammar School may be said to have been the germ of the college. It was opened by Manning in the spring previous to the first meeting of the college corporation in Warren in 1764. It was a Latin school under his charge, and it was his purpose to make the school serve as the basis for collegiate instruction. In 1770 the school was removed to Providence and held in one of the rooms of the brick schoolhouse. In 1772, at the completion of University Hall, the school was placed in one of the rooms. No early records of the school had been kept, and all the notices of the school are supplied by the newspapers. The following is the first notice in the local paper for 1772:

> Whereas several gentlemen have requested me to take and educate their sons, this may inform them, and others disposed to put their children under my care, that the Latin school is now removed and set up in the college edifice, where proper attention shall be given, by a master duly qualified, and those found to be the most effectual methods to obtain a competent knowledge of grammar steadily pursued. At the same time spelling, reading, and speaking English with propriety will be particularly attended to. Any who choose their sons should board in commons may be accommodated at the same rate with the students, six shillings per week being the price. And I flatter myself that such attention will be paid to their learning and morals as will entirely satisfy all who send their children. All books for the school, as well as the classical authors read in college, may be had, at the lowest rate, of the subscriber.
>
> JAMES MANNING.
>
> PROVIDENCE, *July 10, 1772.*

ACADEMIES AND PREPARATORY SCHOOLS.

The early accounts of the school are meager, but Manning wrote to a friend in 1773 that the Latin school under his care had about 20 boys. The next public notice of the school appeared in the Gazette of 1776:

> A grammar school was opened in the schoolroom within the college edifice on Monday, the 11th instant, in which the same mode of teaching the learned languages is pursued which has given such great satisfaction to the inhabitants of this town. The scholars are also instructed in spelling, reading, and speaking the English language with propriety, as well as in writing and arithmetic, such part of their time as their parents or guardians direct.
>
> COLLEGE LIBRARY, *March 22, 1776.*

In 1786 the school was removed to the brick schoolhouse and was in charge of Mr. Wilkinson till 1792. He was considered a successful teacher. His advertisement states the object of the school and the price of tuition:

> William Wilkinson informs the public that, by the advice of the school committee, he proposes removing his school from the college edifice on Monday next to the brick schoolhouse; and, sensible of the many advantages resulting from a proper method of instruction in the English language, he has, by the committee's approbation, associated with him Mr. Asa Learned as an English instructor. Those gentlemen and ladies who may wish to employ them in the several branches of the Greek, Latin, and English languages taught grammatically, arithmetic, and writing may depend on the utmost attention being paid to their children. Greek and Latin at 24 shillings per quarter; English at 16 shillings.
>
> WILKINSON AND LEARNED.
>
> PROVIDENCE, *October 20, 1786.*

From 1786 till 1794 the school seems to have been independent of the college. In 1794 the corporation voted to secure the school again:

> *Voted,* That the president use his influence and endeavor to establish a grammar school in this town as an appendage to this college, to be under the immediate visitation of the president and the general inspection of the town's school committee, and that the president also procure a suitable master for such school.

The school was again opened, and the next notice appears in 1809:

> *Voted,* That a suitable building in which to keep a grammar school be erected on the college lands, provided a sum sufficient to defray the expense of erecting said building can be raised by subscription; that said school be under the management and control of the president of the college, and that Thomas P. Ives, Moses Lippitt, and Thomas Lloyd Halsey, esqs., be a committee to raise said sum and cause said building to be erected, and that they erect the same on the west line of the steward's garden.
>
> *Voted,* That the president be authorized to procure a master to teach the grammar school ordered at this meeting, and that if a sufficient sum be not raised from the scholars to pay the salary of the master the deficiency be paid out of the funds of this University.

Accordingly subscriptions were solicited and the sum of about $1,500 secured. This money was raised chiefly among the citizens of the town. The building was erected on the corner opposite the president's house. An early catalogue mentions an instructor for 1824, but from this time it is uncertain whether or not the school was continued without interruption.

In 1845 Merrick Lyon assumed the charge of the school, with an associate, Henry S. Frieze. Mr. Frieze accepted a call to the Latin professorship at Michigan University in 1854, and his place was supplied by Emory Lyon. The school continued under the principalship of Drs. Merrick and Emory Lyon till the death of the senior principal in 1886.

Dr. Merrick Lyon had entire charge of the classical department, and this school always had a high reputation in the classics. Sixty-three premiums offered by the president of the University for excellence in preparatory Latin and Greek have been taken by members of this school since the present management was assumed in 1845.

The catalogue for 1851-'52 mentions the instructors, Merrick Lyon, Greek and mathematics; Henry S. Frieze, Latin and modern languages. The school numbered 103 students.

In the English department there are classes in algebra and geometry, geography, history, and English grammar. In addition to the above classes regular provision is also made for those who desire to receive instruction in natural philosophy, chemistry, astronomy, and surveying. There are exercises in declamation and English composition once a week. The tuition is $12.50 per quarter. Students from abroad can be boarded in the vicinity of the school at rates varying from $2 to $3.50 per week.

CLASSICAL DEPARTMENT.

Four classes in Latin and three in Greek are constantly in preparation for college. Latin is begun with great advantage by the youngest members of the school in connection with the elementary course. The Latin classes are daily exercised in the Latin grammar or Latin prose composition, while pursuing the study of the Latin reader, and of Cæsar, Sallust, Virgil and Cicero's select orations.

The study of the Greek language commences one year after that of Latin. The course of reading consists of the Greek reader and selections from Xenophon, which are accompanied by daily exercises in the Greek grammar or Greek prose composition.

Ancient history and geography and the Greek and Roman mythology and antiquities are studied in connection with the classical department.

The summary in the catalogue for 1852-'53 shows:

Scholars in attendance	119
Past members of the school	235
Students from this school admitted to Brown University and other colleges	82

The summary for the year 1871-'72 gives the following:

Teachers	18
Students 1871-'72	90
Students 1845-'70	837

ACADEMIES AND PREPARATORY SCHOOLS.

That year there were representatives from Rhode Island, Massachusetts, Connecticut, New Jersey, Japan, and Burmah. In a résumé of the students from 1845 to 1852 there are representatives from Massachusetts, Connecticut, New York, Ohio, Kentucky, Georgia, Vermont, New Hampshire, California, North Carolina, New Jersey, Illinois, Maryland, Alabama, Tennessee, Maine, Pennsylvania, Virginia, Cuba, Würtemburg, Italy and China.

COURSE OF STUDY.

In 1871 the course of study was more elaborate. The tuition for that year was $120 for the older students.

The course of study in the English and classical department is given below. There is also a preparatory department.

ENGLISH DEPARTMENT.

First year.—Bradbury's Eaton's Practical Arithmetic, Greene's Introduction to English Grammar, geography completed, written exercises in spelling and English grammar through the course, Swinton's Outlines of History, French, Monroe's Fifth Reader, spelling continued, writing continued.

Second year.—Arithmetic completed, Wentworth's Elements of Algebra, Greene's English Grammar, Warren's Physical Geography, ancient and modern history, Cooley's Natural Philosophy, French, reading, spelling continued, writing continued.

Third year.—Wentworth's Geometry, Hutchison's Physiology, Collier's English Literature, Wayland's Intellectual Philosophy, Hart's Rhetoric, French.

Fourth year.—Davies's Legendre's Trigonometry, Remsen's Chemistry, English literature continued, Wayland's Moral Philosophy, bookkeeping continued, Andrews's Constitution of the United States, Lockyer's Astronomy, geology, French, bookkeeping.

CLASSICAL DEPARTMENT.

First year.—Harkness's First Year in Latin, Harkness's Latin Grammar, through the course, Harkness's Cæsar commenced.

Second year.—Harkness's First Greek Book, Hadley's Greek Grammar, through the course, Boise's Xenophon's Anabasis commenced, Cæsar continued, Chase and Stuart's Nepos, or Harkness's Sallust's Catiline, Latin composition commenced, reading at sight, ancient geography.

Third year.—Xenophon's Anabasis continued, Greek prose composition commenced, reading at sight, Harkness's Cicero's Orations, Latin composition continued, reading at sight, a review of the studies of the second and third years.

Fourth year.—Anabasis completed. Boise's Homer's Iliad. Greek composition continued: Reading at sight. Frieze's Virgil's Æneid, Lincoln's Ovid, or Chase and Stuart's Bucolics and Georgics. Harkness's Latin Composition completed to Part III: Reading at sight. Baird's Mythology. History of ancient Greece and Rome. A review of the studies of the year.

The above courses of study include all that is usually required for admission to college in our country.

Familiar lectures on the topography, temples, and principal objects of interest in and near Rome and Athens.

Students pursuing the classical course continue their English studies in the grammar and high school departments.

Weekly exercises in composition and declamation are required.

The graduates of this school are admitted to Brown University by certificate without examination.

The school now is in charge of Dr. Emory Lyon and Edward A. Swain (Brown, 1882), assisted by Herbert A. Rice (Brown, 1889).

The effect of a well-organized literary society when supported by the students is a good complement to the routine of school work; at the University Grammar School in 1854 the Hope Debating Society was organized. The motto of the society was *Semper surgamus*. Its object was expressed in the following preamble: "We, the undersigned, desirous to secure to ourselves the advantages of a practical education resolve for the attainment of this object to form an association and adopt a constitution."

The regular meeting was to be held each Friday evening. The committee framing the constitution were Elisha S. Thomas, Arnold Greene, Robert I. Goddard. The active membership included 17 of the students and the honorary membership included the faculty of the school, at that time three in number.

A second society called the "What Cheer Lyceum," was organized December 27, 1856. This society chose for its motto *Patientia et perseverantia omnia vincunt*. Their preamble was the same as that of the Hope Debating Society. The board of officers were Thomas T. Caswell, president; Orville A. Barker, vice-president; G. Lyman Dwight, secretary; James Shimmin, treasurer; John H. Stiness, Richard Waterman, 2d, Henry Pearce, prudential committee. The general management of this society was very similar to its predecessor.

MERRICK LYON.

From personal recollections as a student I can say that he was a genial man and of a kindly disposition. He had a merry twinkle in his eye, and those eyes would shine when a student gave some rule in prosody of particularly exceptional value, or a long list of special words to be used in some particular way. When a student would hesitate on the future of some Greek verb, he would often suggest "Dontknowsomai?" On another occasion, a student in his translation had taken decided liberty with the text. Dr. Lyon laid down his book, and looking at the class, said:

This morning as I was coming to school, one of my friends asked me if it was not very monotonous hearing the same translation over and over again. "By no means," I said, "I never hear the same translation twice." The next may translate that passage.

He knew Greek and Latin, and if the student did not it was his own fault, because the instruction was imparted well and patiently.

Dr. Lyon received his preparation for college in Worcester, at the Hopkins Academy. He was graduated from Brown University in the class of 1841. His life work was teaching, and he taught in Providence. In 1845 he was principal of the University Grammar School. He was a fellow and a trustee of Brown, filling the vacancy in the latter position occasioned by the death of President Caswell. He held offices of public trust, but was especially interested in education, serving for more than thirty years on the school committee board. Dr. Emory Lyon afterwards took the principalship of the school, and the same general policy of the school was maintained. This school is the oldest in the city of Providence, and still is true to its traditions.

KINGSTON ACADEMY.

This academy, although in its palmiest days occupying a high grade among the institutions of learning, and deserving a worthy place in a survey of secondary education, had an early origin, and in the early days was lowly. There are facts in the history of this academy which make it among the most interesting of all. It was situated in South Kingston, in the southern part of the State. From 1819 till 1832, among the list of students, in addition to representatives from Rhode Island, Massachusetts, South Carolina, Connecticut, Louisiana, and North Carolina, are boys from Fayal, Azores, West Indies, Matanzas, and Minorca in the Mediterranean. The fact of these students from other States and other countries coming to this academy will furnish an interesting link between the commercial and educational interests of the State, and will afford opportunity for speculation. The genesis of this academy extends back to the year 1695.

1695. Samuel Sewal, esq., of Boston, for the consideration of a nominal sum, and for the encouragement of literature and good education and the maintenance of a learned, sober, and orthodox schoolmaster, conveyed 50 acres of land in Pettaquamscut, in special trust, to John Walley, for the procuring, settling, supporting, and maintaining a learned, sober, and orthodox person from time to time, and at all times forever hereafter, to instruct the children and youths of the above-mentioned town of Pettaquamscut, as well as English there settled, or to be settled, as Indians, the aboriginal natives and proprietors of the place, to read and write the English language and the rules of grammar.

This is an account of the origin, and some of the language is that of the deed. As showing the estimate in which a knowledge of grammar was held by Sewall, this statement at the end of the deed is interesting: "Signed, sealed, and delivered in presence of —— the words Judith his wife, 'and in the rules of grammar,' being first interlined."

The instructor was to be appointed by Samuel Sewall and his wife Hannah, or their survivors, or by the minister of the Third Congregational Church in Boston and the town treasurer, or their successors. In spite of such a formidable appointing power, nothing was done till 1781, when a schoolhouse was built in Tower Hill. Constant Southworth, Increase Hewitt, John Hazard, William Nichols, Robert F. Noyes, and Benjamin Hill were the schoolmasters till 1819. In that year the academy was moved to Kingston. The next change in the institution was one of name only, when in 1823 the academy was incorporated under the name of "Pettiquamscut Academy." The disposition of the school lands will be seen from the petition to the assembly this same year, 1823.

Whereas Elisha R. Potter, James Helme, Thomas S. Taylor, Robert F. Noyes, and other inhabitants within the Pettiquamscut purchase, in the county of Washington, and trustees of Pettiquamscut Academy, have represented to the assembly that on the 4th of November, 1695, Samuel Sewall, esq., and Hannah Sewall, wife of said Samuel, late of Boston, in the State of Massachusetts, conveyed by their deed of that date 500 acres of land, situate in said purchase, to John Walley, esq., of said Boston, and his heirs, in trust for the encouragement of literature and good education, and the maintenance of a schoolmaster within said purchase, to be appointed by the said Samuel and Hannah, or the survivor of them, after their decease by the minister of the Third Congregational Church, in said Boston, and the town treasurer of said town, and their successors in office forever; and that said persons who have the power of appointing said instructor have in like manner the power of locating the school; and whereas they have represented to this assembly that the trustee, about the year 1775, left the United States and has not to their knowledge returned, and from that period has wholly neglected his trust; that some time since said minister and treasurer located the school at the village of Little Rest, within said purchase, and appointed an instructor who now exercises a superintendence of the school; and that said school is now incorporated by the name of the "Trustees of the Pettiquamscut Academy;" and that said Elisha R. Potter, James Helme, Thomas S. Taylor, Robert F. Noyes, and others have prayed this assembly to authorize the sale of said 500 acres of land, the same now being little productive, and cause the proceeds of said sale to be vested in the funds of the institution and the interest thereof so applied as most effectually to secure the object of the donors.

The petition was granted, and the trustees were authorized to sell the 500 acres and give a bond of $8,000 to the State treasurer that the money arising from the sale would be paid into the school funds. In 1826 the assembly was petitioned that the name be changed to Kingston Academy. This was granted. From the date of the establishment of the academy in Kingston, in 1819, to the end of the school year ending April 26, 1832, there had been 158 students. The principals had been Oliver Brown, A. M.; Nathaniel Helme, A. M.; Alfred Gardner; Hinman B. Hoyt, A. M.; William G. Hammond, A. B.; Asa Potter, A. M.; William Cragg, A. B.; Elisha Atkins, A. B.; Henry M. Davis; Christopher Comstock, esq.; William Gammell, A. B.

The year 1832 marked the beginning of the period of greatest prosperity. For 1832 the number of students was 88; 1833, 137; 1836, 116; 1837, 86. The last catalogue shows an attendance of 78 for the year ending 1854. At the commencement of this prosperous condition of the school in 1832 Elisha R. Potter was the instructor in the classical department, Christopher Comstock in the English department, and Joseph Brayton assistant. The catalogue for that same year indicates the course of study and gives facts of general information regarding the academy.

The school is divided into two departments, a classical and an English, the exercises of which are attended in separate rooms. The books in the English department are Murray's English Grammar,

ACADEMIES AND PREPARATORY SCHOOLS. 41

Olney's Modern and Worcester's Ancient Geography, Daboll and Smith's Arithmetic, Bennett's Bookkeeping, Colburn and La Croix's Algebra, Bowditch's Navigation, Flint's Surveying, Legendre's Geometry, Comstock's Natural Philosophy and Chemistry, Wilkins' Astronomy, Blair's Rhetoric, and Paley's Moral Philosophy.

In the classical department are used Adams' Latin Grammar (Gould's edition) and Goodrich's Greek Grammar, Latin Reader, Historia Sacra, Viri Romæ, Cæsar's Commentaries, Sallust, Virgil, Cicero, Livy, Horace, Greek Reader, Græca Minora, Greek Testament, Græca Majora.

There are two vacations in each year; the first commences on the last Thursday in April, the second on the last Thursday in August.

The price of tuition in English studies is $3, and in Latin and Greek $5 per quarter. The price of board in the family of the English instructor, or in other private families, is $1.50 per week, including washing. The expense, therefore, for a single pupil in the English studies is about $84; in the classical studies, about $91 per year. To this is added the costs of lights and fuel during the winter term, which amounts only to a trifling sum.

THE FRIENDS' SCHOOL.

The prominence of some one man of keen insight into the needs of the times, or some religious denomination, is identified with the beginnings of nearly all the institutions of education. On the part of the founders of Rhode Island colleges and academies we are impressed with their spirituality.

The recognition of a divine dependency by no means prevented the utmost exertion of their own powers. The Friends School was an institution planted by the Quakers, and the preceding remarks apply with especial force to them. Breaking away from all forms and ceremonies, the Friends as a denomination went to the other extreme, and held for their guidance the "inward light" and "truth." With their views on war, with a devotion to what made for the interests of humanity, it seemed as though among them education would be sheltered and fostered.

What a delightful character the Quaker tradition imparted to everything that it touched! A certain grave and sweet simplicity, an air of candor and of plain rectitude, a frank and fraternal heartiness—these were all distinctly Quaker. They were imitated to base ends indeed, and no rogue so roguish as a counterfeited Quaker! No stories of such smug duplicity as those which were told of the smooth knave in drab. But it was only the homage to virtue. Knaves wore the Quaker garb because the Quaker garb was justly identified with honesty. Those whose early youth was identified with Friends, as with them and among them, but not of them, still delight in the recollection and associate with them still a refined superiority.[1]

The Quaker idea of education and the sentiments of our founder can be seen from the following address, which was presented to the yearly

---

[1] George William Curtis.

meeting by a man who had this institution close to his heart and worked for it at all times:

If, therefore, the quarterly meetings could promote a school where boarding scholars might be received and taught in such a manner as to qualify our youth of the rising generation to teach school, we think it would be an acceptable service. It is agreed that, as the school is intended for the education, maintenance, and clothing of children whose parents are not in affluence, that they shall be instructed in reading, writing, and accompts as fully as the time allowed them will permit. Some useful employment may be provided for the boys according as their age, strength, talents, or condition may require. Learning and labor properly intermixed greatly assist the ends of both, a sound mind in a healthy body. The girls will also be instructed in knitting, spinning, useful needlework, and in such domestic occupations as are suitable to their sex and stations. I believe it is the wish of all concerned in this important affair that by gentleness, kind and affectionate treatment, holding out encouragement and approbation to the deserving, exerting the influence of the fear of shame, and prompting the children to every act of kindness and beneficence one toward another, to bring forward into the society and into its service a number of youths who may have been made acquainted, under such tuition, in degree, with the discipline of wisdom.

Though the improvement of the children in learning, their health, and other suitable accommodations are matters of great moment in such an institution as this, yet there is one of a superior nature—to promote a tender, teachable disposition, inuring them to bear that yoke in their youth which will moderate their desires and make way for the softening influence of divine good will in their hearts, fitting them for the faithful discharge of every duty in life, yielding content in affliction, moderation in prosperity, becoming at once the safeguard and ornament of every stage in life from youth to ripe old age.

The man through whose exertions the school was started and continued was Moses Brown. He was born in Providence July 23, 1738. The name of Brown will ever be cherished in Rhode Island annals, not only for what those bearing this name did for her in colonial days, but also in the present. He was the youngest of four brothers, all of whom contributed to the commercial and mercantile prosperity of the State. The catholicity of this man is shown in good words and work. He was instrumental in securing for New England Samuel Slater, who brought with him Arkwright's invention. This was to revolutionize the cotton industry, so that to the music of the loom the walls of many a New England hamlet were firmly upraised. Brown was the intimate friend of those in authority in the Revolution, Governor Hopkins, of Rhode Island, and those who were in the field.

The first blood that was shed in our strife with the mother country was in connection with the capture of the *Gaspee*. Here then was "fired the shot that was heard around the world." When it was quite certain that the persons who had done this thing, or were suspected of doing it, would be sent to England for trial, Moses Brown's committee of correspondence applied to Samuel Adams, of Boston, for advice. He replied to their letter that the occasion "should awaken the American colonies and again unite them in one bond." John Brown furnished the boats for the attack, it is said. Did his firm really do it? Did they own the boats? If so, then Moses Brown was connected with it. Two members of the firm were present—John and Joseph. John was taken to Boston on suspicion and Moses went there and secured his discharge. How and by what means is not known to this day.[1]

---

[1] Moses Brown, by Augustine Jones.

ACADEMIES AND PREPARATORY SCHOOLS. 43

He must have had influence with the authorities to have secured his brother's release, and how he did it would be of great interest. An incident occurred in 1775, which illustrates his deep adherence to what he considered his duty. He and other friends were a committee to send provisions to the noncombatants in Boston at its seige by Washington. He was refused by Washington and also by the British commander, but did not desist. Five hundred dollars were sent in and the committee, entering the city by boats, took in food. This committee was merged into the "meeting for sufferings." Before this meeting were brought any cases needing help. It was before this meeting that the necessity of a school was presented by Brown in 1780.

As a philanthropist he liberated all his slaves in 1773, and as a patriot he was intrusted with a settlement of the boundary question and was instrumental in securing the emancipation act in Rhode Island in 1784. Of chief interest in the consideration of his character are his relations to matters of education. While known for his public and private relations to commerce, industry, and public utility, yet his chief memorial will be the Friends' School. In the year 1764 he was chosen to the assembly and did what he could to secure a charter for Rhode Island College. He was also instrumental, in connection with Governor Hopkins, in securing the location of the college in Providence. He gave the college a donation of books and $1,000.

He was never a member of the corporation, although elected a trustee and repeatedly urged by his associates to accept the position. In 1774, at the age of 36, he became a member of the Society of Friends. Withdrawing at this time from the bustle of commerce and trade, he sought that retirement which was more congenial to his early formed taste for intellectual pursuits. Here, on his beautiful estate in the environs of Providence, in rural quiet and simplicity, he spent a long and useful life, aiding by his judicious counsels and abundant wealth in the promotion of intelligence, piety, and freedom among men.[1]

His assistance henceforth to educational movements is nearly absorbed by his interest in his school, so that the account of what he did for education and the history of the school are nearly identical. In 1780 a subscription was started for a school and his contribution was $575. The work seemed to progress slowly and in 1782, at the "meeting for sufferings," the address before mentioned was composed by him and signed as clerk. The points touched upon in this address were that the Friends should provide their own teachers, for there was great difficulty in securing them; that their own scholars might be kept separate, in order that they might be educated in the Quaker belief; that one school was better than several, and that the expense would be less at a school where the pupils might board.

OPENING OF THE SCHOOL.

The school opened in Portsmouth, R. I., where it existed for a period of four years. The teacher was Isaac Lowton. The school house was

---
[1] R. A. Guild.

a building that was also used for a meeting house. It was two stories high and very plain. Isaac Lowton was an eminent and eloquent minister; his figure was short and lithe; his manners polite and affable, and his conversation intelligent and agreeable. His education was a good one for that day, and as he was fond of reading and had a good memory his store of knowledge was constantly increasing. His favorite authors were Young and Milton, and his sermons were often embellished with quotations from them.

In a set of rules and regulations for the observance of the teacher and scholars by "the meeting for sufferings" they say:

Besides the necessary literary instruction the children are to be taught habits of regularity, of decency, of respectful subordination to superiors, of forbearance, affection, and kindness to each other, and of religious reverence to their maker and those habits of silence and recollection taught and practiced in the ancient schools and inculcated in the holy Scriptures.

The school was discontinued, through lack of funds. The closing of the school was a great blow to Moses Brown, and the small school fund in his possession was scrupulously guarded and increased till the school was again opened in 1819, when it had amounted to $9,300. He also kept the matter before the society. In 1814 he offered to the school a lot of 43 acres in Providence, and a sum of money, which, with all that had been accumulating from the old fund, amounted to $20,000. In 1816 he conveyed the land to the trustees of the school, and buildings were erected, so that the school was again opened in 1819.

LETTER WITH GIFT OF LAND.

The following letter, accompanying the gift of land, will show the interest of the donor:

PROVIDENCE 4TH OF 5TH MO., 1814.

To the Meeting for Sufferings:

DEAR FRIENDS: As my feeble state of health prevents my attending the Meeting at this time, I thought best to inform you that in the course of my confinement by bodily indisposition for some time past, the subject of the Yearly Meeting's School has been renewedly brought under my consideration. And believing that a permanent institution for a guarded education of the rising generation will be promotive of their usefulness in society and the honor of truth, I have, for the furtherance of these desirable objects, concluded to give a tract of land on the west part of my homestead farm, containing about forty-three acres, for the purpose of erecting suitable buildings for the Boarding School thereon; provided the Meeting should consider it an eligible situation, and conclude to carry into effect the establishment of the benevolent institution thereon. If the Meeting should appoint a committee to view the ground, consider of the proposal and report their prospect to the next Meeting for Sufferings, which may be more generally attended, they can then act upon it, as it shall appear to them best. You will however dispose of the proposal in this or any other way that appears to you best. As treasurer of the School Fund, I may for your information mention, that its present amount is about nine thousand three hundred dollars.

With desires that this important subject may be considered, and proceeded in, in conformity to the mind of Truth, that we may hope for its blessing,

I conclude, your affectionate friend

MOSES BROWN.

In addition to this gift, he gave annually $100 to educate poor children, another lot of land, and $15,000 by legacy.

In 1822, his son Obadiah gave the school $100,000. Two interesting facts in connection with this bequest are mentioned. This is said to be the largest sum of money which any institution of learning in the United States up to this time had received, and this money was made by the manufacture of cotton, for which industry the father had done so much in connection with Slater.

Moses Brown died in 1836, 99 years of age. The last seventeen years of his life witnessed the successful operation of the school which was so dear to him. "No monument marks the humble grave of Moses Brown; but his life work is his monument, and it rests upon four foundations: Manufacturing industry, patriotism, education, and philanthropy."

EARLY SCHOOL DAYS.

In 1818, when the new buildings were nearly completed, it was feared that no suitable teachers could be obtained, for there did not appear to be any from the Yearly Meeting who were competent. Two young girls from Nantucket, Mary Mitchell and Dorcas Gardner, leaving pleasant homes, gratuitously gave their services, and entered upon their duties before either of the other teachers arrived. From letters which had been presented by Mary Mitchell, an idea of the school then may be gathered. They left Nantucket in a small sloop, December 30, 1818, via New Bedford, for Providence. One day's sail brought them to New Bedford, and one day's ride in an extra stage brought them, late in the evening, to Moses Brown's door.

Our driver was not acquainted with the road; we had been detained by his repeated calls at houses to inquire the way; our horses were tired and we all longed, when we stopped at Moses Brown's door, to sojourn with him for the night. Robert Brayton alighted and rapped. We could not hear what he stated, but our aged friend came out and said: "Wouldn't the young women better alight? I should be glad to have them stay the night." Tired and dispirited as we were, he seemed like a good old patriarch, and we promptly accepted his kind invitation. He asked us to call for whatever we wanted, freely as we would at home. "A cup of tea," we said, "would be refreshing." Whatever the misgivings of these young assistants might be with regard to their qualifications to teach, they sheltered themselves under the humble name of auxiliaries; and young and sanguine, presumed to present themselves to the scrutinizing eye of Moses Brown. When subsequently asked what he thought of the dress of these young women, he said he saw nothing to object to, but the number of little combs they wore in their hair.

1st mo., 1st, 1819: Proceeded to the school. All is confusion.

1st mo., 4th: Girls' schoolroom. As neither books nor stationery were purchased, it was thought best to defer the opening of school until the following second day of the week.

Afternoon: School over, and such a school! At night we were conducted to the large vaulted lodging room; there were not many beds, as the bedsteads are to be corded when they are needed. Sheets unwashed, just as they came from the hands of those that made them at the sewing bee at Nantucket. No Thomas Howland, no Deborah Hill; there can not be a regular school till the arrival of these teachers.

The red table. Second day, morning. A kind of school. We request and the books come. The Browns and Almys buy whatever we ask for, except a carpet and a telescope; two luxuries we wish the good people of Nantucket would furnish. Moses Brown brings us whatever he can spare from his "garden stores."

3d day: Our two superintendents, two male teachers, three females, 7 girls and 6 boys, all went into the basement story, sat and ate at a long red painted table.

1st mo., 19th: Can not some of the industrious housewives of Nantucket spin the institution a carpet? No matter what the figure, or stars or stripes! None of our floors are painted; none of the walls whitewashed; the ceiling is very high; it is a noble building. All it needs is to be finished. Dr. R. Green says: "Invite the children to eat brown bread; white bread, as constant food, is so prejudicial to health." So we have plates of each kind on the table. Milk we are supplied with by a person who offered to bring the school as much as it needed. We have no cows as yet. No coffee is drunk, shells and Souchong tea are the substitutes. The girls do well. The branches taught are grammar, reading, writing, arithmetic, and geography.

2d mo., 4th: We have 39 scholars. They arrive daily. Our task becomes greater and greater.

2d mo., 10th: 60 scholars. We rise before the sun; collect in the boys' school room for ten or fifteen minutes, until the breakfast bell rings; then go down into the boys' dining room, in which are two tables—one for boys and one for girls. The morning-school holds till 12; then comes dinner. Afternoon school, from 2 till half past four; half an hour remains till tea time, just long enough for a short rest of our limbs by sitting, as we stand much of the time. After tea comes the school for grammar, until half past seven. At eight the little girls go to bed; larger ones at nine.

2d mo., 22d: How were all these boys to be governed? By what authority restrained? Some were bold, some adventurous, some resistant of rule. The institution afforded no precedents, therefore the teachers could quote none. There had never been within these walls a court of decision or appeal. Rules from the Nine Partners' Boarding School were suggested. "Not so," said the younger teacher, "would you anticipate offences by introducing into this infant institution, as yet without record of omission or commission, the rules of an old time-worn establishment in which the rebellious and untoward have had to meet their reward? It is not politic, nor is it Christian—where there is no law there is no transgression." The older teacher assented to the beauty of the theory, but he did not feel sure it would serve long in practice. They concluded, however, if offences *did* come they would endeavor to call the attention of the culprit not to any code of *human* law, but to the dictates of that Divine law which everyone carried in his own breast. A consequence of their experiment was long and private interviews between teachers and pupils, during which expostulation and mild rebuke were patiently tried.

3d mo. 8th: Our visitors, who increase daily, often find substantial meals at tea time. Our long red tables, full of large white bowls, iron spoons, pitchers of milk, and pitchers of molasses, and a large tin bread pan full of hulled corn. We have no talking at these long red tables, except when such friends as Samuel Rodman or James Robinson come.

6th mo.: It was found that the children were sending money to town for books. They bought an elementary work on botany.

The early spring had brought forth within the uncultivated grounds of the school many a little wild flower, which induced one of the assistants to suggest to those under her tuition botanical analyses of them. "Botany!" exclaimed Moses Brown, "why, surely, all knowledge is useful. Let them buy the books."

These extracts will give a good idea of the animus of the school and of the life and discipline. At the reopening in 1819 there were 11 scholars, but the number increased largely before the close of the year.

ACADEMIES AND PREPARATORY SCHOOLS.

Among the interesting reminiscences of the school is a personal letter from O. B. Hadwen, of Worcester. The occasion was the visit of President Jackson and his escort to the school. The President and escort entered the boys' schoolroom from the main building. During the visit the boys were requested to rise and remain standing. The President and party walked through the room, bowing frequently. In returning and passing the teacher's desk, Lewis Cass, then Secretary of War, and wearing his sword, made a military salute. This display of a martial weapon and its noise when thrust into the scabbard made a profound impression on these boys, removed from all scenes and knowledge of war.

The grade of instruction is such as to fit students for any of our colleges, or to broaden their education if they do not enter college. Instruction is given on all the subjects, except international law, that are taught in Brown University. In some cases students from this school have entered the sophomore class at Brown. From 1869 to 1881 Prof. J. Lewis Diman lectured on history, and Prof. J. W. P. Jenks on natural history. Instruction in the modern languages is given, and a very high grade is maintained in this department. In general, it may be stated that the studies required for admission to modern colleges are here taught, and are carried to about the equivalent of the freshman year in these colleges. In order for a student to pass in his examinations a standard of 90 per cent is required, and students are admitted to colleges upon certificate.

For the twelve years preceding 1885 the average number of pupils was 205, the percentage of Friends being but 37½. The membership in 1889 was 261, including representatives from eighteen of our States and of all religious denominations. The percentage of Friends was 26; of the instructors one-half are Friends.

PRESENT STATUS.

The present status of the school is progressive; the standard is high and in accord with modern educational ideas. Until within comparatively recent years the Quaker ideas as to music and art were in vogue, but nearly ten years ago the ground was taken by the present principal that instruction in music and art were needful to a well-rounded education; that without these an education could not be liberal. To-day "musical education receives careful attention and instruction is given by excellent teachers on the pianoforte and in singing. Not only is the musical training made subservient to education, but it is the means of bringing pupils in touch with the people of the city. Quoting from the Providence Journal of March, 1889:

> It is a pleasant custom for the authorities of the Friends' school to give during the year at least one evening with the music of the best authors. Thereby not only do the young gentlemen and ladies of the school get a glimpse into the most impor-

tant branch of culture, but many lovers of music without the walls have the opportunity to hear music of a kind Providence affords all too little of. The concert was delightful and doubly so, as being the only one of its kind that the 120,000 or 130,000 people of Providence will have any opportunity to hear this season.

It has been the practice to give at least one of such concerts each season. The one here referred to was given by talent from Boston, and not by the students. In the department of art "instruction is given in mechanical, pencil and crayon drawing, and painting in oil and water colors. The aim is to educate the mind to the essential principles of art and to train the eye and hand to its successful practice." Scattered through the various rooms of the building, but especially in those rooms where the students spend most of their time, are paintings and etchings. The institution is the fortunate possessor of two busts executed by Theed, of London; one of John Bright and the other of Elizabeth Fry. Between these two is hung a portrait of the "Quaker Poet" Whittier, to whom this school is dear, and whose name is reverently honored within its walls. Said Robert C. Winthrop in an address, speaking of these two marble busts and this portrait:

Eloquence, poetry, and philanthropy will form an inspiring group for your scholars to have ever before their eyes, and may lead them to emulate what they admire.

So much for the art side. For industrial training during the past few years there has been established "a department in the practical use of tools in wood and metal work, including wood carving." This is optional and is under a competent instructor. The display of this department at the close of the year 1889 was creditable and the work well done. One piece found a ready sale at $100. Not only are the boys interested in this department, but also the girls.

The library consists of about 6,000 volumes, with a rare and valuable collection of material relative to Friends. "Familiarity with libraries and books, acquired by daily contact and use, is an exceedingly important part of school work. Knowledge where information may be obtained is next to possessing it." Liberal methods are pursued with regard to the library.

The discipline of the school is on a broad basis. The good discipline of the institution demands unqualified obedience to its rules. But its moral and social training, the most important matter in education, teaches individual responsibility and obedience to personal conviction of right and duty.

This method lies at the foundation of true character and is the educator's most delicate and difficult field of service. The end to be attained is that the child shall stand safely and firmly when the fostering influences of school and home are withdrawn.

Special attention is given to the care and guidance of the pupils, for we are impressed with the conviction that education is derived not merely from the acquisition of knowledge, but to a still greater extent from that potent and shaping influence which comes from contact of youth with mature minds. The endeavor is, by constant intercourse and watchful care, by precept and example, to mold and form as well as instruct; to prepare the pupils to become not only accurate scholars but noble men and women. To the attainment of this end the discipline is mainly directed. Although the organization of the school is of such a character that the personal influence of all the teachers is felt to a considerable extent, yet the immediate care of the scholars is committed, under the general direction of the principal, to two officers, whose special duty is to exercise a constant and controlling influence over the pupils at all hours. For the attainment of this same end, i. e., the refining and molding influence upon character, the boys and girls recite together and sit at the same tables in the dining hall, over each of which a teacher presides; occasionally, also, the officers and pupils meet for social intercourse in the public hall. Experience has shown that the benefit arising to both girls and boys from such coeducation can hardly be overestimated. It is no longer a matter of experiment, and is shown to be quite as beneficial to the girls as to the boys.

Such is the present status of the school. The progressive spirit here obtaining, and characteristic to a greater degree of Friends in general, is well summed up by George William Curtis:

> The muses were but pagan goddesses to the older Quakers. James Naylor and George Fox would have put aside the sweet solicitations of color and of song as St. Anthony avoided the blandishments of the lovely siren whom he knew to be the devil. But gently the modern Quakers have been won over. That grim austerity, as of the Puritan, has yielded to kindly sympathies, and the wholesome gayeties and the refining graces of life are not disowned by the Quietists. Nay, even in a severer day was there not a certain elegance of taste in Friends' raiment? If the bonnet were rigidly of the Quaker type was it not of exquisite texture? Was not the fabric of the dress as delicate and soft as if woven in Persian looms? Was a sense of Quaker aristocracy unknown, and has no Quaker equipage been seen which rolled with an air as superior as that of a cardinal's carriage?

SOCIETIES.

Among valuable contributory sources to education are the literary societies formed for purposes of improvement and debate. Many of the Greek-letter societies in our colleges maintain a debating society as a part of their literary training. At a recent reunion in Providence of one of the Greek-letter fraternities of Brown, an eminent lawyer said:

> To my training and practice in my society debating club, I owe very much of my success in pleading and appearing before the public.

The Lyceum Phœnix was established at the Friends' School in 1833. Regular meetings are held and conducted in accordance with the rules of parliamentary usage. Debates are held and literary exercises of a more general character. This society published a pamphlet called "The Phœnix Echo." The work is like the annuals published in so many of our colleges, and for the good taste and subject matter will compare favorably with the best of them. There is one other society of a similar nature, called "The Athenæum," founded in 1874. The membership in each is open to both the young men and ladies of the school. There are two literary societies of which the membership is composed entirely of the young ladies: The "League," of which the motto is "*Animi cultus humanitatis cibus,*" and the Tennyson Club, "*Better not* to be at all, than not be noble." The average membership in each is about 15. There is also a Young Men's Christian Association.

COURSE OF STUDY.

The present faculty numbers 16. The course of study is so planned that it will meet the requirements of those who wish to enter college, or will give an all-round education to those who will pursue their studies no farther than the courses here offered. With the exception of Brown University, the Friends' School offers the most advanced courses. There are two courses, the classical and the literary and scientific.

Classical course.

First year.—First term: Latin, beginner's book; algebra; English analysis. Second term: Latin, beginner's book; Cæsar, 13 chapters, Book I; algebra, to complete 19 chapters of Wentworth; Roman history.

Second year.—First term: Cæsar, Books II and III; Greek grammar; Greek lessons; Greek history; English composition. Second term: Cæsar, Books I and IV, or Sallust and Cæsar, Book IV; Greek grammar; Greek lessons; Anabasis, 3 chapters; Latin composition; geometry; 6 books.

Third year.—First term: Virgil—Æneid, Books I and II; Cicero, 3 orations; Anabasis, Books I and II; Latin composition; Greek composition. Second term: Virgil, Books IV, V, and VI; Cicero, 4 orations; Anabasis, Books III and IV; Latin composition; Greek composition.

Fourth year.—First term: Homer—Iliad, 3 books; Livy, Book XXI, or French; Latin composition; Greek composition; mathematics reviewed; Xenophon; Hellenica (optional). Second term—Virgil—Eclogues, or Ovid (optional); Cæsar, Cicero, and Virgil, including Book III, reviewed;[1] Anabasis reviewed;[2] mathematics reviewed; reading Greek and Latin at sight.

Literary and scientific course.

First year.—First term: Elementary algebra; reading and composition; United States history; Latin, beginning book; mental arithmetic. Second term: Reading and composition; algebra, to complete 19 chapters of Wentworth; physical geography; Latin, beginning book; and Cæsar 13 chapters; mental arithmetic.

Second year.—First term: Geometry, 6 books; history of England; reading and composition; English grammar; Cæsar, Books II and III. Second term: English analysis; botany; reading and composition; Cæsar, Book I; physics.

Third year.—First term: English literature; rhetoric and English analysis; trigonometry and astronomy; reading and composition; Virgil, Books I and II; civil government. Second term: German or French; advanced American history; reading and composition; civil government; chemistry; Shakespeare.

Fourth year.—First term: Old English and Anglo-Saxon; German or French; composition; mental philosophy; geology. Second term: English poetry; history of civilization; German or French; physiology.

Attention will be given throughout the course to elocution, English composition, and the Scriptures.

---

[1] Instead of these reviews, 4 books of the Odes of Horace may be substituted.
[2] Instead of this review, 50 pages of Herodotus and 1 book of Homer's Odyssey may be substituted.

Mineralogy, zoology, logic, evidences of Christianity, bookkeeping, ancient history, surveying, and drawing will be elective studies in the second and third years, and Latin in the fourth year. Should students desire to pursue a more extended course in the classics and mathematics (for which provision is made), a longer time than four years will be necessary.

BUILDINGS.

It seems eminently fitting that an institution of learning should be located in the midst of pleasant surroundings. Many of the academies of Rhode Island are situated on the shores of her bay, but the Friends' School is located in Providence on ground of about 50 acres in area. Beautiful groves and walks are at the immediate service of the student. From the cupola of the main building can be seen every town in the State with the exception of New Shoreham on Block Island.

The main building was the original structure erected under the supervision of Moses Brown. This building is 220 feet in length, three stories high, and contains recitation rooms, dormitories, the girls' schoolroom, parlor, and dining room.

To this building has been added a wing 50 by 40 feet, containing the boys' schoolroom and dormitories. Alumni hall forms the right wing of the main building. This is the treasure house of the building, for here are the two marble busts of John Bright and Elizabeth Fry, and the portraits of Whittier and Moses Brown. In this hall are held all the public entertainments and lectures. Opening out from this hall is the library. Here, too, are rooms containing the scientific and chemical apparatus and the geological and mineralogical cabinets. In the upper stories are the girls' dormitories. Reference has been made to the artistic decoration of the various rooms. In connection with each wing is a gymnasium.

The astronomical observatory, situated upon the grounds in the rear, contains an achromatic telescope, equatorially mounted, with $4\frac{1}{4}$ inch object glass, a transit instrument, and an astronomical clock, all superior instruments. These are used for class and general instruction, under the direction of the teacher of higher mathematics.

LIST OF PRINCIPALS.

The foundation of an institution which has sent from its walls students to the number of 10,000 into all stations in life must be on a solid basis. The early principals were called superintendents. From the reopening of the school in Providence, in 1819, the following have been in charge: Matthew Purington, 1819-1824; Enoch Breed, 1824-1835; Seth Davis, 1835-1836; Enoch Breed, 1836-1837; Rowland Rathbun, 1837-1839; Allen Wing, 1839-1844; Olney Thompson, 1844-1847; Silas Cornell, 1847-1852; Charles Atherton, 1852-1855; Gertrude W. Cartland, 1855-1860; Albert K. Smiley, 1860-1879; Augustine Jones,

1879 to the present time. The school has numbered among its academic staff men famous as educators and scholars. Moses A. Cartland; Lindley M. Moore, of New York; John Griscom, Prof. Gummerie, Prof. Moses C. Stevens, Caroline Cartland, Sarah Alice Cornell, John F. Rowell, Mary Ann Stanton; Prof. Alonzo F. Williams, Brown University; Charles Brownell, Charles H. Parkhurst; Stephen A. Chase, of Salem; Pliny E. Chase, of Haverford College, and President Thomas Chase, of Haverford College.

Such are a few of the better-known educators who have comprised the personnel of the school in days gone by. There are others who, if not so well known, have done faithful and conscientious work, thereby making an integral part in the sum total of the grand result. Its graduates have gone into all professions and pursuits, and a glance at the representatives of their commencement exercises and reunions will show who they are. Here again a few must suffice: Hon. Jonathan Chace, U. S. Senator; Abraham Barker, of Philadelphia; Dr. Henry Wood, Johns Hopkins University; Dr. Samuel B. Tobey, of Providence. Many graduates have come back here to teach and have won reputation.

WASHINGTON ACADEMY.

Washington Academy was founded in response to a demand for increased advantages in higher education. In 1800 Brown was the only institution where a higher education could be obtained. The Friends' School had been organized in 1784, but after its removal to Providence, was suspended till 1814. There was a demand for an institution where young men could be trained for the position of teaching. Accordingly, those who were interested in Newport, Providence, and Warwick decided to found an academy and locate it at Warwick. The movement was actuated by the public spirit of the founders, and represented a great amount of self-sacrifice. As was usual then, a part of the expense was defrayed by a lottery. Shares at $20 each were offered, and subscriptions were solicited. Unfortunately the records are in a bad state of preservation.

The first meeting under the articles of association was held at the house of Oliver Spink, in Wickford, March 10, 1800. A committee was chosen to draft a charter and see that the necessary steps were taken to secure it. The purpose of those who were interested in this academy can be shown by the following selections from the charter:

Whereas institutions for liberal education are highly beneficial to society, by forming the rising generation to virtue, knowledge, and useful literature, and thus preserving a succession of men qualified for discharging the offices of life with usefulness and reputation, they have therefore justly merited and receive the public attention and encouragement of every wise, polished, and well-regulated State;

And whereas an academy erected in North Kingstown, in the county of Washington, in this State, would be advantageous to this Government;

And whereas Lodowick Updike, Peter Phillips, Benjamin Fowler, George Thomas, Thomas Rumreill, Daniel E. Updike, Benjamin Reynolds, Philip Tillinghast, William

Ellery, Robert N. Auchmuty, Samuel Elam, John I. Clarke, Thomas P. Ives, Christopher G. Champlin, William Hunter, Walter Channing, Daniel Lyman, and Asher Robbins appear as undertakers in this design; and thereupon a petition hath been presented to this assembly praying that full liberty and power may be granted unto them to found, endow, order, and govern said academy; and that they may be incorporated into one body politic, to be known in the law with the powers, privileges, and franchises necessary to the purposes of said institution.

Then follow provisions for subscription to the stock, the number of trustees (twenty-five), the election of new trustees, the government of the academy, and the four following enactments:

And, furthermore, it is hereby enacted and declared, That into this liberal and catholic institution shall never be admitted any religious tests; but, on the contrary, all the members hereof shall forever enjoy full, free, unmolested, and absolute liberty of conscience; and that the places of principal and other instructors shall be free and open to all denominations; and that the youth of all religious denominations shall and may be freely admitted to the equal advantages of this institution, and all receive alike fair, generous, and equal treatment during their continuance therein, they conducting themselves peaceably and conforming to the laws and statutes thereof.

And it is hereby ordained and declared, That in this academy shall no arts or methods be practiced to allure and proselyte or insinuate the peculiar principles of any one or other denominations into the minds of the scholars.

And it is thereupon declared, constituted, and established, That everything of this nature shall be accounted a misdemeanor, be avoided, and by all denominations disdained and discountenanced as beneath the dignity and foreign from the true intention of this institution, the main design of which is to sow in the minds of the rising youth the seeds of useful literature, to cultivate and improve good morals, and thus to make them useful to themselves and to their country.

And, furthermore, for the greater encouragement of this seminary of learning, we do grant, enact, ordain, and declare that the estate of this academy, the estate, persons, and family of the principal instructor for the time being, lying and being within this State, with the persons of other instructors and scholars, during their belonging to said academy, shall be freed and exempted from all taxes, serving on juries, and menial services, and from bearing arms, impress, and military service.

The charter provided that the first meeting of the trustees should be held August 27, 1800. The following officers were chosen: Samuel Elam, president; Peter Phillips, vice-president; Benjamin Fowler, treasurer; Daniel E. Updike, secretary.

At this meeting the land, consisting of 4 acres, was presented for the site of the academy. This gift was made by Mr. Nicholas Spink and Ann, his wife, Mr. John Franklin and Hannah, his wife. An additional gift of $100 was made by Mr. Samuel Elam, who, according to the tradition, wished the name of the institution to be Elam Academy, but through the persistency of one of the trustees the original name of Washington Academy was retained. Towards the latter part of 1800 the building committee announced that the work was nearly completed, but that there was a deficiency in the treasury. This was met by a new subscription, and early in 1802 the school opened with seven scholars, under the preceptorship of Alpheus Barker, of Newport. The building was divided into four rooms, two of which were used as recitation rooms; during the absence of the principal or assistant from the room a monitor was appointed. As there were no catalogues the course of study must be gathered from reminiscences of those who were students. The ordinary rudiments were taught, as well as the higher mathematics, navigation, surveying, and astronomy. The town of Wickford was just entering upon a period of commercial activity. From her wharves sailed merchantmen for the African trade, for the East Indies, and the coasting service. Wickford was the market for a large agricultural district, from which the produce was sent abroad. In this town a large part of the young men followed the sea till they were about 25. By that time many had so risen that they had fair prospects of securing the command of a vessel, or of ranking among the officers. At this juncture they wanted a course in navigation, which they could now get at home in their own academy. Before 1840 Washington Academy had fitted no less than fifty men for practical navigation.

CORRESPONDENCE.

A very good insight into the educational methods and the subjects taught at the higher academies of the first part of this century may be gathered from a brief sketch of one of the Washington Academy boys. There were two other academies then, Kent and Warwick, so that some of the correspondence is connected with them. Jeremiah G. Chadsey, a graduate of Washington Academy, of North Kingston, went to Plainfield, Conn., to school, because there was none of a high grade in his own State, Rhode Island. As soon as the academy was opened in Wickford he returned. Here he was instructed in astronomy, navigation, and surveying, how well may be seen from the fact that for his own gratification he made an almanac computing all the calculations for that year. As a surveyor he was employed by the probate court as one of the commissioners to lay out any land that might be in dispute. As a navigator he taught navigation successfully for several years. The following letter will show how his scholarship was regarded by the principal of the academy where he had just completed his last year of study:

WASHINGTON, *January 20, 1803.*

DEAR SIR: If you can consistently call on me some evening this week I should be glad, as I wish to have some conversation with you concerning your becoming an assistant in W. Academy.

Yours, personally,

A. BAKER.

Mr. JEREMIAH CHADSEY.

On the same note appears the reply as follows:

I was previously engaged when I received this.

J. G. CHADSEY.

The engagement was the acceptance of a position of assistant at Kent Academy, where he remained nearly four years. The next letter will show his success as a teacher, and the reply of the committee at the Central School in Warwick, to his application for the position.

EAST GREENWICH, *January 31, 1807.*

GENTLEMEN: Being informed that your Central School is without a teacher, I take the liberty to recommend Mr. Jeremiah G. Chadsey to your notice. He is possessed of all the necessary abilities to teach the English language grammatically, all the branches of arithmetic and mathematics. He has taught reading, writing, arithmetic, algebra, surveying, navigation, geography, and astronomy in our Kent Academy with the applause of all who were concerned in it, and universal satisfaction of the gentlemen who have attended his examinations.

I sincerely regret his withdrawing his useful instruction from this academy, and I fear we shall not be able to fill the place he quits with equal abilities. He has a very happy faculty of giving instruction and obtaining the love and esteem of his pupils. He is modest, mild, inoffensive and unassuming, and able to give complete satisfaction to his employers. With sincere wishes for the prosperity of your Central School,

I am, gentlemen, your most obedient, humble, servant.

PETER TURNER.

To the CENTRAL SCHOOL COMMITTEE,
Warwick.

WARWICK, *Feb'y 5th, 1807.*

SIR: We, the committee of the Warwick Central School Society, having met and noticed your application, do inform you that there will be a vacancy for a preceptor in our school on the first of April next, and having examined your several recommendations, which perfectly meet our approbation with respect to your literary knowledge and other competent qualifications for a preceptor, do grant to you the privilege of filling the same should your terms of tuition meet our approbation.

We are, with much esteem and respect, yours, &c.,

JOSEPH ARNOLD (S. C.).
CHARLES BRAYTON.
GEORGE ARNOLD.

Mr. J. G. CHADSEY.

A bill rendered by Mr. Chadsey to one of the patrons of the school will show the current charges.

Mr. Christopher Greene, Dr.

1807.		
April 27.	To cash delivered to his son Sam'l	$0.12
July.	To 1 quire paper for Nath'l	.25
Sept. 3.	To 1 lb. candles	.22
Sept. 28.	To boarding his son Sam'l 24 weeks, at $1.25	30.00
	To his tuition and contingents the above time	6.14
	To schoolhouse rent do.	.67
	To boarding his son Nath'l 9¼ weeks, at $1.25	11.88
	To teaching him navigation the above time	4.00
1808.		
Mch. 2.	To cash delivered to Nath'l	.25
Mch. 28.	To boarding his sons Nathanael and Richard (from Dec. 28 to March 28) 7 weeks, at $1.25	8.75
	To their tuition the above time	1.75
	To schoolhouse rent, firewood, &c	.39

A letter from Mr. Chadsey shows his reasons for leaving this school at Warwick and some of his ideas regarding the profession. The first part of the reply of the committee has been torn from the original letter, but it was evidently a short sentence, as what follows contains the greater part.

GENTLEMEN: I now have the offer of another school, which I conceive to be more lucrative than yours, and as the support of my family depends entirely upon my earnings I feel it a duty which I owe to myself and family to embrace the opportunity, and therefore must beg leave of being discharged from your institution, but not without expressing to you my gratitude of the kind treatment you have ever manifested to me, and through you must return my sincere thanks to my employers in general. I am sorry that it was not in my power to give you earlier notice; but I can assure you, gentlemen, that I had not the least idea of leaving you till within two days past, and that I have no other object in going but that of increasing my pay. When you consider the length of time that I have been in your service, and that a shift of instructors is necessary for the discipline of a school (for by a long acquaintance between the master and scholars a familiarity is formed which ends many times either in a negligence to govern or an unwillingness to be governed), I say, gentlemen, when you take these things into consideration you will think that my removal is as necessary as it is hasty, and therefore will pardon my precipitate determination. That your institution may flourish under the care of all instructors, and become a nursery of information to the rising generation, is the ardent wish of
Your most obliged and very humble servant,
J. G. CHADSEY.
Messrs. JOSEPH ARNOLD, HENRY REMINGTON, CHARLES BRAYTON,
Warwick Central School Committee.
FRIDAY MORNING, *April 20, 1810.*

We add that we are very sorry that you are about to leave the academy when so much of the respectability it now holds is greatly owing to your unwearied attention to the improvement of the scholars at all times. It has always been our wish that the principal of the academy should have been willing to have allowed you such a part of the profits of the institution as would have made it an object for you to have continued in it, knowing from long experience how much depends on a good second in such an institution. We part with you with great reluctance, and add that you may depend and calculate upon us at all times as your friend.
ELIHU H. GREENE.

Mr. Chadsey is at liberty to show the above to whom he pleases.
E. H. GREENE.
Mr. J. G. CHADSEY.

RENEWAL OF CHARTER.

About thirty years after the founding of the academy the interest in it seemed to decrease. It may have been that other academies were then in successful operation in the State, or that more of the young men engaged in business or commerce, for at this period the commercial activity of Wickford was at its height. The teachers during this period were Wilbur Tillinghast, Linden Fuller, Amanuel Northup, Carr Northup, Barton Ballou, Mr. Wood, and Francis Chappel. The terms which these gentlemen held their position varied from six months to eight years. In 1833 a crisis in the affairs of the academy was reached. The buildings were in such a condition that repairs must be made at once if they were to be saved. Accordingly, on April 13, 1833, the friends of the institution came to its support, and a petition was made for a revival of the old charter of 1800, with the amendment that failure to hold annual meetings should not invalidate it. Among the names of the new board of trustees were those of Nicholas Brown, Daniel E. Updike, Pardon T. Hammond, Thomas P. Ives, Jeremiah G. Chadsey, Jonathan Reynolds, Joseph C. Sanford, and John Brown Francis. Under the new charter the following were chosen as the officers: John Brown Francis, president; Jonathan Reynolds, vice-president; Pardon T. Hammond, secretary; Joseph C. Sanford, treasurer.

By subscription a sum was raised for the repair of the buildings. The first teacher after the reorganization was William D. Upham. A salary of $100 was given him and one-half of the proceeds from tuition. He received for the first year $427. Miss Caroline Whiting was his assistant. Several students from adjoining towns attended, and the interest was maintained for about three years. From this time till 1848, when the academy was leased to the school district, there were frequent changes in the teachers. Only inferior teachers could be engaged, because the income from tuition was used to meet the expenses, and the attendance now was very small. At a special meeting of the trustees, held May 27, 1848, it was voted to lease the academy to the school district for a public school.

KENT, LATER EAST GREENWICH, ACADEMY.

PETITION FOR A CHARTER.

Educational methods are various and the contributory sources are numerous. In many of the colonies the surroundings were favorable to educational development. Rhode Island has been the scene of many a hard-fought battle for principle, civil and religious. The towns situated on her bay have witnessed stirring scenes, and the recollections of these events have aroused dormant feelings of patriotism and pride. In Narragansett Bay was captured the *Gaspee*, and the first blood in the Revolution was shed. Vessels with the rich freight of the Indies came to the wharves of Providence and Newport. The locations of institutions of learning in this State were well chosen, and many of them had a rich historic setting which could not fail of inspiration. Kent Academy at East Greenwich, on Narragansett Bay, is one of these favored institutions. In this township and vicinity lived men who were famous for their part taken in the Revolution, and who aided the cause with counsel and money. The stirring times of war and the excitement incident to the close of the century had passed. Prudent men were determined to provide increased facilities for education. The definite shape which the movement took is best set forth in the preamble and articles of association drawn up by Hon. Ray Greene.

EAST GREENWICH, *Oct. 8th, 1802.*

Ethan Clark, William Arnold, Mathewson and Mowry, and Peter Turner, all of East Greenwich, and State of Rhode Island, and Ray Greene, Elihu Greene, and Christopher Greene, all of Warwick, anxious to promote the happiness of posterity and to continue the blessings of a free and equal Government, which this country enjoys in as great a degree as any other nation, and believing that well-conducted seminaries of learning in which youth may acquire knowledge, with the advantages of places of public worship to incline their minds to morality and religion, are the most probable means to effect their design, have associated for this (as they consider) laudable purpose and have purchased a lot of land in East Greenwich containing an acre and twenty rods, upon which they intend (with the assistance of others that may be equally disposed to promote the good of mankind) to erect a building about sixty feet long and thirty feet wide, two stories high, and convenient for the accommodation, and, when properly regulated, suitable for the instruction of a considerable number of youth in such branches of education as may be thought most to their advantage. They also please themselves with the idea that such an institution will be productive of the advantage to East Greenwich and its vicinity of introducing a settled minister of the gospel to preach in the meeting house which is now so seldom improved.

This place (in East Greenwich) being central in this State, and possessing so many advantages, will induce many persons to place their children here for education, where they can visit them with convenience and be frequent spectators of their improvement. To complete the contemplated plan very considerable expense will be required, much more than is reasonable for a few to bear; but we flatter ourselves that there are others, who, believing as we do the dissemination of literature, information, and religion is amongst the first duties of society, and the most productive of order and good regulations in republican governments, will become subscribers to this plan, and adding their names to these already mentioned will lend their assistance to support the society. * * *

In accord with this design, the articles of incorporation were granted in 1802. How far the ideas of the incorporators were met will appear from the extracts from the charter.

CHARTER OF KENT ACADEMY.

AN ACT to incorporate certain persons by the name of the Proprietors of Kent Academy.

Whereas the establishment of public institutions for the promotion of literature and general diffusion of knowledge is an object of the highest importance to society by affording the means to the rising generation of gaining instruction in the principles and practice of virtue, and of acquiring that knowledge and wisdom which is necessary to qualify them to fill with usefulness and honor the various stations and offices of life; and

Whereas an academy founded in East Greenwich, in the county of Kent, would be highly beneficial to that place and advantageous to the Government; and

Whereas a number of persons have undertaken in this design, and have by their committee preferred a petition to this general assembly, praying that full liberty and power may be granted unto them to found, endow, and govern said academy, and that they may be incorporated into one body politic by the name of Proprietors of Kent Academy, with all the powers, privileges, and franchises necessary for the purpose of said institution. * * *

Then follow the sections pertaining to the holding of property, board of government, duties of the officers, and the general management of the academy. Section 7 is of interest because therein "it is further enacted that, for the greater encouragement of this institution of learning, the estate of this academy lying and being within this State shall be exempted from all taxes."

Such was the purpose of the founders. The realization of their wishes will be seen in the men who were educated there.

The beneficent influence of the academy was more decidedly in the direction of general improvement of the community in character and acquirements and in inspiring higher aspirations generally than in affording very many conspicuous examples of brilliant careers. Very many men and women of sterling and substantial qualities owed the groundwork of their education to the old Kent Academy.[1]

The institution was established in its present location in the year 1802, as the Kent Academy. From its founding to the year 1839 it was conducted as a stock academy. It then passed for a few months into private hands, but upon the organization of the Providence (now New England Southern) Conference of the Methodist Episcopal Church, in 1841, it became the property of the conference by purchase. Finally, in 1884, it was repurchased by a stock company, but in 1888 the stock was surrendered. It is now conducted by a board of thirteen directors, six of whom are selected by the corporation, six by the conference, and one by the alumni.

During all the transfers and changes in the academy, by common agreement the same grade of work was continued, so that the purpose of the founders was maintained.

EARLY HISTORY.

The first teacher was Mr. Abner Alden, and his assistant, Jeremiah G. Chadsey. From the record kept by Mr. Chadsey of the attendance the following will show the number of scholars:

Quarter beginning December 31, 1804, 72; April 1, 1805, 122; July 1, 1805, 133; September 30, 1805, 109; December 30, 1805, 83; March 31, 1806, 101; June, 1806, 127; September 30, 1806, 100; December, 1806, 95.

Mr. Chadsey was a graduate of Washington Academy, and has been mentioned more fully in connection with that institution. The following contract will show how the expense of the assistant was to be met.

This is to certify that Jeremiah Chadsey agrees to assist me in teaching the school in Kent Academy, for which I, the subscriber, promise to give him two-fifths of the amount of the bills of tuition when collected. This contract to commence at the beginning of the second quarter, August 20, 1804, and to continue as long as I agree to employ him and he agrees to serve me.

ABNER ALDEN.

---

[1] Historical address by Dr. Henry E. Turner.

Mr. Chadsey also served as a secretary and treasurer. One of the bills from his account book will give an interesting comparison of prices:

Dr. Henry Niles.	Per Contra Cr.
1804.	1805.
Dec. 17. To the tuition of his son 22 weeks and contingent $3.88	May. By ploughing 1 lot..............
1805.	June. By cash paid Mr. Alden .... .32
To do. from Dec. 31 to Mch. 20 and firewood 2.40	Nov. By .... qts. milk ....
	1806.
	Mar. By 1 load wood 1.75
	Apr. By 1½ doz. eggs........... .17
	May By 12¼ lbs. veal at 4 .... .50

Mr. Alden was a man of good qualifications as a teacher and succeeded in establishing a good school. Said one of his pupils:

The influence of Mr. Alden in forming the morals and manners of his pupils, if a boy under 10 years of age can judge, was not inferior to his power of imparting knowledge. To my mind, and I knew him well in after years, he was the ideal schoolmaster.

For tuition in 1808 the rates were, for reading and spelling, $2; reading, writing, and spelling, $2.25; arithmetic, with bookkeeping, $2.50; English grammar, $3; composition and speaking, $3; Latin and Greek languages, $3; the principles of astronomy and geography, with the use of the globes, $3.50.

The following extract appears from the records of 1816:

Resolved, That the committee, collectively and individually, attend at least once in the week at the academy, and if necessary give the preceptor the friendly and candid advice respecting the government and instruction of the academy.

Resolved, That the Rev. Daniel Waldo be requested to call occasionally at the academy, to afford to the scholars of the institution such advice and instruction as his duty as a clergyman and parental kindness may dictate.

Till 1820 the institution seems to have been no pecuniary gain to the proprietors. That same year it was—

Resolved, That the secretary's account for the sum of three dollars be paid to him for recording the proceedings of the trustees from the founding of the institution to 1820.

In 1822 Nathan Whiting was elected preceptor.

There has never been a school before or since where the scholars enjoyed such perfect happiness as they did under the administration of Mr. Whiting. Although he was a fine classical scholar, possessing an abundance of general knowledge himself, he had very little faculty to communicate it to others. Being rather absent-minded and very unwilling to punish disobedience or neglect, unfair advantage of these failings was taken and enjoyed supremely. Occasionally, on pleasant summer afternoons, pupils were allowed, during school hours, to sit on the front steps of the academy, under the pretense of studying in the open air, where they would amuse themselves in composing satirical poetry on their teachers' eccentricities, and squibs on each other. Yet in spite of all this, some learned more in certain branches of knowledge during Mr. Whiting's administration than ever before, particularly geography and general knowledge of the world. Previous to this all the information acquired was from Morse's geography, which was committed to memory and then recited, but Mr. Whiting taught by using the atlas and demonstration with the terrestrial globe.[1]

---

[1] History of East Greenwich, Dr. D. H. Greene.

EAST GREENWICH ACADEMY.

ACADEMIES AND PREPARATORY SCHOOLS. 61

TEXT-BOOKS.

From the first catalogue, issued in 1840, the list of teachers is taken. Rev. David G. Allen, principal; J. Newhall, A. B., languages and mathematics; Miss Lucy G. Eldridge, preceptress; Miss Hannah C. Eldridge, drawing and painting; Miss Anna S. Burge, music. The course of study is not stated, but can be inferred from the list of text-books, which is here given.

Smith's grammar, geography, Adams' arithmetic, Davies' arithmetic, Legendre's geometry, surveying, Bailey's algebra, Olmsted's school philosophy, Guy's astronomy, Colt's bookkeeping, Mrs. Lincoln's botany, Parley's school history, Smellies' natural history, Jamieson's rhetoric, Abercrombie on the intellectual powers, Jones' chemistry, Worcester's third and fourth reading books. French—Bugard's practical teacher, translator. Latin—Goodrich's Latin lessons, Adams' Latin grammar, Latin reader, Virgil. Greek—Goodrich's Greek exercises, Fisk's grammar, Greek reader.

Italian and Spanish.—The common introductory books to these languages. For more advanced scholars in Latin and Greek the books vary to accord with their after-course of study. Those used thus far have been Livy, Horace, Tacitus, Xenophon's Anabasis and Memorabilia.

In this year, 1840, the above were the text-books, giving an idea of the grade of work done. The catalogue shows an attendance of 108: males, 52; females, 56. There were 4 teachers in addition to the principal.

From 1840 various principals have had charge of the academy. In 1847 the academy closed with only 7 students, but the next year there was a return to its old-time prosperity. From the list of principals some names will appear which have more than a local reputation. Abner Alden, A. M.; Joseph L. Tillinghast, A. M.; Aaron Putnam, A. M.; Ezekiel Rich, A. M.; James Underwood, A. M.; Rev. Daniel Waldo; Benjamin F. Allen, A. M.; Nathan Whiting, A. M.; Charles H. Alden, A. M.; Rev. Ebenezer Coleman; Christopher Robinson, A. M.; Rev. Henry Edes; Pennel Corbett, A. M.; George W. Greene, A. M.; Joseph Harrington, A. M.; Joshua O. Coburn, A. M.; Thomas P. Rodman, A. M.; Rev. James Richardson; Rev. Daniel G. Allen; Rev. Benjamin F. Teft; Rev. George F. Pool; Rev. Daniel G. Allen; George B. Cone, A. M.; Rev. William Bagnall; Rev. Robert Allyne; Rev. George W. Quereau; Rev. Micah J. Talbot; Rev. Bernce D. Ames; Rev. James T. Edwards; Rev. David H. Ela; Rev. Francis D. Blakeslee.

The academy buildings are situated on an eminence overlooking East Greenwich Bay. The grounds contain 5 acres, and here are Winsor House, the academy, and the boarding hall. In the academy building are the recitation rooms, library, and chapel. In this building are the botanical, mineralogical, and geological cabinets. The rooms vary in size, according to the departments for which they are needed. The chapel is commodious, and contains a pipe organ. In this hall the public exercises and entertainments are held.

PROMINENT GRADUATES.

A fair estimate of the work of an institution may be obtained through the men who have been graduated. Among the graduates of this academy have been men in representative departments of public and professional life. Hon. Nelson W. Aldrich, U. S. Senator; William Sprague, U. S. Senator, and one of the war governors; in State politics, Governor William Greene, of Warwick; Chief Justices Charles Matteson, of Coventry, and Pardon E. Tillinghast, of Pawtucket; Hon. Henry T. Sisson, lieutenant-governor, and Hon. Enos Lapham, the present lieutenant-governor. In the professions, Rev. Charles H. Payne, D. D., at one time president of Ohio Wesleyan University; William F. Warren, president of Boston University; Samuel F. Upham, of Drew Theological Seminary; Prof. Eben Tourjee, of the Boston Conservatory of Music; Prof. Alonzo Williams, of Brown University.

Among names prominent in local reputation appear Hon. Samuel H. Cross, Hon. Frederic C. Sayles, Hon. Robert Henry, Hiram B. Aylesworth, and the celebrated boatbuilders, of Bristol, Charles F. Herreshoff and Charles F. Herreshoff, jr. Any such roll must be incomplete, but this institution seems to have received grateful recognition at the hands of its graduates, testifying that their mature judgment approves the educational methods and advantages of their youth.

COURSE OF STUDY.

The course of study provides for the classical, English, elocution, art, music, commercial, and normal departments. The instruction in the commercial course is made as practical as possible, by having one part of the room arranged as in bankers' and brokers' offices. The students take charge of these, thereby getting training by object lessons. Pupils are here prepared for college, and the studies taught are those of preparatory schools. A rounded education is afforded in case the student does not intend to pursue his education beyond this institution.

College preparatory—Latin scientific.

The three following courses are as comprehensive and thorough as those of most female colleges. Gentlemen, as well as ladies, who may wish to take a systematic academic course can pursue either of these to graduation and receive a diploma. This course is arranged to give a preparation for the Latin scientific course in college.

	Fall.	Winter.	Spring.
Junior year.	Latin grammar and lessons .... 5 Algebra .... 5 United States history ..... 5 English readings and spelling 1	Latin grammar and lessons .... 5 Physics or physiology ..... 5 Algebra .... 5 English readings and spelling 1	Latin, Cæsar .... 5 Algebra .... 5 Modern history ..... 5 English readings 1
Middle year.	Cæsar, Cicero, and Latin .. 4 French or German .... 5 Geometry .... 5 Roman history ..... 1 English readings 1	Cicero and Latin prose .... 5 French or German .... 5 Geometry .... 5 English readings 1	Cicero and Latin prose ...... 5 French or German .... 5 Rhetoric or astronomy ...... 5 English readings 1
Senior year.	Cicero .... 2 Æneid and eclogues .... 5 Roman history .... 4 Ancient geography .... 1 Constitution of the United States 5	Æneid .... 3 Georgics .... 5 Mathematical review ...... 3 Chemistry 5	Æneid .... 5 Latin review .... 5 Mathematical review .... 5 English readings 1

College preparatory—classical.

Wesleyan and Brown universities and other colleges admit our students without examination upon certificate from the principal.

	Fall.	Winter.	Spring.
Junior year.	Latin grammar and lessons .... 5 English grammar .... 5 United States history ..... 5 English readings and spelling 1	Latin grammar and lessons .... 5 Arithmetic, mental and written .... 5 Physics or physiology ..... 5 English readings and spelling 1	Latin, Cæsar .... 5 Modern history ..... 5 Arithmetic completed ...... 5 English readings 1
Junior middle year.	Cæsar, Cicero, and Latin prose .... 4 Greek grammar and lessons .... 5 Algebra .... 5 Roman history ..... 1 English readings 1	Cicero and Latin prose .... 5 Greek grammar and lessons .... 5 Algebra .... 5 English readings 1	Cicero and Latin prose ..... 5 Greek, Anabasis .... 5 Algebra .... 5 English readings 1
Middle year.	Cicero .... 2 Anabasis and Greek prose. 3 French .... 5 Geometry .... 5 English readings 1	Virgil's Æneid .... 3 Anabasis and Greek prose. 2 French .... 5 Geometry .... 5 English readings 1	Æneid .... 5 Anabasis .... 4 Rhetoric .... 5 Grecian history 2
Senior year.	Æneid and eclogues .... 5 Homer .... 5 Roman history .... 4 Grecian history .... 1 Ancient geography 1	Georgics .... 5 Homer .... 5 Mathematical review ...... 3 Roman history .... 1 French review .... 1 English readings 1	Latin review .... 5 Greek review .... 5 Mathematical review .... 5 English readings 1

College preparatory—scientific.

This course is arranged to give preparation for the scientific course in college and for schools of technology.

In this department special attention is paid to practical work in the laboratory. The students themselves perform most of the experiments in physics and chemistry, and pursue more or less of original investigations in geology, botany, and astronomy.

	Fall.	Winter.	Spring.
Junior year.	United States history. Algebra. Constitution of the United States. English readings and spelling (1).	Physics. Algebra. Physiology. Free-hand drawing.	Modern history. Algebra. Rhetoric. Free-hand drawing.
Middle year.	French or German. Geometry. Zoology or physics. English readings (1).	French or German. Geometry. Chemistry. English readings (1). Mechanical drawing.*	French or German. Logic or trigonometry. Astronomy. English readings (1). Mechanical drawing.*
Senior year.	Geology or surveying. Mental philosophy. English readings (1).	English literature. Evidences of Christianity or analytical geometry. Political economy. English readings (1).	Moral philosophy. Botany. Applied physics. English readings (1).

* Not required for graduation.

Academic.

	Fall.	Winter.	Spring.
Junior year.	Latin grammar and lessons. Algebra. United States history. English readings and spelling (1).	Latin grammar and lessons. Algebra. Physics or physiology. English readings and spelling (1).	Cæsar. Algebra. Modern history. English readings (1).
Middle year.	French or German. Geometry. Zoology. English readings (1).	French or German. Geometry. Chemistry. English readings (1).	French or German. Logic. Rhetoric. English readings (1).
Senior year.	Geology. Mental philosophy. Constitution of the United States. English readings (1).	English literature. Evidences of Christianity. Political economy. English readings (1).	Moral philosophy. Botany. Astronomy. English readings (1).

Art.

The studio is large and well lighted. It is furnished with all needful appliances for the successful prosecution of the studies of this department.

Occasional lectures on art and an occasional visit to the art galleries of Boston will be accorded the students in this department.

	Fall.	Winter.	Spring.
Junior year.	Arithmetic. Geography. Drawings from patterns and casts. English readings and spelling (1).	Arithmetic. English grammar. Drawing from casts. Perspective drawing. English readings and spelling (1).	Arithmetic. English grammar. Perspective drawing. Architectural drafting. English readings (1).
Middle year.	French or German. Drawing from nature. Water-color painting. Illumination and lettering. English readings (1).	French or German. Water-color painting. Drawing from life. Crayon portraiture. English readings (1).	French or German. Oil painting. Drawing from life. Botany. English readings (1).
Senior year.	United States history. History of fine arts. Oil painting. India ink and sepia drawing. English readings (1).	English literature. History of fine arts. Oil painting. Drawing in colored crayons. English readings (1).	Rhetoric. Art criticism. Oil painting. Drawing from life. English readings (1).

Essays upon art will be written during the second and third years.
Another language may be substituted for French or German.
China decorating and waxwork are taught independently of the course.

Elocution.

This course is designed to so train the mind, voice, and body as to secure naturalness and effectiveness in delivery, and to prepare the student for any position in which elocutionary excellence is desirable. Personal instruction is made a special feature of the course. Frequent opportunities are given for the recitation in public of illustrative selections.

	Fall.	Winter.	Spring.
Junior year.	Vocal technique. Speech, defects and remedies. United States history. English readings.	Vocal technique. Physical harmony. Physiology. English readings.	Vocal expression. Studies in emotion. Modern history. English readings.
Middle year.	Vocal gymnastics. Analysis of gesture. French or German. English readings.	Vocal effects. Gesture. French or German. English readings.	Forensic oratory. Personation. French or German. English readings.
Senior year.	Delsarte philosophy of expression. Dramatic studies. Moral philosophy. English readings.	Principles and methods of teaching. Criticism of authors. English literature. English readings.	Applied methods. General review. Rhetoric. English readings.

Normal.

The object of this course is to furnish instruction, in both the theory and practice of teaching, to those who can not well pursue a full course in a regular normal school. A thoroughly qualified and experienced teacher, a graduate of one of the first normal schools of the country, has charge of this department. The intermediate department of the academy furnishes surperior opportunities for practice in teaching, under the direction of this normal teacher, such as is afforded by the very best State normal institutions.

The course of study is definitely outlined and adapted to those for whom it is designed. A certificate is given to those, who, in the judgment of the faculty, are thoroughly qualified to teach.

A community where an institution of learning is located should be the better for its presence and is justified in securing what it can from it. At the academy what are called "oratoricals" are held each Friday evening. It is the regular rhetorical exercise of those in that department, and to these the townspeople are invited. In addition to this a course of lectures and literary and musical entertainments are maintained through the winter. By such means the people feel that they are welcome to the advantages which such an institution can share with them, and its sphere of usefulness is so much the more increased.

SMITHFIELD SEMINARY, LATER LAPHAM INSTITUTE.

SMITHVILLE SEMINARY, 1839-1863. LAPHAM INSTITUTE, 1863-1875, NORTH SCITUATE.

Smithville Seminary, afterwards Lapham Institute, was founded by the Rhode Island Association of Free Baptists. It was designed to give a liberal education to youth of both sexes. At the time of its founding in 1839, the Free Baptists had only two academies—one in Maine and the other in New Hampshire. The Rhode Island Association was desirous of having an academy in this State. To secure this object, the Rev. Hiram Brooks was called from the West and was empowered to solicit subscriptions. His faith in the prospects of the new institution as a paying investment was far stronger than his business methods; for while he was successful in raising the sum of $20,000, the manner in which it was done was unfortunate. He secured subscriptions from people of small means, who gave him nearly all their savings and who were promised a return of at least 7 per cent, possibly 10 per cent. The money raised was invested at once in the necessary buildings, and it was impossible to obtain any such return on the capital. Subscribers never received any dividends, and the knowledge of the manner in which the money was raised hampered the institution when it needed help in later years. The buildings are three in number; one large central building, with two wings separated nearly 20 feet from the central one by connecting halls. The recitation rooms, offices, dining room, and apartments for the faculty are in the central building, and the wings are the dormitories for the boys and girls, respectively.

HOSEA QUIMBY.

In the autumn of 1839 the school opened. The corporation consisted of a board of trustees and an examining committee. The first principal was Rev. Hosea Quimby, who came from the Maine Academy.

He was assisted by Mr. Weld, Miss Johnson, and Miss Weld. In a short time it was found that the first three named instructors could do all the necessary work, so the academic staff was reduced to that number. For the next four years that was the corps of instructors. In 1845 Quimby had as the assistant in the male department A. R. Bradbury, and in the female, Caroline L. Bradbury. Two other teachers had the primary department, and Mr. A. L. Meader the music. The institution was now well started, and the next few years represented as high a period of prosperity as the school ever attained. The catalogue for the year 1845 shows an attendance of 132 in the male, 101 in the female, and 87 in the primary department. Outside of Rhode Island there were representatives from Massachusetts, Connecticut, New Hampshire, Pennsylvania, New Jersey, and New York.

COURSE OF STUDY.

The catalogue for the year 1845 states that this institution presents to those youths, who may resort here, an opportunity for studying the Greek, Latin, French, Spanish, German, Hebrew, and Italian languages, the various branches embraced in English literature, the different natural sciences, mathematics, metaphysics, etc. Instruction is also given in drawing, painting, instrumental and vocal music. The design is to afford means for fitting students to enter college, or for giving those who do not take a collegiate course the privilege of getting a thorough, practical education. The institution takes rather a medium stand between a college and a common academy; hence, several of the regular college studies, as well as the more common branches, are here pursued, giving good opportunity to all who wish to fit themselves for the great duties of life.

The following books were used:

Greek: Goodrich's Greek grammar, Anthon's Greek reader and lessons, Greek Testament, Xenophon's Anabasis, Donnegan's Lexicon.

Latin: Andrews and Stoddard's Latin grammar, Andrews's Latin reader, Ainsworth's or Leverett's dictionary, Cæsar's Commentaries, Anthon's Sallust, and Cicero, Virgil (Cooper's), Horace, Livy, Ovid, etc.

French: Surault's grammar, Belliger's phrases, first class book, Life of Washington, Racine, Boyer's or Meadow's dictionary, etc.

Spanish: Sale's grammar, El Traductor Español, Novelas Españolas, Don Quixote, Neuman's dictionary.

Italian: Bachi's grammar and tables, Prose Italiane, Moralle Novale, Il Tesoreto, Dello Scolare, Italiano, Bachi's phrases and dialogues, Graglia's dictionary.

Hebrew: Seixa's manual, Stuart's grammar and christomathy, Gibbs's Lexicon, Gesenius's Lexicon, Hebrew Bible.

Mathematics: Sherwin's algebra, Davies' algebra, and Legendre, Bowditch's navigation, Flint's survey.

Natural Sciences: Comstock's elements of chemistry, natural philosophy, mineralogy and geology, Mrs. Lincoln's botany, Burritt's Geography of the Heavens, Poe's conchology, Combe's physiology.

English: Fisk's grammar, Porter's rhetorical reader, Pope's Essay, Young's Night Thoughts, Davies' arithmetic, Emerson's third part, Smith's geography, Harris's bookkeeping, Goodrich's History of the United States, Worcester's history, American Expositor, Webster's dictionary.

Intellectual and moral sciences, etc.: Watts on the Mind, Upham's mental philosophy, Newman's rhetoric, Hodge's logic, Wayland's moral philosophy, Wayland's political economy, Paley's Evidences of Christianity, Paley's Theology, with Paxton's notes.

Rhetorical exercises, etc: Besides a weekly rhetorical exercise, consisting of composition and declamation, there are various benevolent and literary societies designed to promote the moral as well as the intellectual welfare of the youths who may wish to enjoy their benefit.

EXPENSES.

For tuition in English grammar, arithmetic, reading, writing, geography, Watt's history, rhetoric, moral science, or political economy, $4 were charged. For each of the higher branches and languages, 75 cents were charged until amounting to $5.50, but no student was required to pay more than that, however many studies he might take, except in case of music, drawing, and painting. The expense of these varied according to the expense the institution incurred in furnishing them. At present 50 cents is charged for vocal music and $6 for instrumental, including the use of piano.

For board those who sit at the cold-water table were required to pay $1.12½ per week, at the other $1.32. (The table at which was furnished a vegetable diet and cold water was called "the cold-water table." At the other were served tea, coffee, and meat.) To those young ladies who take care of their own rooms an allowance of 12½ cents is made per week, so that to them the board comes to $1 per week at one table and $1.20 at the other. Hence, those females who are disposed to engage in domestic labor, such as to keep their own rooms in order and wash and iron for themselves, will save on their expense, and therefore actually earn, from 25 to 50 cents per week. The arrangement when first going into operation was to allow males the privilege of taking care of their own rooms as well as the females, but it was soon found that this would not answer, as they, not generally being accustomed to such kind of business, could not attend to it so as to keep their part of the building in proper order. Many would be enabled to do this, but generally to the contrary.

For room rent and furniture, students are charged from $1.50 to $2.50 each per quarter. Those who have their washing done by the seminary pay 3 cents per piece. Students furnish their own lights and pay for warming their rooms, the actual expense of this being apportioned among them. The design is to bring all the bills as low as will comport with having such a school as the wants of the community require. The whole expense of a student will vary from $18 to $26 a quarter.

For the express benefit of those who are to go out for the purpose of common-school teaching, especial instruction will be given in the fall terms, and at other times if required. The class will receive a course of lectures on the subject of school keeping.

The year is divided into 4 terms, of twelve weeks each, commencing as near as practicable with the different seasons of the year.

Quimby continued the school till 1854 when it closed with only about 20 students. He is described by one who taught with him as a man of generous and benevolent disposition, who did all in his power to help needy and deserving students. In his own affairs, he saved little if anything for himself, but spent it on the school. He was a fine mathematician, but had no taste for the languages. He rented the school property to Samuel P. Coburn, who became the principal. The school again flourished and for the year ending 1855 the catalogue records an attendance of 77 males and 55 females. There were 6 assistants. The expense of tuition was a little higher. English branches, per term $5.00; higher English branches $5.50; Latin and Greek, $6.50; board at the seminary, $1.90 per week, or board and washing (allowing 7 pieces per week) $2.10. He kept the school for two years, when it was closed for a number of years.

From the foregoing résumé it will be seen that the curriculum was practical and of a high grade. The results were shown in the admission of its graduates to the New England colleges. This high standard could not be maintained from the natural income of the school. The institution had no endowment fund, because all the money raised at the outset had been invested in buildings and furnishings. In 1850 the property, which was owned by the bank, and was in debt to the amount of $5,000, was put up at auction. There was an arrangement made by twenty-five of the Free Will Baptists to subscribe $200 each and secure the property. This movement was not carried out, for Mr. Quimby, the principal, bought the property himself. Quimby was assisted by six teachers at the close of the year ending July 17, 1851. The number of pupils was 152; males 79, females 73. There was the same grade of work as in 1845, and civil engineering was added to the course.

The period of the greatest prosperity of the school appears to have been under the management of Mr. Quimby, from 1844 to 1848. The revival of this institution commenced with the year 1863, when the school took the name of Lapham Institute.

CHANGE OF NAME.

In 1861 one of the former teachers, who had left the school to enter the ministry, came back to Providence. He was interested in the old seminary and inquired into its existing status. This he found was not encouraging, for the buildings had been standing unoccupied and were each year falling more and more into dilapidation. He called to see some of the prominent men of the Free Baptist Association, but they took a gloomy view of the situation. In thinking over the problem the idea occurred to him of having what he called a "jubilee meeting," at which the old teachers and graduates should assemble and consult for the best advancement of the seminary.

He suggested the idea to the Rev. George T. Day, and was asked by him when he would purpose to have such a jubilee. "The Fourth of July," he replied. "No, sir," said Mr. Day, "that won't do. We must have the institution opened and in running order by the 1st of August." It was decided to hold a meeting the 22d of February, 1863. Addresses were to be made by Rev. George T. Day and Prof. Thomas L. Angell on behalf of the alumni, and Mr. Quimby was to represent the teachers. The 22d of February that year was a very stormy day, and such a severe snow storm prevailed that there was no suitable conveyance to the seminary, which was located 10 miles from Providence. The exercises were accordingly postponed to the next day. When the company then assembled it was announced that the Hon. Benedict Lapham had offered to buy the property if the association would put it in repair. The offer of Mr. Lapham was accepted, and $5,000 was raised by the association. In recognition of this action on the part of Mr. Lapham the name of the seminary was changed to Lapham Institute.

Under the new régime Rev. Benjamin F. Hayes was chosen principal, and the school was successfully conducted by him. He was called to the chair of mental and moral philosophy at Bates College. At the close of his last year the attendance was 207. In the catalogue for that year an interesting footnote is made on the subject of expense, that "in consequence of the high prices now prevailing, 10 per cent is for the present added to the term bills."

Prof. Hayes was succeeded by his assistant, Thomas L. Angell, he, too remaining but two years, leaving to accept the chair of modern languages at Bates College. The next principal, George H. Ricker, remained seven years, and under him the school enjoyed an enviable reputation for the admirable classical training it afforded. He, too, was called away, to accept a professorship in Latin and Greek at Hillsdale College, Michigan. It speaks well for the grade of the academy, that three successive principals had been called to professorships in colleges. Prof. Ricker left in 1874. He was followed by A. G. Moulton, who died soon after the close of his first year.

DEPARTMENTS OF STUDY.

The last catalogue issued under his principalship offered the following courses and departments of study: (1) A college preparatory course; (2) A ladies collegiate course; (3) an English and scientific course; (4) a department in painting and drawing; (5) a music department.

The summary of students in these courses were: Classical, 14; English, 70; musical, 27. The same grade of instruction was maintained, but a more modern series of text-books had been introduced.

The last man to have the charge of the school was W. S. Stockbridge, who remained until the school was closed, nor has it been resumed since. At this school nearly 1,500 students have been educated for all pursuits and professions. The class of students which it gathered within its walls appreciated the advantages of an education, because they had to work for them. For them there was no royal road to learning.

As is usually the case, the majority of the graduates have made for themselves a local reputation, but among those more widely known are James B. Angell (Brown University '49) president of Michigan University; ex-Governor Henry Howard, of Rhode Island, and his brother, lieutenant-govenor; Prof. Thomas L. Angell, of Bates College; Rev. George T. Day.

The private schools for boys have maintained a high grade in the State, and many of them have prepared students for college. Some of those schools receive only day pupils and others are boarding schools. Among the former is the English and classical school in Providence. Since its organization, in February, 1864, the whole number of boys admitted has been 2,150, of whom 250 were fitted for college and nearly 100 went directly to scientific, medical, and law schools. This school is the largest. Among the others was the Union Hall School, under the management of Samuel Austin. This was established in 1847 and flourished till 1867. In 1852 girls were admitted. The Fruit Hill School, with Mr. Stanton Belden as its last proprietor, was a successful boarding school for boys and fitted students for the New England colleges, besides offering instruction in navigation and surveying.

The Rev. Charles H. Wheeler had a private school for boys and prepared students for Brown and the New England colleges. There were other private schools for boys in the State, but they were on a smaller scale.

SMITHFIELD ACADEMY, UNION VILLAGE, 1810-1813.

The beginning of this academy was due to the labors of Elisha Thornton. He was one of the associates of Moses Brown in his establishment of the Friends' school, in 1784, at Portsmouth. Thornton taught at his academy for thirty years, and removed to New Bedford about the beginning of this century. Till 1808 the educational movements were spasmodic. In that year was incorporated "The Smithfield Academic Society," Nicholas Brown being one of the incorporators. The labors of Thornton in the preceding generation were now producing results in the petition of Peleg Arnold, Richard Steere, Ezekiel Comstock, Joel Aldrich, John W. C. Baxter, and David Aldrich to be made a body corporate by the name of the "Trustees of Smithfield Academy." This petition was granted at the February session of the assembly, 1810. At the first meeting of the trustees the following officers were elected: President, Peleg Arnold; vice-president, Joel Aldrich; treasurer, Richard Steere; secretary, David Aldrich.

As usual in those days, the money was raised by lottery. Two attempts were unsuccessful, but an arrangement was made with Joel Aldrich so that the necessary funds were raised. The building was of two stories, the scholars being in the main room. When the school increased the assistants had their special classes in the small rooms.

This school was more than an academy in name, and its grade was that of the preparatory school for the New England colleges. From 1835 to 1850 the school was very strong in science under the impulse given it by Prof. Bushee. There was an attendance of many scholars who on leaving would complete their education; hence for such there was an all-round course of study. The first teacher was David Aldrich, followed by Josiah Clark. Then John Thornton, the son of Elisha, had the school for six years. Among other teachers were Ward Wilson, George D. Prentice, and Christopher Robinson. At one period of the school previous to 1830 there was no settled teacher, and various ones tried it. The year 1830 marks the beginning of the period of greatest prosperity. The interest of the Society of Friends in the academy may account for the fact that students came here from the South. From 1831 there were arrangements made for those scholars who wished to board in the principal's home and in the homes of some of the townspeople. The price of tuition was $9 per quarter, and board $2.50 per week.

In the case of Smithfield Academy, as of so many others, its success is largely due to the energy of one man, who came to the academy in the autumn of 1830. It had had successful teachers before, but from his interest and long connection with the school he brought it up to its highest standard.

PROF. JAMES BUSHEE.

He was born in Smithfield October 15, 1805. Till his eighteenth year his education was obtained at the public school in his native place. He wanted a higher education, so he spent two years at the Friends' school. On graduation he obtained a position to teach in Somerset and also in Fall River. In 1830 he returned to Woonsocket and opened a public school in Union Village, in the Smithfield Academy. The next year he opened at the same place a boarding school. His connection with the Smithfield Academy is of chief interest.

From personal recollections by his old pupils he is described as being a man of spare stooping form, giving an impression of greater height than he really had:

He reminded one much of Abraham Lincoln, both in the style of features and in the fact that acquaintance with him invariably removed the impression at first sight unfavorable and left a far fairer one produced by a knowledge of the noble mind and true Christian charity of the character that was behind it. His kindliness of heart often inclined him to help those scholars who were anxious to attend his school but could not pay full tuition. I know of several cases where he charged them nothing, and others not more than half the regular price for tuition, when at the same time the money was much needed. A longing for education was always enough to enlist his sympathy and aid.

Regarding his moral character:

I wish to add my tribute of appreciation and praise for the precepts which I received at his hands of a moral character. You, sir (the professor), taught me the importance of discriminating between right and wrong; you, sir, taught me the importance of being truthful and upright; you, sir, taught me to honor character; and if I have accomplished anything thus far in life it is due in no small degree to this instruction.

Towards the end of the daily session he would tell the school to put away their books, for he wanted to have some play. The play was a list of figures which he would give the scholars to add, and the one who was the first to give the right answer would be considered the smartest; but the one who was first, yet had the wrong answer, was very careful next time, because of the publicity of the failure. Said one of the bank presidents of Pawtucket: "I regard that fifteen minutes' daily practice in addition as one of the best features of my education while at the academy. To-day I can add up a long column of figures quickly and accurately."

The professor was a self-taught man, and was particularly happy in imparting information. He was an educator, for he could draw out what was in the dull and backward. He was quick to see the benefit of the conversational method for instructing and helping those who could not express themselves, and used this method in the sciences. The sciences were always a delight to him, especially astronomy. To him was due the credit arising from the statement that at Smithfield Academy the cabinets of minerals, chemicals, and philosophic apparatus were equal to those of Brown University. It was his purpose to write a text-book on natural philosophy, but he never did. He composed a treatise of nearly 200 pages on mathematical mechanics. In his passion for knowledge he would use all the money he had to buy the necessary appliances, and was often in debt. He had no time to make money, but his life work was a constant study how he could gather knowledge by which he could help his fellow-men.

REMINISCENCES.

His discipline was parental. He appealed to the student's sense of what was right and fitting. He seemed to treat his pupils as if they were on an equality with himself. If a rule was broken he would show the offender the reason for the rule and the result that would follow from its violation. He would also show the student that infraction of the rules would cause the principal sorrow, and such was the affection for him that the pupils would not wittingly do anything to hurt his feelings.

He was a member of the Society of Friends, but characterized as a man of progressive ideas. Music was taught in his school. He would allow the students to assemble whenever they pleased in his parlor to sing the "Old Granite State," such was his love for that hymn.

One night one of the boys who boarded in his family, as he was falling asleep, began to hum some kind of a tune. Coming to the foot of the stairs the professor listened till he located the voice. Then asking, "Sonnie, is thee sick?" "No, sir;" replied the lad. "Well, I thought thee must be sick from the distressing noise I heard."

Prof. Bushee did more than simply labor in the station where his life work was cast. His interest in the instruction of the masses was keen. When the lecture system came into vogue, he was first to organize a course in Woonsocket. He was also actively interested in the antislavery movement. He was one of the founders of the Worcester Natural History Society, and served as one of its officers for nine years. In August, 1866, a large number of his pupils held a reunion in Worcester. The speeches and reminiscences show the esteem and veneration in which their professor was held. His educational work covered more than half a century and he entered into his rest December 20, 1888. Perhaps no better impression can be given of this man than from his own words, at a reunion of his old pupils in the celebration of his eightieth birthday.

The eightieth anniversary of the birthday of Prof. James Bushee, which took place at his home in Union Village, deserves more than a passing notice, as there were nearly 200 persons present, a large number of whom had at some time during the past fifty-eight years been under the instruction of the professor. As early as 2 o'clock the guests began to assemble, and it was a pleasing sight to witness the meeting of old friends and schoolmates, who had not seen each other for years. In places here and there, small groups might be seen discussing incidents of their school days and relating the little tricks they played on the professor. But his side of the story generally unfolded to the interested listeners a new side to the question, which seemed to confound the relators then as well as of old. Soon all assembled in the schoolroom and every seat was occupied. Prof. Bushee then called the school to order as follows:

LADIES AND GENTLEMEN: It is now my pleasant duty to welcome you. I heartily welcome you to our hearts and homes; welcome you again to the old academy, where you have, as students, so often assembled in your youthful days; to this old academy, dear to you as well as to me. I have experienced many grateful things; none as grateful as the present. It is a pleasing task for me to extend to you all a heartfelt greeting amidst these hallowed scenes. We have here the bell which tolled here half a century ago to summon you to your recitations, and it has been thought fit to call you together to-day with this same bell, on the occasion of my eightieth birthday. This is my fifty-eighth year in teaching—twenty-eight in Massachusetts and thirty in Rhode Island—but I have finally returned to the old academy, a most fitting place for my years. I wished to have this present gathering take place on the old academy grounds. It is meet, after so long a time, after the lights and shadows of so many years, for the old pupils to commune together, to speak of the thorns and crosses scattered along their paths, and to relate how they have passed their time. This is the bell that called you to your duties as students. This is the Bible with which the morning services were commenced. This morning the bell was rung as usual, but never before has it called together such a number of pupils. The Bible was read, but never to such a number. Allow me to read a few appropriate verses, which you have so often heard from this long-since familiar book.

The professor then read a few verses from the Book of Psalms, "Blessed is the man that walketh not in the counsel of the ungodly."

Mr. Bushee was the last one in charge of the academy, and when he withdrew its career was terminated.

PART III.

EDUCATION OF WOMEN.

A chapter on the education of women has been deemed essential to the complete survey of the history of higher education of the State. There have been no colleges for women in the State, but the private schools and the academies have prepared students for such institutions and have been of a high grade. All the phases of female education have been developed from instruction in the elementary branches to the courses of lectures delivered by Prof. Diman to classes of ladies. At a time when institutions of learning for women were comparatively rare and educational methods were crude, the history of a seminary like that in Warren, where nearly 1,500 young ladies received a good education, or of a school like Mr. Kingsbury's, where a smaller number were graduated but the same high grade of work maintained, is of value. The greater part of the education for women was given by the private schools and academies. These schools have been under the direction of good teachers and have maintained a high grade in what they have offered.

A place has been given to the normal school in this chapter because its character as a normal school has been varied, and because it was one of the institutions offering advanced education for young women and young men. The institutions which have been traced in detail are the oldest and most important. While these were exclusively for the higher education of girls, there were many young ladies who received a similar training in academies and schools like the Friends' School or the Kent Academy. The private schools of the State have offered thorough and effective education for young women.

YOUNG LADIES' HIGH SCHOOL.

YOUNG LADIES' HIGH SCHOOL, JOHN KINGSBURY, PRINCIPAL, 1828-1858

The investigator of the history of education finds many phenomena in his researches, and must chronicle many changes. To-day long vacations are in vogue; the school hours are shorter; the buildings for schools are planned with a view to all the modern improved ideas, so called; but perhaps there is no greater change to-day than in the department of education for women, especially in their higher education. There are such colleges as Bryn Mawr, Vassar, Smith, and Wellesley, which are entirely devoted to the higher education of women, and many of the universities are opening their doors to women. Women are taking courses in medicine, and there is being erected in Chicago an institution where women may receive theological training. Nearly all the educational advantages which are open to men are also open to women, while nearly all the professions have admitted women.

The Young Ladies' High School was the pioneer in the institutions at Providence for higher education. At that time the name high school was not used to indicate the highest grade in the public schools, but signified an institution of higher education. As illustrating the change in the ideas of education of women in the beginning of this century and to-day, the following account, in Mr. Kingsbury's own words, will be of interest. This account was given by him at the close of his connection with this school, in 1858:

To those who are familiar with public sentiment with regard to education now, but who know, except as a matter of history, little of the change which has taken place during the past thirty years, the establishment and successful operation of a school like this may seem a small affair. Could we, however, place them at the beginning of this series of years and with them trace all the circumstances adverse to success it would be much easier to make that impression which is so necessary to a perfect understanding of the subject. Allow me to give two or three illustrations for this purpose. At that period the range of studies in female education was very limited in comparison with the present. In addition to the elementary branches a little of history, a smattering of French, and a few lessons in painting or embroidery were thought to be sufficient for the education of girls. The study of the Latin language, of algebra, of geometry, and of the higher English branches was introduced into few schools out of the city of Boston, and it was thought visionary to attempt the study of them here. In fact, it was hardly possible to escape ridicule in making the experiment. Even the boys in the street were sometimes heard to say in derision, "There goes the man who is teaching the girls to learn Latin."

The subject of vacations will furnish another illustration. Thirty years ago the public schools were allowed the Friday after each quarterly examination. Thus the enormous amount of just four days in the year, in addition to the Fourth of July and Thanksgiving, was allowed for vacation. Private schools generally had no vacation at all. Such was the state of public opinion that in the organization of this school it was not deemed politic to take more than four weeks' vacation at first, and this was thought by some persons to be an unwarrantable liberty. The same public opinion will not now be satisfied with less than eight weeks' vacation even in public schools.

Again, the terms for tuition in private schools will furnish another illustration. Thirty years ago the price of tuition in the highest classical school in this city was $5 a quarter. I had the temerity to charge $12.50 for the same time, or $50 a year; and what is most marvelous, teachers were most offended at the innovation.

It may be proper here to speak of the schoolroom and furniture. At the outset it was deemed important to arrange and furnish the schoolroom in such a manner that the transition from well-furnished homes to places of study should not present the wretched contrast which had been too common previous to that period. Frequently a room set aside as unfit even for trade or mechanical purposes was selected and fitted up in the cheapest manner as the place where the daughters of our richest and most respectable people were to be instructed. Therefore, in order to avoid this mistake, a building which had been used by the venerable Oliver Angell, of this city, for a schoolroom was procured and entirely refitted for the purpose. The old desks and seats were removed, the walls were neatly papered, the whole floor was carpeted—a luxury till then unknown in this country, so far as I have been able to learn—

and the room was furnished with desks covered with broadcloth, and with chairs instead of stiff-backed seats. Some very excellent people lifted up their hands in astonishment, and said it would be a pity to have so much money wasted; that this furniture would need to be renewed so often that the expense could not be sustained. The novelty of such a schoolroom attracted many visitors, not only from this city but from abroad. One gentleman from Kentucky, being in Hartford, came here solely to see it. The old room was low studded and badly ventilated. Therefore, at the end of twenty years and in accordance with the increased knowledge of physiology and school architecture, the old building gave place to the present structure, which for beauty, convenience, comfort and health, is surpassed by few, if any, in the country. And here it may be proper to say that the desks and chairs, which were thought to be an expenditure so extravagant and wasteful at the organization of the school, are still standing in the new building. After having been used thirty years they are so good that with proper care they may last many years longer.

The estimate of higher education for women has been noted, as well as the difficulty in its attainment. Brown University did very much to raise the educational standard in the community, and the public school system was in its infancy; hence there was a demand among the people for increased educational advantages for their daughters. It was in response to this demand that Mr. Kingsbury opened his school. In his own words, in the circular which was printed to announce the opening of this department of the High School—the only advertisement of any kind ever set forth to secure public attention—the following language was used to express the leading idea:

Our object in the establishment of this department is to afford young ladies such facilities for education that they will be under less necessity of spending abroad the most important period of their lives, a period in which a mother's judicious care is so necessary to the formation of character. In this undertaking we look for support only among those who wish their daughters to acquire a thorough education. No attempt will be made to gain the approbation of such as would prefer showy and superficial accomplishments to a well-regulated mind.

The number of scholars was at first limited to 36, but, the accommodations allowing it, the number was soon increased to 40. Three more were added after the erection of the present building, and 43 has been the fixed number ever since. No pressure of circumstances has ever induced me to add a single one beyond the prescribed number, except when by some mistake or misapprehension a member of the school was on the point of being excluded. In such a case the individual has been received as a supernumerary and gratuitous scholar. At the end of six months the complement of scholars was full. Since this period there has always been a list of applications in advance of the full number varying from 20 to 60. When I decided to bring my connection with the school to a close there were 32 names on the list. The admissions for the whole period have been 557.

The founder of this school deserves more than passing comment. Too often the professional man is guilty of the charge of narrowness, because he can not get out of the ruts which he has worn for himself. It is gratifying to describe a man like Kingsbury, who was possessed of such a liberal and catholic spirit that President Wayland could say, while addressing the ladies of this school:

Though you, ladies, have had so much, you have not had all of John Kingsbury. While he has thus labored for you there has hardly been a benevolent effort in this city which has not felt the benefit of his wise and disinterested efficiency. Whether a university was to be endowed, or a church to be established, or an association to be lifted out of difficulties, or a society of young men to be aided and directed in their labors to promote the cause of Christ, John Kingsbury was the man to do it. *Nihil tetigit quod non ornarit, quod non ædificavit.* Such has been, and is, your honored instructor, and we come here to unite with you to-day to testify to the appreciation he is held by all good men in the city of Providence.

John Kingsbury was born in Connecticut May 26, 1801. He was educated by his own exertions, for he was the son of a farmer in moderate circumstances. The education of his early years was what he obtained at the district school till he was 15. By teaching he obtained the money to take him through college, although he also taught while in college. He graduated from Brown University in 1826 with the honor of salutatorian. After leaving college he taught in a private school in Providence for two years, and then organized his own school, over which he presided for thirty years. While teaching he had a class in the Richmond Street Congregational Church, where many young men came within the influence of his thought and teaching. He also actively allied himself with the Franklin Lyceum, a scientific association. He was its secretary for some time, and also president. He was one of the founders of the American Institute of Instruction in 1830, and continued to be actively interested in it.

Said Mr. Barnard, the retiring commissioner of public schools, in 1849:

To the uniform personal kindness of Mr. Kingsbury, to his sound practical judgment in all matters relating to schools and education, to his prompt business habits, to his large spirit, to his punctual attendance and valuable addresses in every meeting of the institute which has been held out of the city, and the pecuniary aid which his high character and influence in this community has enabled him to extend to the various plans which have been adopted by this department, I desire to bear this public testimony and to make my grateful acknowledgements, both personal and official

As showing the confidence reposed in him it will be only necessary to mention the institutions with which he was connected: The American Board of Commissioners for Foreign Missions, corporate member; Butler Hospital for the Insane, trustee; Brown University, trustee; afterwards one of the board of fellows and secretary of the corporation. In addition to these duties he secured the greater part of the subscriptions for a new religious society, the Central Congregational Church. He was also a very prominent member of a committee, in 1850, to raise $125,000 for the more complete endowment of Brown University. He closed his labors as a teacher to accept the position of commissioner of public instruction. From this brief sketch, almost a mere catalogue of the offices of trust he held, may be seen the esteem in which he was held by his fellow citizens. Nearly all of these duties he fulfilled while he was teaching.

In a letter from one who knew Mr. Kingsbury the following statements are taken:

It was the good fortune of many of the young men who, for the first time away from their father's house, and now freshmen in Brown University, were honored with an introduction to John Kingsbury, and who, through membership in his Bible class at the Richmond Street church, entered upon an acquaintance that ripened into a life-long friendship. Apart from the advantage that came from a careful and discriminating study of the scriptures, always made to bear upon actual contact with life's conflict, there was that in the man himself which was motive power for good. His was a wonderfully attractive power, and by its very winsomeness quickened in many of us a desire to be such a man as he. So direct and positive was this that it was invidiously said of one young man by some of his classmates that he was "trying to be like Mr. Kingsbury," and the writer on hearing it, was conscience stricken as possessed of a similar ambition for so high an honor. Mr. Kingsbury so identified himself with the good of every young man as that those whom he approached were drawn to him as to a father. He helped with living sympathies and friendly tokens. His influence, all unconsciously wielded in little, quiet ways, has long and always been retained. "Go home," he once said to the writer as vacation was approaching. "Go home as often as you can while your parents are living. Make them glad by your presence and your devotion." This was said in a tone that fell like music upon the ear, and started chords that vibrate still in the homes we are always slow to leave. On another occasion, when it came to his knowledge for the first time that the son of a classmate was in Brown University, and was dishonoring his father's name, he said: "If the father of this young man had only attended the annual commencements and kept me informed of his son's intentions and coming I would gladly have sought him out and helped him to a better way." Such was John Kingsbury, and such the help he rendered to one and another young man as successive classes entered the university. The very sound of his name brings only pleasant memories to every student who enjoyed his acquaintance and friendship. Though not one of the faculty of the university he was an educator of the young men who came to his Bible class and his home, none the less pronounced and none the less gratefully appreciated than they.

With such a man as Kingsbury at the head of the school, and the high standard which he set up, it is no surprise that the institution was eminently successful. How this success was realized can be inferred from the reunion which was held at the close of his connection with the school, when the leading citizens assembled to bear grateful recognition of his services and labors. The success was also due to the following characteristics, which Mr. Kingsbury aimed to maintain:

(1) To have the moral sentiment of the school always right.

(2) To have the scholars feel that no excellence in intellectual attainments can atone for defects in moral character.

(3) To form exact habits, not only in study, but in everything.

(4) To have all the arrangements of the school such as are adapted to educate women.

(5) To educate the whole number well rather than to elevate a few to distinction.

(6) To train them to happiness and usefulness by a harmonious cultivation of all the powers of the mind rather than to render them remarkable for genius or intellect.

(7) To make them intelligent and efficient without being prone to ostentation or pretension.

(8) To make them feel that common sense is more valuable than literary or scientific culture.

(9) To make elementary studies prominent throughout the course,

so that spelling—old-fashioned spelling—and the higher ancient classics have sometimes been contemporaneous studies.

Such was the standard of his school, and those who knew the man can testify that in so far as he was able he strove for the accomplishment of his high purposes. To show how he strove in this direction he states the following with reference to himself:

(1) Unremitting labor from the beginning to the present time.

(2) Never being so satisfied with past or present success as to indulge a tendency to inactivity.

(3) Beginning every term with the same strong desire to make some additional improvement, as I felt at first for success itself.

(4) Adopting every real improvement in education, whether it was demanded by public sentiment or not.

(5) Rejecting everything which did not approve itself to my judgment after examination and trial, though it might be demanded by public sentiment.

(6) Never allowing the public to become better acquainted than myself with educational interests, especially such as related to the education of young ladies.

(7) Daily seeking the special aid of heavenly wisdom and guidance.

These truly are lofty and noble purposes and could be taken as models by every educator in the land. It is gratifying in the extreme to note that a school with a lofty purpose could and did succeed, and that, too, with no glittering announcement from catalogue or circular.

The occasion of the close of Mr. Kingsbury's relations to his school was celebrated by a reunion of his pupils in the chapel of the college. The corporation had offered the use of this building. The whole tone of the gathering was such as to deeply impress the principal that his work had been appreciated, and that his friends and pupils had come to do him honor. President Wayland presided, and the governor of the State, the mayor of the city, professors from the university, and clergymen were among those assembled.

Said President Wayland, after explaining the reason of the reunion:

To me this gathering possesses peculiar interest, for I have known this institution from its commencement, and have observed its progress to the present hour. It arose as the sun frequently arises on the morning of a most brilliant day, amidst clouds and mist. The greater part of our citizens looked at the attempt as very public-spirited but very chimerical. Our population was about one-third of its present number. It was seen that such schools as we needed could be sustained in Boston, New York, and Philadelphia, but very few believed we could sustain one in Providence. Mr. Kingsbury thought differently. He knew us better than we knew ourselves. Mr. Kingsbury determined to have a ladies' school which should be an honor to Providence, or he would have none at all. He has realized his idea and the results are spread before the world. There is hardly a family amongst us, which, in some of its branches, does not acknowledge with gratitude the benefit of his instructions and personal influence. Five hundred of his pupils look upon him with gratitude and veneration and at this very moment are returning thanks to the man whose whole life has been so successfully devoted to labors for their intellectual and moral improvement.

YOUNG LADIES' SCHOOL. (PROF. LINCOLN.)

Upon the withdrawal of Mr. Kingsbury from his school it was taken by Prof. J. L. Lincoln and continued under the name of the Young Ladies' School. In September, 1857, Prof. Lincoln took charge. At that time it was the only private school for young ladies in the city, and as the applications for admission were always in excess of the number which could be accommodated, the school was select. There were seats for fifty students. In addition to that number, Prof. Lincoln had special classes that came in for English literature, or the sciences. There were always two regular assistants. Prof. Chace lectured on geology, Prof. Appleton on chemistry, and his brother, William, on history. The principal of the school had the classics. The course of study embraced a period of four years, and the young ladies received such an education as would have prepared them for entrance to colleges like Vassar or Smith. In some branches, such as physics and philosophy, mental, moral, and natural, they were further advanced than the preparatory studies. There were no colleges for women then, and it was the aim of the school to give a young lady a training that would enable her to follow the profession of teaching, or to occupy herself in any station of life which might present itself.

But the influence and power of the school can not be estimated by numbers. As indicative of the character of the school, it will be sufficient to say that the standard marked out by the founder was followed. While maintaining his school Prof. Lincoln also had some classes at the university. In 1867, feeling that he could not sustain the duties incumbent upon him, at the college and in his school, he ceased his connection with the school and devoted himself exclusively to his professorship at the university.

In answer to an inquiry as to the number of pupils he had, Prof. Lincoln said:

I find the names of 214 pupils registered during the eight years (1859-1867) of my school. During the first year I had 42 desks in the school, but as there were more on my list waiting for admission, I put in 8 additional desks and after that 50 was the regular number. But besides these 50 pupils, I had older girls who came in for lessons; so that sometimes there were 70 pupils in the school. During these years there were 33 who may be said to have graduated, having stayed long enough to complete the course which I contemplated for the work of the school.

Upon the withdrawal of Prof. Lincoln to the college Rev. John C. Stockbridge took the school. The previous traditions of the school and the same grade of work were maintained. The school continued under the management of Mr. Stockbridge till 1877. During that period 250 young ladies received their education in whole or in part at this school. Several were prepared for Vassar, so that the school still offered instruction in advanced work.

The colleges for women having been founded at a comparatively recent date, higher education was acquired at the private schools. These were of a high grade. In addition to those described in detail there was a private school organized in 1858 in Pawtucket by Mrs. William B. Read. This school was continued ten years.

In 1866 Miss Mary R. Shaw opened a private school in Providence, and continued in charge of it till 1874, when it passed into the hands of Miss Josephine L. Abbott. Since the opening of colleges for women young ladies have been prepared for these institutions at this school. Among other schools in Providence were the Young Ladies' School, 1865-1878, Miss Eliza Weeden; School for Young Ladies, 1871, Mrs. Fielden and Miss Chace; and several boarding schools for young ladies. In Pawtucket there were the Young Ladies' Seminary, 1875-1880, Mrs. Thomas Davis; and the School for Girls, 1881, Miss L. A. Greene.

WARREN LADIES' SEMINARY.

This school was situated in Warren, one of the seaport towns. When the commercial and maritime history of the State shall be written, it will be found that the activity of towns like Warren, was an important factor in its development. In addition to the communication which the town had with other centers, through the coming and going of the West India men and coasters, Warren was favored in the community of the interests of the inhabitants. Nearly all were related to each other by ties of kindred, and a high degree of public spirit characterized the people. A town or community which is commercial is always characterized by more public spirit than manufacturing or industrial centers. The school was ever the pride of the town, and contributed greatly to the honor of the community. In Warren the college had been organized in 1764.

The seminary was organized in 1834, May 7, and nearly all the membership of the school for that year was from Warren. The whole number of students was 75, and of these but 12 were from other towns. The following were the instructors: Robert A. Coffin, principal and teacher in the classical and philosophical departments; Mrs. Coffin, teacher of drawing, painting, and ornamental needlework; Miss Mary Ann Reed, teacher in the historical and descriptive department; Miss Julia Ann Arms, teacher of French and mathematics; Miss Adeline Croode, teacher of music.

Mr. Coffin was a good teacher, and Miss Reed was for a long period connected with the school, proving herself a most excellent and popular teacher.

There were 5 proprietors of the school, and a board of visitors, of 7 members.

As this was one of the early boarding schools for girls and the only school of the kind at that period in Rhode Island, the prospectus, taken from the first catalogue is of interest.

"A building has been prepared for the accommodation of the school containing a large hall, recitation rooms, lecture room, chemical laboratory, together with the usual accommodations for a family and nine students.

"The course of study is intended to be systematic, liberal, and thorough; systematic, based on the laws of the human mind; liberal, giving access to varied sources of knowledge and aiming at the development and improvement of all the mental powers; and at thorough training of the mind to habits of careful investigation, accurate reasoning, and patient, persevering research. The recitations are not the mechanical repetition of a set of words previously committed to memory, but the free expression of thought and feeling on the part of both teachers and scholars. Nor are the pupils confined to the lessons contained in their books. They are encouraged to seek for knowledge in the operations of nature and in the exhibitions of human character, and to apply the principles of science to the occurrences of life. The religious influence exerted in the school is intended to be positive and efficient, but not sectarian.

"The regular course of instruction in the English branches is intended to occupy three years. Before entering on the course, it is expected that ladies will be acquainted with the first principles of grammar and arithmetic and with some system of geography. There are in each year three terms of study, consisting of fifteen weeks each."

COURSE OF STUDY.

First year.

First term.—Smith's Arithmetic, Malte Brun Geography, Parley's First Book of History.

Second term.—Arithmetic continued, Second Book of History, Mason on Self Knowledge.

Third term.—Lincoln's Botany or Good's Book of Nature, Book of Commerce, Grund's Geometry.

Exercises through the year in reading, spelling, definition, grammar, and composition.

Second year.

First term.—Legendre's geometry, ancient history, Dillaway's mythology, Watts on the Mind.

Second term.—Legendre continued, Comstock's natural philosophy, Whatley's Logic.

Third term.—Ecclesiastical history, Comstock's chemistry, Newman's rhetoric.

Exercises through the year in reading, grammar, and composition.

Third year.

First term.—Vose's astronomy, political class book, Abercrombie's intellectual philosophy.

Second term.—Bailey's algebra, Paley's natural theology, McIlvaine's Evidences of Christianity.

Third term.—Algebra continued, Eaton's geology, Parkhurst's moral philosophy.

To those who wish for a more extended course than the above, instruction will be given in either or all of the following branches: Campbell's philosophy of rhetoric, Cheever's Studies in Poetry, Gambier's Moral Evidence, Smellie's philosophy of natural history, logarithms, trigonometry, practical astronomy, the Latin, Greek, and

French languages, drawing, painting, ornamental needlework, and music on the piano.

The seminary is furnished with apparatus for illustrating the principles of natural philosophy, astronomy, and chemistry; and lectures on these subjects are given every term. In the spring lectures are given on school-keeping. Occasionally lectures are given on other subjects. A course of 24 lessons in penmanship is given every term without any extra charge.

Prices of tuition.

	Per term.
Reading, grammar, geography, and arithmetic	$3.75
Other branches in the regular course	5.00
Languages and English studies in the extra course, extra charges	7.50
Lectures	1.00
Drawing and painting	3.00
Ornamental needlework	1.00
Calisthenics	1.00
Music	10.00
Use of piano	3.00

Price of board $1.50 per week, or $1.75, washing included. Fuel and light extra.

The parents and guardians of the pupils, and others who are interested in the cause of female education, are invited to visit the institution whenever they may find it convenient. The arrangements are such that frequent visits will cause no interruption in the school and no deviation from the usual course of instruction.[1]

The catalogue of the year 1836 shows a membership of 116, of which 44 were pursuing the regular course of three years. A larger proportion of students were coming from neighboring States, particularly from Massachusetts. Three came from Vermont and 2 from Georgia. The boarding house in connection with the seminary had accommodations for 30. For the year 1838, 94 students were enrolled, with representatives from 3 different Southern States. Southerners were induced to place their daughters in the school because their sons were at the college in Providence, only a few miles distant, and because the school was attracting attention by the excellence of its courses. Till 1842, when there was a change in the management of the school, caused by the incorporation of the governing board and other alterations, the successors to Mr. Coffin had been the Rev. Josiah P. Tustin, D. D., of Philadelphia, and Rev. John C. Stockbridge, of Providence.

In 1842 a change was made in the school. The school property, which was owned by Shubael P. Child, Henry H. Luther, John Luther, and Jeremiah Williams, was capitalized by them and offered in 30 shares at $200 each. Those who took the shares, and the original proprietors, became the guardians and trustees. It was considered wise for the best interests of the school that the institution should be incorporated. Accordingly, in 1845, a charter was received from the legislature, and in November of the same year, under its provisions, the permanent organization was effected. Shubael P. Child, president; Henry H.

---

[1] Catalogue of the Warren Ladies' Seminary, 1834.

Luther, vice-president; Charles Randall, treasurer; Thomas G. Turner, secretary.

The board of directors consisted of Otis Bullock, G. M. Fessenden, Josiah P. Tustin, Samuel Hunt, John Norris, William H. Church, and A. M. Gammell.

In 1842 A. M. Gammell was the principal, with five assistants. The school grew and acquired a reputation in the immediate vicinity, and also in New England. Girls were not received under 15 years of age, and some were at the school who were well advanced in the twenties. For the year 1845 the catalogue shows the membership of the school to be 120; 1846, 154; 1847, 172; 1848, 149; 1850, 132; 1851, 148; 1853, 125; 1855, 185; 1857, 114. In 1855 there were representatives in the school from New York, Georgia, Massachusetts, Illinois, Ohio, Maine, Connecticut, Nova Scotia, New Jersey, Pennsylvania, Florida, and Indiana. The funds which had been secured from the sale of shares in 1845 were devoted to additions to the building. In 1855 and 1856 it was clearly evident from the increasing patronage that the accommodations were too limited. In the next year there was an issue of 20 shares, at $200 each. These were chiefly taken by the principal, Mr. Gammell. The avails of this new issue were also devoted to the enlargement of the building. There was one more issue of 15 shares, not all of which were taken. The total number of certificates was 60.

The seminary continued to prosper, but in 1857, during the vacation, the buildings were burned. There was an attempt to revive the institution, but the loss of the buildings was a blow from which it did not recover. The faculty for the last year of the seminary consisted of 9 instructors and 2 matrons. The board, including washing, fuel, lights, and tuition in the English branches, including lectures, vocal music, and calisthenics, was $175 for the academic year of forty-two weeks.

The catalogue for the same year was called an "historic catalogue," because it contained the names of all the instructors and pupils from its establishment in May, 1834, to July, 1856. The instructors and matrons were 60, and the pupils 1,259. This number did not represent all the pupils who received instruction, as appears from the report of the board of directors to the board of trustees, where it was stated that more than 1,500 received "the elements, and many of them the accomplishments, of a finished education."

The school was also instrumental in contributing to the prosperity of Warren and thus to the State. As has been stated, the townspeople were, very many of them, related, and many of them followed the sea. Wherever they might go they could speak well of the school. Such, doubtless, was true in the case of students who came from Havana and Matanzas. The commencements and public exercises always drew many people to the town, and the Baptist church, where the exercises were held, was crowded. The institution was in touch with the college, for some of the faculty were on the board of examiners and were also lecturers in special subjects.

This seminary at Warren was an important factor in the education of women. A great many of the students were preparing themselves to teach, and had their training here. The normal school was not established till 1854, so that in a measure, its lack was supplied. The reputation which the seminary had for its instruction enabled many of the graduates to obtain positions as teachers, and thus to transmit methods which had been employed so successfully there. The sphere of its influence was a wide one, for nearly all the States were represented among the students. Many came from the South, because there were few such schools there, and because in many cases their relatives were at the college in Providence.

With an able corps of instructors possessing the confidence and best wishes of the townspeople, and furnishing a truly liberal education for the young ladies of the day, the Warren Ladies' Seminary is justly entitled to an honorable position in the history of education for women.

NORMAL SCHOOL.

This school has furnished a good indication of the public opinion regarding advanced and improved ideas in education in this State. The history of normal schools in the United States may be traced to the early part of this century.

On the 2d of July, 1839, Mr. Mann wrote in his diary:

> To-morrow we go to Lexington to launch the first normal school on this side of the Atlantic. I can not indulge in an expression of the train of thought which the contemplation of this event awakens in my mind. Much must come of it, either of good or of ill. I am sanguine in my faith that it will be the former. But the good will not come of itself. That is the reward of effort, of toil, of wisdom.

The next day he records:

> Only three persons presented themselves for examination. In point of numbers this is not a promising commencement. What remains but more exertion, more and more, until it must succeed?

What Horace Mann did for education in Massachusetts, Henry Barnard did for Rhode Island. Said he:

> I have aimed everywhere to set forth the nature, necessity, and probable results of a normal school, so as to prepare the public mind for some legislative action toward the establishment of one such school.

After his election as school commissioner, in the school act which was prepared by him he inserted this clause:

> To establish one thoroughly organized normal school in the State, where teachers and such as propose to teach may become acquainted with the most approved and successful methods of arranging the studies and conducting the discipline and instruction of the public schools.

Accordingly he used all his influence toward arousing public interest in favor of a normal school. He organized conventions and associations of teachers and delivered lectures. He used the columns of the daily papers and issued numerous pamphlets which were distributed among the people.

In 1845 a bill consolidating the various educational provisions was passed by the assembly. This included the establishment of one normal school. The act was passed, but it was unavailing, because no appropriation was made. The friends of such a school did all in their power to keep the question before the public, but nothing was done till 1850. That year the university was reorganized, and it was announced that there would be a normal department or a professorship of didactics. Samuel S. Greene, who was the city superintendent of schools, was chosen to this professorship. Good work was done, but the public needs were not met, because the instruction was not sufficiently popular. To meet this demand the normal school was opened on October 24, 1852, by Prof. Greene as a private school. He had three assistants, among them Dana P. Colburn. The first normal classes were held in the old Providence High School building, which is now the permanent home of the normal school. The school now was so successfully established that public sentiment in favor of securing its permanency was such as to induce the school committee to pass this resolution:

Resolved, That, in the opinion of this committee, the time has arrived when a normal school for the education of teachers should be added to our system of public instruction, and that it be recommended to the city council to establish such a school, either separately, for the exclusive benefit of the city, or in connection with the government of the State of Rhode Island, for the joint benefit of the city and the State, as in their wisdom they may deem best.

The school was continued by Prof. Greene through April, 1854.

In accordance with the above resolution, appropriations were made and measures taken to reorganize the school. Prof. Greene was fully occupied at the university, so Dana P. Colburn was chosen principal, at a salary of $1,200. Thus, after nine years, did the work which was inaugurated by the wisdom of Mr. Barnard find realization.

A notable event of this period was the holding of a special session of the school, beginning April 7, 1856, and continuing for three weeks. "It was attended," says Mr. Colburn, "by nearly 150 teachers, and is believed to have been in a high degree successful." Of the gentlemen who gave instruction and lectures are found the names of Rev. Robert Allyn, who succeeded Mr. Potter as commissioner in 1854; Mr. Barnard, Rev. Dr. Barnas Sears, then president of Brown University, Profs. Alexis Caswell, Robinson P. Dunn, James B. Angell, George I. Chace, William Gammell, and Albert Harkness; Rev. Dr. Edward B. Hall, Rev. George T. Day, Rev. E. M. Stone, Rev. Thomas H. Vail, Rev. John Boyden, Rev. Dr. S. A. Crane, Rev. T. D. Cook, Hon. Welcome B. Sayles, Gen. Joseph S. Pitman, and Mr. Levi W. Russell.

In 1857 there was a proposition made on the part of Bristol that the school be removed from Providence to that town. This offer would relieve the State from the expense of the school. The proposal was accepted. There had been some dissatisfaction that the State treasury should bear so much of the expense, and it was thought by others that a change was necessary for the greater success of the school. In May, 1857, the normal school was incorporated, and its removal to Bristol approved. Mr. Colburn was still in charge, and to him was due, in a large measure, the success of the school. Two years after the removal of the school Mr. Colburn died. He had been well known among teachers and all the friends of public education in New England. His biographer said:

> There can be no doubt that the great work of Mr. Colburn's life was his instruction in normal schools. For ten years he consecrated to this vocation his ripest powers of mind and heart, and by his success in it the value of his brief life must be estimated. The normal school was his workshop, whence emanated his most positive influence on the surrounding world and where his loss will be longest felt.

The death of Mr. Colburn was a heavy blow to the school. In addition the next few years brought the confusion and uncertainty of the civil war. The location of the school at Bristol, a small town, was prejudicial to its growth. The academic staff of the school was good and the exertions made by the faculty were scholarly and able, but of no avail. In 1865, at the close of the spring term, the school adjourned for a period of five weeks, and in July the trustees suspended it indefinitely. The next five years were a period of trial and suspense for the friends of the school. An act was passed in 1866 to provide instruction in the special preparation of teachers. Accordingly nearly 150 were trained at the Providence Conference Seminary in East Greenwich and at the Lapham Institute in Scituate. The expense to the State was nearly $2,500.

But the need of a normal school was just as imperative as ever, and extracts from the educational reports from the various towns for the year 1869 show that the schools were sadly crippled in their efforts, because there was an insufficiency of trained teachers. In that same year Thomas W. Bicknell was appointed commissioner of education. He fully realized the need of a training school for teachers. The methods he used were on the same general plan as those employed by Mr. Barnard. The Rhode Island Schoolmaster, the educational paper of the State, was suspended in 1868, but Mr. Bicknell revived it. He also began the organization of teachers' institutes and educational lectures for the public. The efforts of his predecessors had not lost their effect, and as a result of the new interest the board of education and the commissioner were made trustees. An appropriation of $10,000 was voted. The opening exercises were held in September, 1871. One hundred and fifty applicants for admission presented themselves, and certificates were given to 106. Before the end of that year the number of students was 115, of whom 8 were young men. Prof. James C. Greenough was principal.

Among the last important links in the history of the school was the appropriation of $40,000 by the May session of the legislature in 1877 to provide a permanent home for the school. The old high school estate was secured, and is now the home of the normal school. Since the reorganization the normal school has maintained its standard and has held its rank at the head of the public-school system of the State.

The account of this school has been inserted under the chapter of education for women, because the personnel of the school is almost entirely of women.

PART IV.
BROWN UNIVERSITY.

The university now bearing the name Brown University is the only one which has had more than a chartered existence. It was founded in Warren in 1764, and its original name was Rhode Island College. This change was made in accordance with a provision in the charter, to the effect that at any time thereafter a more particular name in honor of the greatest and most distinguished benefactor might be given. Built by the self-sacrifice and personal exertions of the founders, with the exception of a few years during the revolution, its existence has been uninterrupted, although its history has been varied. It has had periods of prosperity and periods when the friends of the university trembled and anxiously awaited the outcome; but the very storms have served but to strengthen the university in the principles of a worthy endurance.

The graduates of Brown are in every station in life, and gratefully acknowledge their debt of gratitude to those who taught and guided them in their university career. Brown has been fortunate in the good and noble men who have shaped its policy and assisted at its councils. The names of Manning, Wayland, Sears, Caswell, Dunn, Diman, and Gammell will recall men whose lives were consecrated to the highest good of their fellows. The influence of such men is more than local; it lives in the lives of the students who came in contact with it, and the whole world of letters is better for the lives of these Christian scholars. In a smaller college the student has an advantage in that he can come in contact with professors during nearly all his course.

The location of Brown in Providence, the largest city in the State, has given the university prominence, and it has availed itself of the opportunity for making its influence felt in the community. The leading men of the university have been characterized by a public spirit, which has led them to respond to the call of the municipality or of the State. Not only at home but also abroad the academic staff have won distinguished merit and recognition by their public services. Brown University, which is already in possession of an honorable past, is now girding itself for still greater usefulness in the future. The period now opening with the academic year of 1894, is one of greater prosperity than that of any preceding, and the policy of the present administration is so shaping itself that this opportunity may be utilized to the utmost.

PRESIDENT MANNING, 1764-1791.

Those who write the history of the institutions of learning of the last two centuries must go behind the final movements which resulted in the establishment of the college or academy. The political and social environment of the leaders must be closely studied, for they were men of strong personality. Those who came to the front were characterized by broad views, except in some cases where there was a denominational bias. The relation between church and state was close, and the civic leader needed the ecclesiastical aid. The man who in its beginning may be said to have been the college was James Manning. If some of the later administrators are entitled to be called saviors of their college, to him belongs the title of father of the college. With him the college was ever present; whether in the halls of the colonial or of the State legislature; in all, either public or private, he was ever planning how he might best promote the interests of Rhode Island College. The biography of Manning in his later years is the story of the institution, so closely was he identified with it. The history of the foundation reflects his life.

OBJECT OF THE COLLEGE.

The first president of Rhode Island College, afterwards Brown University, was James Manning. The design of the college originated with the Philadelphia Baptist Association, and they decided to place it in Rhode Island. Manning, who had been selected by the association as its agent in the matter, came to Rhode Island and began the establishment of a college. The Baptists, then a small denomination, felt the need of an institution where their youth could be trained in their belief. There was the academy at Hopewell, N. J., a preparatory school, but the denomination desired a college.

Among the early documents of the university is one which states the very object of the institution. In order to explain this document, the account of the change of location must be very briefly anticipated. The first location was at Warren, in 1764; six years later, after much discussion, the university was removed to Providence. A movement was at once started by those who had wished the location to be at Newport, to secure a charter for a new college at that town. The corporation of Rhode Island College at once decided to petition the general assembly for the rejection of the new charter. A memorial was prepared and a committee chosen to present it in the assembly. This document will clearly show the reason for the establishment of the college.

To the honorable the general assembly of the colony of Rhode Island, to sit at Newport on the first Wednesday in May, 1770.

The remonstrance of the trustees and fellows of the corporation of the college in said colonies humbly showeth—

That the several denominations of Baptists residing in most of the British northern colonies are, taken collectively, a considerable body of Christians; and these people having of late years taken into consideration that there are no public seminaries for the education of youth where those of that persuasion can enjoy equal freedom and advantages with others, were thereby induced to form a resolution to erect a college and institute a seminary for the education of youth somewhere in North America, to be effected chiefly, if not. altogether, by the application and at the cost and expense of the Baptist churches. That, having proceeded thus far, they began to inquire after the most convenient place for executing their design, and on deliberation, finding that the colony of Rhode Island was settled chiefly by Baptists, that a very considerable part of the inhabitants are still of that persuasion, and that a universal toleration of liberty of conscience hath from the beginning taken place in it, they had great hope it would prove a proper place for founding a college, and in which the infant institution might be most encouraged; and accordingly they applied to the general assembly of said colony for a charter of incorporation, which they thankfully acknowledge was freely granted them.

That in forming this charter care was taken that, notwithstanding the burden of expense was to fall chiefly on the Baptists, yet no other Christian society should be excluded from the benefits of it, and, accordingly, a sufficient number from each of the principal of them was taken in to be trustees and fellows in the corporation as might be able to take care of and guard their interest in it in all time to come. And the youth of every denomination of Christians are fully entitled to and actually enjoy equal advantages in every respect as the Baptists themselves, without being burdened with any religious test or complaint whatsoever.[1]

SKETCH OF JAMES MANNING.

James Manning was born in Elizabethtown, N. J., October 22, 1738. His father was a farmer. Of his mother it was said " she exemplified in her daily life the happy and sanctifying influences of the Christian religion." In later years Manning was said to have preeminently good sense, and there is no doubt but that he owed much of it to his home training. Of his schoolboy days but little is known. Said the editor of his published letters: " I have not found in the whole series of letters one misspelled word." That fact indicates some degree of diligence and application in the elementary education which he received. He entered a preparatory school at Hopewell, where an academy had been opened " for the education of youth for the ministry." At the age of 20 he was admitted to membership in the freshman class of the College of New Jersey. The information with reference to his college days is meager, but he is said to have been characterized by diligence and devotion to his studies. He excelled in rhetoric, eloquence, moral philosophy, and the classics. He was also fond of athletics. He was graduated with the second honor in a class of 21. Shortly after graduation Manning made preparation to enter upon the ministry, the profession which was to be his life work. In the sketch of the early days of the college the preliminary steps in its establishment were described. Manning, after graduation, had made a tour through the southern colonies and had come to Rhode Island to found a college. From his account of the college, which he never completed, it is seen

---
[1] History of Brown University from Illustrative Documents. R. A. Guild. Pp. 205, 206.

that he was very prominent in the work of organization. The charter was secured in February, 1764, but no home for the college had been provided. It seemed desirable that the location should be in some place where the president could preach, in addition to the work of instruction. The two churches in Newport had competent preachers and there were reasons why a settlement at Providence was undesirable at that time. In April of the same year Manning removed with his family to Warren, where he opened a Latin school, preliminary to collegiate instruction. This Latin school founded by him has continued till the present time, and is known as the University Grammar School. Manning at the second meeting of the corporation held in Newport, September, 1765, was elected "president of the college, professor of languages and other branches of learning, with full power to act in these capacities at Warren, or elsewhere."

Manning from the very beginning of his connection with the college had its welfare deeply at heart. He knew nothing which was paramount to the state of religion in the country and Rhode Island College. The details of his life henceforth are so closely identified with the phases and crisis of the college that they will be given in their appropriate place.

CORRESPONDENCE.

Manning was an active correspondent with all whom he thought could assist the college. In nearly all of his letters, in some way or other, he makes reference to the needs of the college. In one letter to Rev. John Ryland, of England, he says:

> What think you of an application to England, by some suitable person, in order to augment our little and insufficient fund, as Mr. Edwards made but a partial application; or would a well-concerted scheme of a lottery to raise £1,000 or £2,000 meet with encouragement by the sale of tickets in England?

The reply to this part of the letter is as follows:

> As to raising money by a lottery, I dislike it from the bottom of my heart. 'Tis a scheme dishonorable to the supreme head of all worlds and of every true church. We have our fill of these cursed gambling lotteries in London every year. They are big with ten thousand evils. Let the devil's children have them all to themselves. Let us not touch or taste.

In justice to the sentiments of Manning on the subject of lotteries he continues to the same friend in reply:

> Your opinion of lotteries coincides with mine; but some of our friends urged me to mention the subject, as they could not see a prospect of supplies in any other way. Besides, I believe there have not been such iniquitous methods used in this matter with us as in the State lotteries at home. They have been used to promote good designs.

In another letter to a friend in England he says:

> Do you think it would be worth while for an American Indian, as we are generally deemed, to visit England on the errand of collecting some more money for our college?

BROWN UNIVERSITY—FRONT CAMPUS.

A list of "worthy men of learning and character who desire the honors of Rhode Island College" in England had been sent to Manning. Before honoring them thus it was the wish of the faculty to know if they had been consulted personally, and if they desired the honors, otherwise they feared the bestowal of the honor would do the college harm. Manning, who had conducted the correspondence, was informed in reply by Ryland:

> For me to ask any of those gentlemen I nominated in my letter whether he would please to accept a degree from your college would spoil all the honor and delicacy of conferring it. Its coming *unsought*, yea *unthought* of, constitutes its chief excellence and acceptableness to men of fine feelings. For my own part I would not have given you a single farthing, or so much as a thanks, for a feather if I had it not in my power with the utmost truth to say, "I neither sought it nor bought it, nor thought for a moment about it."

Letters of acceptance of gifts to the college, urging its claims on the friends of the denominations, notes of condolence, and letters discussing mooted points in theology occur at frequent intervals till 1779, when Manning left the city for awhile to visit his friends. From the wide range of topics which came under discussion his ability and devotion to the college were recognized.

FUNDS AND LOCATION OF THE COLLEGE.

The charter had been secured for the new college and James Manning had been chosen to the presidency. The college opened with one student. Although there was but this one college in the State, it was practically in charge of a single denomination. The charter was such that other denominations were to be represented, but the management was vested in the Baptists. When the question arose how funds were to be raised, the corporation naturally looked to their own denomination, not only in this country, but in Europe. Among the friends of the college in its immediate neighborhood, the sum of a trifle more than $1,000 was raised. The corporation furnished credentials to the Rev. Morgan Edwards, who offered to go to England and Ireland, in order to see what could be done there for the seminary. Wales was his native country, but he had received his education in Ireland. He had the indorsement of many of the clergy of his denomination, and from the assistance of friends of the cause raised $4,500. Writing from London to President Manning he says:

> If I were to stay in London ever so long I believe I should get money, but it comes so slowly and by such small sums that I can not spare the time. However, I may depend on the friendship of two or three when I leave the Kingdom, who have promised to solicit for us, and do not doubt but what they will do more than I shall be able to accomplish, as they may watch convenient seasons. There have been no less than six cases of charity pushed about this winter, viz: Two from Germany, two from the country of England, and two from America. The unwearied beneficence of the city of London is amazing

At the South, by vote of the corporation, Rev. Hezekiah Smith was empowered to solicit subscriptions. He was absent from home a little

1123 R I——7

more than eight months, and traveled through Georgia and South Carolina. The friends in these provinces came to the help of the cause he pleaded and he reported to the corporation the sum of $2,500. The funds raised by Edwards were devoted to an income for meeting the salary of the president, and those raised by Smith were devoted to building purposes. In the South these subscriptions ranged from £100 to 10 shillings, and represented a large number of subscribers, but were not sufficient to sustain the college. Before steps could be taken to raise more money, another question arose. This was a point involving the location of the college, whether it should remain at Warren, or be removed to some other part of the State.

Morgan Edwards, one of the early chroniclers of the college writes:

> To the year 1769 this seminary was for the most part friendless and moneyless, and therefore forlorn, in so much that a college edifice was hardly to be thought of. But Mr. Edwards making remittances from England, some began to hope, and many to fear that the institution would come to something and stand. Then a building and a place for it were talked of, which opened a new scene of troubles and contentions that had well-nigh ruined all. Warren was at first agreed upon as a proper situation, where a small wing was to be erected in the spring of 1770, and about £800 raised towards it. But soon afterwards some who were unwilling it should be there, and some who were unwilling it should be anywhere, did so far agree as to lay aside the said location and propose that the county which should raise most money should have the college. Then the four counties went to work with subscriptions.

The four counties were Bristol, Kent, Newport, and Providence, although at the outset the contest lay between Warren and East Greenwich.

At the annual meeting held for the first time in Warren, a committee of four, with the president, reported that the college be located in some part of the county of Bristol, and it was so voted. Soon after that meeting a notice appeared in the Providence and Newport paper that—

> Application has been made by the gentlemen of Kent County setting forth that they have opened a subscription for founding and endowing said college, on condition that the edifice be erected in the county of Kent; and desiring an opportunity for assigning their reasons to the corporation for a reconsideration of their vote at their last meeting, for erecting the edifice in the county of Bristol. The meeting of the corporation was called to meet at Newport November 14, 1769, at which time and place the gentlemen concerned in securing subscriptions for the different places are desired, by themselves or their committees, to appear, present their several subscriptions, and offer their reasons in favor of the respective places.

This notice at once brought the matter under discussion again. Moses Brown appears to have been the first to suggest that the college be located in Providence. At the meeting of the corporation memorials were presented from the towns that were striving to secure the prize. How far their zeal was influenced by a desire to secure the best welfare of the institution can not be determined. The arguments, however, are interesting. In the memorial from Providence the following were alleged as reasons why the college should be placed there:

> First, that it is absolutely necessary that there be money enough collected for erecting the college edifice and other buildings. Sensible of this the inhabitants

we represent generously subscribed £800, upon principles of regard and esteem for so useful and necessary an institution.

The principal benefit to a college is the number of students, which may rationally be supposed to be greater at Providence than at either of the other places proposed. Reference was made to the catholicity and liberality of the charter and the argument advanced that students of various denominations could find churches of their own order at Providence.

There was also the central situation, the free, cheap, and easy communication between the northern colonies and the several towns in this and the neighboring governments. To this may be added the greater plenty and cheapness of all kinds of provision, fuel, clothing, and cheapness of board.

The ease and convenience with which parents may visit their children to see their proficiency, as well as in case of sickness or accidents, where the best physicians and remedies are at hand. * * *

We have a public library which, in the infant state of the seminary, must be very useful to all the scholars, and particularly for those who may incline to the study of law or physic (either before the first or between that and their second degree). We have not only large and useful libraries in both these faculties, but gentlemen of eminence, who would be very useful in the prosecution of such studies.

We have two printing offices, which will much contribute to the emoluments of the college, there being thus published a weekly collection of interesting intelligence, which not only tends to the enlargement of the minds of the youth, but which will give them early opportunities of displaying their genius upon any and useful subjects, and which must excite in them an emulation to excel in their studies.

In the memorial from East Greenwich:

The county of Kent is the most proper place for erecting said college edifice.

First. It is situated nearly in the center of the colony. This will more effectually accommodate each respective county, and therefore if the corporation should ever petition for the aid and assistance of government, it is more probable they will unite in forwarding and promoting such grants.

Secondly. The local subscriptions of Kent, united with the several general subscriptions, are sufficient to build and complete said college, and those temporary subscriptions will be found altogether insufficient for keeping up and perpetuating the institutional expenses. * * *

Thirdly. As institutions of this kind have been found by experience not to prosper in popular towns, we think the town of Providence too large now in its present condition. As it is a place well calculated for trade, it is altogether reasonable from thence to conclude that the growth and enlargement of it in a very few years will render it quite unsuitable for seminaries of learning to be placed in. The town of East Greenwich, on the contrary, is well situated as to pleasantness, the town being large enough to accommodate the students effectually, and situated upon the post road, so that an easy correspondence might be had with any part of the continent, there being likewise a post-office in town, and every other advantage as to communication with other governments that Providence can urge.

Furthermore, as it has been strongly argued, this institution is founded upon the most Catholic plan, therefore they say they have singular advantages over Kent as to the accommodations of the different religious denominations. In answer to this we can say, in behalf of Kent, we have a Friends' and a Baptist meeting house nearly situated to the place where the college is proposed to be set; also a meeting-house of the Separates within 3 miles of East Greenwich, upon a good road, free from ferries; and it is highly probable, if the college is fixed at Kent, there will be a church and a Presbyterian meeting house built soon.

From Newport these claims were urged:

From the smallness of the college funds it is certain that the principal and surest support must arise from the number of students; and whoever considers the number of inhabitants in Newport, the reputation of the island for health and pleasantness, the easy communication we have with all parts of this government, and with the Western and Southern colonies, and the cheapness with which pupils may be boarded, must confess that no place in this colony is so proper to fix the college in, nor so likely to afford a sufficient number of students, as this town of Newport.

Besides, a considerable advantage may be derived to the professors and students from the library (The Redwood) in this town. A library calculated for men of learning, consisting of a great number of well-chosen books upon all arts and sciences, as well as a very great number in the learned languages, the use of which may be allow'd the pupils, under the discreet care of the president and tutors. This, in the infant state of the college, must be allowed to have great weight.

Such was the tone and such were the arguments used by the memorialists, although the memorials have not been given in full. In the light of the present day the arguments urged, in some cases appear amusing, but the different claimants were all in earnest to secure the location. The meeting called for November 14, 1769, continued three days. Wednesday morning it was resolved:

To recede from the vote of the last meeting to erect the college edifice in the town of Bristol.

In the afternoon it was voted:

That the business of the corporation be not postponed to a distant adjournment.

Thursday morning it was resolved:

That the place for erecting the college be now fixed. But that, nevertheless, the committee, who shall be appointed to carry on the building, do not proceed to procure any other materials for the same, excepting such as may be easily transported to any other place, should another hereafter be thought better, until further orders from this corporation, if such orders be given before the 1st of January next; and that in case any subscription be raised in the county of Newport, or any other county, equal or superior to any now offered, or that shall then be offered, and the corporation be called in consequence thereof, that then the vote for fixing the edifice shall not be esteemed binding, but so that the corporation may fix the edifice in another place in case they shall think proper.

The last meeting of the corporation to decide the question of location was held at Warren, February 7, 1770. Says Manning in one of his letters:

The dispute lasted from Wednesday last, 10 o'clock a. m., until the same hour on Thursday p. m. The matter was debated with great spirit and before a crowded audience. The vote was put, recede or not. It went not, by 21 against 14. In the course of the debates there was sometimes undue warmth, but upon the whole it subsided, and all parties seemed much more unanimous than I expected in after business. Many of the gentlemen of Newport said they had had a fair hearing and had lost it; but their friendship to the college remained, and they would keep their places, pay their money, and forward to their utmost the design.

Thus ended the controversy, and the location was decided in favor of Providence. A petition was made to the assembly for a charter for a college in Newport. It was favorably received in the house, but indefinitely postponed by the Senate.

FIRST COMMENCEMENT.

The historian Arnold wrote of the first commencement, September, 1769:

> Four years had elapsed since the college at Warren was organized, and the graduating exercises of commencement day now opened a new era and established the earliest State holiday in the history of Rhode Island. It was a great occasion for the people of the colony, and as each recurring anniversary of this time-honored institution of learning calls together from distant places the widely scattered alumni of Brown University we do but renew on a more extended scale the congratulations that crowned this earliest festival of Rhode Island college. The first graduating class consisted of 7 members, some of whom were destined to fill conspicuous places in the approaching struggle for independence. It was noticed as a significant fact that all who participated in the event of the day, from the president to the candidates, were clothed in American manufactures.[1]

The members of the class were Charles Thompson, valedictorian, and afterwards a chaplain in the Revolutionary army; Richard Stiles, salutatorian; Joseph Belton, Joseph Eaton, William Williams, William Rogers, afterwards a chaplain in the Revolutionary army, and James Mitchell Varnum, afterwards a brigadier-general in the Revolution, an eloquent member of Congress from Rhode Island, and finally judge of the Northwestern territory. From 1 pupil (William Rogers) at the

---

[1] Contrast with the above, the following account of the commencement of June, 1878, by Prof. Diman:

Among the great festivals which break the rapid and unending round of the seasons there is none that brings with it the peculiar associations which belong to that which we celebrate to-day. There are others more closely connected with household memories, or with the great events of ecclesiastical or civil life; but commencement calls back the buoyant feelings of the early days when hope was bright and when aspiration was high, and the long procession with which it fills our streets, lead by the alert and eager step of youth and closed with the tottering steps of age, is a solemn panorama of human history. There are other processions which have more to attract the attention of the crowd, but there is none more impressive to a thoughtful observer. Year by year for more than a century it has pursued its accustomed route; each year some familiar form is missing from it, yet each year the vacant places are filled and it grows larger and larger with the sturdy growth of the ancient university, each season bringing its new accessions, one day in turn to become gray-haired and pass away. We can not but think that some wholesome lessons are conveyed by such a spectacle, and that few can walk to-day in this long line, in which successive generations are thus represented, without having reflections tinged with a more sober coloring. It must be a benefit once a year to turn aside from the accustomed associations, which so often are centered in selfish and limited aims, and which, when eagerly pursued, so often withdraw us from a wide sympathy with our fellows, and revive the generous aspirations of youth and renew the cordial fellowship which is the distinctive note of a liberal culture. It is easy to understand the feeling which restrained many, especially the older graduates, from taking part in this annual academic festivity. The thinned ranks of the classes that close the procession mingle a bitter drop in the joy with which the survivors greet each other. Yet we can not but think that they act more wisely who keep green in old age the recollections of youth, and who once a year make themselves young again among their old college classmates.

opening of the college, it had grown to the number of 7 at graduation. From the daily paper is taken the order of exercises:

1. The salutatory oration. Richard Stiles.
2. The Americans, in their present circumstances, can not consistent with good policy affect to become an independent state; a forensic dispute. James M. Varnum and William Williams.
3. An oration on benevolence. William Rogers.
4. Materia cogitare non potest. A syllogistic disputation in Latin. William Williams, Joseph Belton, Joseph Eaton, William Rogers, James M. Varnum.
5. The oratorial art; an oration with the valedictory addresses. Charles Thompson.

The following account of the first commencement appeared in the Providence Gazette and County Journal:

On Thursday, the 7th instant, was celebrated at Warren the first commencement in the college of this colony. About 10 o'clock a. m. the gentlemen concerned in conducting the affairs of the college, together with the candidates, went in procession to the meetinghouse. After they had taken their seats, respectively, and the audience were composed the president introduced the business of the day with prayer. Then followed a salutatory oration in Latin, pronounced with much spirit, by Mr. Stiles, which procured him great applause from the learned part of the assembly. He spoke upon the advantages of liberty and learning and their mutual dependence upon each other, concluding with proper salutations to the chancellor of the college, governor of the colony, etc., particularly expressing the gratitude of all the friends of the college to the Rev. Morgan Edwards, who has encountered many difficulties in going to Europe to collect donations for the institution and has lately returned.

To which succeeded a forensic dispute, in English, on the following thesis, namely: "The Americans, in their present circumstances, can not, consistent with good policy, affect to become an independent State." Mr. Varnum ingenuously defended it by cogent arguments handsomely dressed, though ho was subtly but delicately opposed by Mr. Williams, both of whom spoke with emphasis and propriety. As a conclusion to the exercises of the forenoon the audience were agreeably entertained with an oration on benevolence by Mr. Rogers, in which, among many other pertinent observations, he particularly noticed the necessity which that infant seminary stands in of the salutary effects of that truly Christian virtue.

At 3 o'clock p. m., the audience being convened, a syllogistic dispute was introduced on this thesis: "Materia cogitare non potest"—Mr. Williams the respondent; Messrs. Belton, Eaton, Rogers, and Varnum the opponents—in the course of which dispute the principal arguments on both sides were produced toward settling that critical point. The degree of bachelor of arts was then conferred on the candidates.

A concise, pertinent, and solemn charge was then given to the bachelors by the president, concluding with his last paternal benediction, which naturally introduced the valedictory orator, Mr. Thompson, who, after some remarks upon the excellence of the oratorical art and expressions of gratitude to the patrons and officers of the college, together with a valediction to them and all present, took a most affectionary leave of his classmates. The scene was tender, the subject felt, and the audience affected.

The president concluded the exercises with prayer. The whole was concluded with a propriety and solemnity suitable to the occasion. The audience (consisting of the principal gentlemen and ladies of this colony and many from the neighboring governments), though large and crowded, behaved with the utmost decorum. In the evening Rev. Morgan Edwards, by particular request, preached a sermon, especially addressed to the graduates and students, from Phil. III: 8 : "Yea, doubtless, and I count all things but loss for the excellency of the knowledge of Christ Jesus my Lord," in which (after high encomiums on the liberal arts and sciences,) the superior knowledge of Christ, or the Christian science, was clearly and fully illustrated in several striking examples and similes, one of which follows: "When the sun is below the horizon the stars excel in glory; but when his orb irradiates our hemisphere their glory dwindles, fades away, and disappears."

Not only the candidates, but even the president were dressed in American manufactures. Finally, be it observed that this class are the first sons of that college which has existed for more that four years, during all which time it has labored under great disadvantages, notwithstanding the warm patronage and encouragement of many worthy men of fortune and benevolence, and it is hoped, from the disposition which many discovered on that day and other favorable circumstances, that these disadvantages will soon, in part, be happily removed.

The custom which was then begun of having a sermon on commencement was continued until Dr. Wayland's administration in 1828. Its place has been taken by the president's levee, held on the evening of commencement. The sermon to the graduating class is delivered the Sunday before commencement. Commencement has been changed from September to the third Wednesday in June. Class day occurs on the Friday before commencement.

In 1786 these two resolutions were passed by the corporation:

Resolved, That in future the candidates for bachelor degrees, being alumni of the college, shall be clad at commencement in black flowing robes and caps, similar to those used at other universities.

Resolved, That an exclusive right of furnishing such robes and caps, for the use of the candidates, be granted and confirmed to an undertaker for the space of fifteen years.

COURSE OF STUDY.

The colleges and universities of this country were founded upon the model of those in the mother country. There the universities were established for those who were intended for the professions of divinity and law. The courses of study were strong in the classics or in mathematics. There was nothing in the early history of the college like a course of study as it is understood to-day, but from a revision of the laws made in 1783 some idea of the curriculum can be gathered:

The president and tutors, according to their judgments, shall teach and instruct the several classes in the learned languages and in the liberal arts and sciences, together with the vernacular tongue.

The following are the classes appointed for the first year, namely: In Latin, Virgil, Cicero's Orations, and Horace, all in usum Delphini; in Greek, the New Testament, Lucian's Dialogues, and Xenophon's Cyropædia. For the second year, in Latin, Cicero de Oratore, and Cæsar's Commentaries; in Greek, Homer's Iliad, and Longinus on the Sublime, together with Lowth's Vernacular Grammar, rhetoric, Ward's Oratory, Sheridan's Lectures on Elocution, Guthrie's Geography, Kaime's Elements of Criticism, Watts and Duncan's Logic. For the third year, Hutchinson's Moral Philosophy, Doddridge's Lectures, Fenning's Arithmetic, Hammond's Algebra, Stone's Euclid, Martin's Trigonometry, Love's Surveying, Wilson's Navigation, Martin's Philosophia Britannica, and Ferguson's Astronomy, with Martin on the Globes. In the last year, Locke on the Understanding, Kennedy's Chronology, and Bolingbroke on History, and the languages, arts, and sciences studied in the foregoing years to be accurately reviewed.

Two of the students, in rotation, shall, every evening after prayers, pronounce a piece upon the stage; and the members of the college shall meet every Wednesday afternoon in the hall, at the ringing of the bell at 2 o'clock, to pronounce, before the president and the tutors, pieces well committed to memory, and that they may receive such corrections in their manner as shall be judged necessary.

It is not permitted anyone, in the hours of study, to speak to another except in Latin, either in the college or in the college yard.

MANAGEMENT.

The management of the university is vested in a corporation which consists of two branches—that of the trustees and that of the fellows—with distinct, separate, and respective powers. The trustees are 36 in number, of whom 22 are forever to be elected of the denomination called Baptists, or Antipædobaptists, 5 of the denomination called Friends, or Quakers, 5 of the denomination called Episcopalians, and 4 of the denomination called Congregationalists. These were the denominations of New England a century ago. The number of the fellows, including the president, who must always be a fellow, is 12, of whom 8 are forever to be elected of the denomination called Baptists, and the rest indifferently of any or of all denominations. The president must forever be a Baptist. Once in three years the corporation, at its annual meetings, must chose from among the trustees a chancellor of the university and a treasurer, and from among the fellows a secretary. The office of chancellor is merely to preside as moderator of the trustees, the president, or in his absence, the senior fellow, being the moderator of the fellows. The instruction and immediate government of the college is, and must forever continue, to rest in the president and fellows, or fellowship, to whom, as a "learned faculty," belongs exclusively the privileges of adjudging and conferring the academical degrees.

PROMINENT MEN.

Among nearly all the men of that day who were farseeing and who appreciated the advantages of education for their own and for succeeding generations, the college made friends. It also received the support of those who were not directly engaged in literary pursuits, but were in business or in commerce. This was the period of great activity in the colony, as her magnificent bay afforded a means of distribution for all New England, so that the benefits of commerce might be realized and appropriated. The connection between commerce and education finds many illustrations in our colonial history. The interest on the other side of the Atlantic has been seen, in the success which Edwards met in securing funds for the college. Then too, at the South, there was displayed the same zeal.

In Governor Hopkins the college had a firm friend, and his interest was recognized by his election as chancellor. He was an advocate of the location of the college at Providence, and by his extensive learning and genuine love of literature proved a most efficient coadjutor of President Manning, in all the plans and efforts of the latter, for the efficiency and usefulness of the college. The Browns, from one of whom the university takes its name, have ever been deeply interested in this seat of learning.

In 1866 Mr. Ives resigned the treasurership. For nearly a century the affairs of the college had been managed, as we have seen, with uncommon wisdom and skill, by the representatives of a single family. It is doubtful if a similar instance can be found in the history of any other college, and it is certain that there can not be found four successive treasurers thus related, who have displayed such remarkable munificence, ability, and zeal in promoting the welfare of an institution of learning. For this the names of John Brown, Nicholas Brown, Moses Brown Ives, and Robert Hale Ives will be held in everlasting remembrance by the graduates and friends of Brown University.[1]

In colonial days appear the names of Dr. Ephriam Bowen, Governor Joseph Wanton, Hon. James Honeyman, of Newport; Nicholas Easton, a prominent merchant of Newport; Governor Samuel Ward, Dr. Joshua Babcock, of Westerly; Judge Daniel Jenckes, Rev. Samuel Stillman, of Boston; Rev. John Gano, of New York, and Jabez Bowen. Many, by self-sacrifice, sent their sons to the institution, thereby recognizing its usefulness; others, when the university was inveighed against, defended her good name. It is gratifying to think that many of them lived to see the institution established on a firm basis and to see the sons of Brown rising up to call her blessed.

DISCIPLINE.

Regarding the early discipline of the college we have the ideas of Manning himself, in a set of rules which he prepared in 1783:

And whereas, the statutes are few and general, there must necessarily be lodged with the president and tutors a discretional or parental authority; therefore, where no statute is particularly and expressly provided for a case that may occur, they are to exercise this discretionary authority according to the known customs of similar institutions and the plain, general rules of the moral law. And in general the penalties are to be of the more humane kind, such as are at once expressive of compassion for the offender and of indignation at the offence, such as are adapted to work upon the nobler principles of humanity, and to move the more honorable springs of good order and submission to government.

College life then was regulated more on the basis of the family. The professors and the tutors lived under the same roof with the students, and daily visits of inspection were a part of their duties. The following correspondence will illustrate the parental care and duties of the president:

The late Judge Peleg Arnold, when about 18 years of age, in going to mill, heard, as he approached Friends' meeting-house at Upper Smithfield, a great noise like the breaking in of windows, and, being desirous of ascertaining the cause, rode up the hill to within about 20 rods of the house, when he discovered two young men on horseback, each with a club, smashing in the front windows of the meetinghouse.

Immediately on seeing him they wheeled and rode off at full speed. He being a vigorous young man and determined to ascertain who they were, in order to bring them to justice, threw his bag of corn in the road and started in pursuit. The race was a sharp one and continued for 6 miles, when the judge came up with and stopped

---

[1] Brown University, by R. A. Guild, p. 335.

them on Cumberland Hill. After learning their names and places of residence he permitted them to proceed. One of the young men proved to be a student in the college, and the president, being informed of the circumstance, wrote to the clerk of the monthly meeting the following letter:

PROVIDENCE, *December 12, 1770.*

SIR: You may think strange that I, a stranger to you, should address you by this epistle, but will excuse me when I give the reason, which is an information that I have received that one Scott, a youth under my tuition, some time ago, riding through Smithfield (in company with one Dennis, of Newport), rode up to and in a most audaciously wicked manner broke the windows of the Friends' meeting-house in said town, of which meeting I understand you are clerk. Upon the first hearing of this scandalous report I charged him with the fact, which he confessed, with no small degree of apparent penitence; whereupon I thought good to inform you, and by you the meeting, that they shall have ample reparation of damages and such other satisfaction as they shall think proper, being determined to punish with the utmost vigor all such perverse youth as may be entrusted to my care, as I hold such base conduct in the greatest detestation.

You will be so good as to let me know when the first meeting of business is held, that I may send him up to appear before them, and make not only reparation, but such a confession before the meeting as shall be fully satisfactory. I choose to mortify him in this way, and should be very glad that some of the heads of the meeting would admonish him faithfully, and show him the evil of such doings, if this would be agreeable to them; but I speak this, not to direct them in the matter, but what would be agreeable to me. When this is settled, we shall discipline him with the highest punishment we inflict, next to banishment from the society; and with that, if he does not comply with the above.

The youth has been but few months under my care, is a child of a respectable family in Kingston, Massachusetts Bay, and had his school learning at New Haven. I am sorry for his friends, and that it happened to fall to my lot to have such a thoughtless, vicious pupil; but am determined this shall be the last enormity, one excepted, of which he shall be guilty while under my care. I hope the meeting will inform me how he complies with these injunctions, if they think proper to take these or any other methods. Please, by the first opportunity, to favor me with a line in answer to the above requests and you will do a favor to a real friend.

JAMES MANNING.

Mr. THOMAS LAPHAM, JR., *in Smithfield.*

In reply to which, as requested, Thomas Lapham, jr., sent him the following letter:

SMITHFIELD, *the 17th of 12th mo., 1770.*

RESPECTED FRIEND: These may inform that I received thy letter of the 12th inst., concerning one of thy pupil's base conduct, in breaking the windows of our meetinghouse, and agreeably to thy request therein, I hereby inform, that our meetings for business are held on the last fifth day of every month; so that our next will be on the last fifth day (or Thursday) of this instant, at the house where the windows were broken. A meeting for worship begins at 11 o'clock, and commonly holds two hours; then begins the meeting for business. Therefore, if the youth appear before us, I intend to send thee an account of his second progress. I am glad to hear such proper methods proposed for the settling of his scandalous deed, and that the affairs of the college may be so conducted as to be a means of promoting virtue and piety, which are far preferable to arts and sciences, is the real desire of one who wishes well unto all.

THOMAS LAPHAM, JR.

The young man, according to the direction of the president, appeared before the next monthly meeting for business, and informed the meeting what he had done, made a suitable acknowledgment, paid the damage done to the windows, received some wholesome admonition and advice, and returned to his college duties, it is to be hoped, a better man.

LAND AND BUILDINGS.

The first of the college buildings erected in Providence was University Hall. This was modeled after Nassau Hall of Princeton. Perhaps none of the college buildings has undergone more changes than this. Here was the chapel, and here was the dining hall when "commons" was in vogue; during the Revolution, barracks and a hospital were made from the hall; its rooms were used for dormitories and for recitations. The old student in returning to Brown to-day would not recognize the buildings; of the original plan all that remains are the walls. The interior has been fitted up in suites of rooms, and the entries which were formerly the scenes of midnight revelry have been divided and changed.

The first reference to a building is on the records of the second meeting of the corporation held in 1765, from which it appears $1,992 was subscribed for the building and for endowing the college. A committee was chosen with instructions to take the matter in charge, but before a decision was reached the question regarding the permanent location of the college arose. As soon as that was settled, by the vote of 1770, which brought the college to Providence, it was voted that the college edifice be built according to the following plan, viz: That the house be 150 feet long and 46 feet wide, with a projection of 10 feet on each side (10 by 30), and that it be four stories high.

The lot selected for the building comprised originally about 8 acres, and included a portion of the "home lot" of Chad Brown (who was one of the original proprietors after the native Indians of whom it was purchased). It was for this reason purchased through the agency of the Brown family, in order that the college might stand on the "original house-lot or home share, so called, of their pious ancestor"[1]

Describing the location at that time, Mr. Edwards writes regarding it as "remarkably airy, healthful, and pleasant, being the summit of a hill pretty easy of ascent and commanding a prospect of the town of Providence below, of the Narragansett Bay and the islands, and of an extensive country, variegated with hills and dales, woods and planes, etc. Surely this spot was made for a seat of the muses." This building and the president's house were carried along together. The amount expended was $9,480. "Sundry supplies" were furnished by Nicholas Brown & Co. The account which was rendered of them as well as the money expended by the building committee, shows some of the customs and of the current prices of that day.

---

[1] Brown University with illustrative documents. R. A. Guild, 232. The cost of the land was $730.

1770.	£	s.	p.
Jan. 1. To cash paid for the postage of a letter to the corporation		1	6
May 23. To 3 pts. rum allowed John Jenckes for the scow men		0	10
May 25. To one-half day's work of Earle's negro		1	6
May 25. To cash paid Comstock for one-half day's carting with three creatures		3	0
June 1. To one wheelbarrow, new, but broke to pieces in the service		10	6
June 19. To ½ gall. West India rum for the digging of the well		2	0
Aug. 25. To 4 galls. West India rum, very good and old, and 1 lb. sugar, third floor		15	7¼
Oct. 13. To 3 galls. West India rum when raising roof		10	6
1771.			
Feb. 7. To 1 box glass for president's house	3	3	0
Mar. 8. To cash paid Ebenezer Leland for painting the college and president's house	9	0	0

REVOLUTIONARY PERIOD.

Rhode Island, together with the other colonies, had felt the oppression which brought on the Revolution; the sentiments of the young men as expressed in their graduating speeches indicated a strong patriotism. In June, 1775, the following extract appeared in the Providence Gazette:

> To the reverend president, honorable professor, and rest of the honorable corporation of Rhode Island College—the dutiful petition of the senior class:
>
> MOST WORTHY PATRONS: Deeply affected with the distress of our oppressed country, which now, most unjustly, feels the baneful effects of arbitrary power, provoked to the greatest height of cruelty and vengeance by the noble and manly resistance of a free and determined people, permit us, gentlemen, to approach you with this, our humble and dutiful petition, that you would be pleased to take under your serious consideration the propriety of holding the ensuing commencement in a public manner, as usual; whether such a celebration of that anniversary would be in conformity to the eighth article of the association formed by the grand American Congress, and which all the colonies are all religiously executing, and that you would be pleased to signify unto us your resolution respecting the same, that we may govern ourselves accordingly.
>
> JOSIAH REED,
ANDREW LAW,
JAMES FULTON,
Committee in Behalf of the Senior Class.
>
> COLLEGE IN PROVIDENCE, *June 8, 1775.*

The corporation recognized the patriotism of the class and the sacrifice that would be entailed by the omission of the commencement exercises. This was a great sacrifice, for the commencement then was an important event in the life of the student. The day was a holiday in the city, and many went to the exercises to do the young men honor. Concluding the reply to the petition, it was said:

> Institutions of learning will doubtless partake in the common calamities of our country, as arms have ever proved unfriendly to the more refined and liberal arts and sciences; yet we are resolved to continue college orders here as usual, excepting that the usual commencement, by the advice of such of the corporation as could conveniently be consulted, will not be public.

BROWN UNIVERSITY—UNIVERSITY HALL.

The graduating class numbered ten, and theirs was the last commencement till 1782. In December, 1776, the city was in control of the British and the college was closed, the following notice appearing in the papers:

> This is to inform all the students that their attendance on college orders is hereby dispensed with until the end of the next spring vacation, and that they are at liberty to return home or prosecute their studies elsewhere, as they think proper, and that those who pay as particular attention to their studies as these confused times will admit, shall then be considered in the same light and standing as if they had given the usual attendance here.
> In witness whereof I subscribe,
>
> JAMES MANNING.
> PROVIDENCE, *December 10, 1776*.

Accordingly, till May, 1782, the course of studies was suspended. In 1769 there were 13 students, and the whole number from that date to the year 1776 was 197. In 1780 a meeting of the corporation was called, to see if the college could be revived. Money was very scarce, so Manning offered to accept £60, or $300, for his salary instead of £100, which he had been receiving. This was in April. On a Sunday in June the college building was seized, in accordance with a council of war, for a hospital for the French troops. It had been seized before and used as barracks.

In the journal of an aid-de-camp of Count de Rochambeau, who visited Providence, reference is made to the city and the college:

> Providence est une assez jolie petite ville, très commerçante avant la guerre, il n'y a rien de curieux qu'un hôpital de la plus grande beauté.

At the meeting of the corporation in 1782 provision was made for the immediate instruction of the youth. The building was in a very bad condition, from its occupancy as barracks and as a hospital. The money for its repair was raised by the corporation. The public commencements were resumed in 1783, but the next was not held till 1786, because, on account of the suspension of the college exercises, there were no students to graduate.

Manning felt the need of instruction in the French language, and a memorial to the French King was drawn up, in which his assistance was solicited toward securing a professor and a collection of books. In the words of the memorial:

> Ignorant of the French language, and separated as we were by more than mere distance of countries, we too readily imbibed the prejudices of the English—prejudices which we have renounced since we have had a nearer view of the brave army of France, who actually inhabited this college edifice; since which time our youth seek with avidity whatever can give them information respecting the character, genius, and influence of a people they have such reason to admire—a nation so eminently distinguished for polished humanity.
> To satisfy this laudable thirst of knowledge nothing was wanting but to encourage and diffuse the French language; and that not merely as the principal means of rendering an intercourse with our brethren of France more easy and beneficial, but also for spreading far and wide the history of the so celebrated race of kings, statesmen, philosophers, poets, and benefactors of mankind which France has produced.

This address was given to Thomas Jefferson to present to the king, but in his judgment it was thought inopportune. As the matter had been intrusted to him his opinion was accepted.

Manning was constantly writing to get his friends in England interested in the college. To Thomas Llewelyn, of London, he wrote, suggesting that he make such a subscription to the college as would entitle it to be called by his name: "Cambridge College was so fortunate as to attract the attention of a Hollis, New Haven of a Yale, and New Hampshire of a Dartmouth, who have given their names to these seats of learning. We should think ourselves no less happy in the patronage of a Llewelyn. Llewelyn College appears well when written, and sounds no less agreeably when spoken."

At the March session of the assembly, in 1786, Manning was chosen unanimously to represent Rhode Island in the Congress of the Confederation. At first he was averse to accepting the election on account of his connection with the college, but a feeling of public spirit and devotion to the college influenced him to accept. That the latter was the chief reason appears in one of his letters of that year:

Pray don't be alarmed should you hear that I am in Congress. The motive of my accepting this most unexpected, unsolicited, but unanimous appointment of the State to that office was the recovery of a considerable sum due to the college for the use taken of the edifice and the damage done to it by the public in the late war. It was thought by those most acquainted with the state of our application to that honorable body that my presence would facilitate that grant; more especially since none of the persons likely to be elected would greatly interest themselves in that business.

Manning did not succeed in this, and it was fourteen years after before any recognition of the claim was made by Congress. The sum received in compensation was stated by Dr. Benedict to be $2,000. Manning said that the just due was more than £1,000.

While in Congress he took no active part on the floor except to reply to an attack which was made against New England. It was said that he must have given himself to much business then, and that he was master of all the important questions which had been debated, being able to give the arguments pro and con. In a letter to a friend he says:

I am treated with respect by Congress and the heads of Departments. The present Congress possess great integrity and a good share of abilities, but for want of more States on the floor the public and important business is from day to day neglected. We are, however, in daily expectation of a fuller delegation.

His views on the inadequacy of the Confederation and the necessity of union were in accord with what the succeeding events showed to be the wise policy of the Government. When the question of the ratification of the Constitution was being discussed by Massachusetts he attended the debates and proceedings of the convention. He himself said that Massachusetts was the hinge on which the whole must turn.

By this time he had been relieved of the greater part of his pastoral duties and was enabled to devote his whole attention to the college. This, however, did not prevent him from assuming occasional pastoral duties and keeping fully posted on all the important movements of the day.

CLOSING YEARS OF MANNING.

From this period till the close of his life he was active in his zeal for the college and in the aid which he could give his State. He was ever interested in what pertained to common-school education, and was on the school committee for many years, serving as chairman.

In April, 1791, he preached his farewell sermon to his people, and at a meeting of the corporation of the college held the same month he requested them to find a successor to him. He seemed to have a presentiment that his days were numbered. Sunday, July 24, he was seized with an apoplectic fit while conducting family prayers, and lived till the following Fiday.

Many a man of sterling worth, in a few words delineating the character of another man, has sketched his own. So was it with Manning. Admirably fitting to his own character are the qualities which he said must be sought for in the choice of a successor to his charge: "A man of letters, politeness, strict piety and orthodoxy, of popular talents, possessed of a good share of human prudence, and no bigot; in a word, a truly Christian orator." The entire community felt that a great man had fallen, and all possible respect and reverence were paid to his memory. His portrait is in the possession of the university. From an obituary notice in the Providence Gazette this extract is taken:

In his youth he was remarkable for his dexterity in athletic exercises, for the symmetry of his body and gracefulness of his person. His countenance was stately and majestic, full of dignity, goodness, and gravity; and the temper of his mind was a counterpart to it. He was formed for enterprise. His address was pleasing, his manner enchanting, his voice harmonious, and his eloquence almost irresistible. Having deeply imbibed the spirit of truth himself as a preacher of the Gospel, he was faithful in declaring the whole counsel of God. He studied plainness of speech and to be useful more than to be celebrated. The good order, learning, and respectability of the Baptist churches in the Eastern States are much owing to his assiduous attention to their welfare. The credit of his name, and his personal influence among them have never, perhaps, been exceeded by any other character.

Of the college he must, in one sense, be considered as the founder. He presided with the singular advantage of a superior personal appearance, added to all his shining talents for governing and instructing youth. From the first beginning of his Latin school at Warren, through many discouragements, he has by constant care and labor raised this seat of learning to notice, to credit, and to respectability in the United States. Perhaps the history of no other college will disclose a more rapid progress or greater maturity in the course of about twenty-five years.

PRESIDENT MAXCY, 1792-1802.

Under the administration of President Maxcy the college was sustained in all the departments, and continued to graduate a fair number of students. Undue stress is too often laid on an administration characterized by brilliancy and new departures, but those which have merely conserved the growth of the institution are likewise of importance. Without the latter it would have been difficult for succeeding administrations to have won their reputation. It was doubtful if the period succeeding the death of President Manning called for an aggressive policy. The college did not resume its exercises till 1782, the break between 1776 and that date being occasioned by the revolutionary struggle. The two buildings, university hall and the president's house, were intact, although sadly in need of repair, and a small number of students were returning. To hold the ground and, in a sense, to broaden the new foundations which had been again laid by Manning when the college opened in 1782, may be said to be the policy of the incoming president. Then, too, Manning was a man widely known in his denomination and by the public. On his preaching tour during the years of the suspension of the college, he was widening his reputation in the colonies. He was a man of marked ability and he did probably what no other man could have done for the college, hence the new president was to step into a large place. Maxcy was a young man, with his spurs yet to win as the leader of a college. At the first commencement after his inauguration, during the illumination of the college, a transparency was placed in one of the upper windows displaying his name with "President, 24 years old." His policy then was to conserve what had been gained, and he seems to have accomplished it. This, then, may account for the fact that no record can be made during his administration of new buildings or of large bequests. It was said of his presidency:

He was one whose name and fame are identified with its reputation and whose mildness, dignity, and goodness, equaled only by his genius, learning, and eloquence, subdued all envy, made all admirers friends, and gave him an irresistible sway over the minds of those placed under his care. Under his administration the college acquired a reputation for belles-lettres and eloquence inferior to no seminary of learning in the United States. His pupils saw in him an admirable model for their imitation, and the influence of his pure and cultivated taste was seen in their literary performances.[1]

SKETCH OF PRESIDENT MAXCY.

President Maxcy was born in Massachusetts September 2, 1768. His father is mentioned as one of the most respectable inhabitants of the town; but it seems to have been to his mother that he owed those traits of piety and mildness which characterized his more mature years.

His mother, says his biographer, was a woman of strong mind and devoted piety, and beautifully exemplified the practical influence of the Christian religion, by the uniform consistency which marked the whole tenor of her life. Upon her devolved the delightful duty of implanting in the mind of her son those seeds of truth and righteousness, which should in after years bud and blossom into usefulness.

In early years he gave promise of talent and of maturity of intellect. It is of interest to note that when a boy he was fond of speaking and

---

[1] President Maxcy's Remains, by Romeo Elton, p. 15.

some of his oratorical efforts even then were creditable. In view of these early indications, his parents decided to give him a liberal education, and he was sent to the Wrentham Academy, kept by William Williams, one of the first graduates from the college. He entered Brown, or Rhode Island College, as it was then called, in 1783, at the age of 15. His conduct in college was such as to win the esteem of instructors and classmates. From the discipline of college his mental powers were stimulated and invigorated. It is said his writings were recommended as models to his classmates; that they were eminent for delicacy of taste, and that his conceptions were embodied in language of classic purity. He was graduated with the highest honors of his class. A position of tutor becoming vacant in the college, it was offered to him, and was accepted. For four years he filled this position with satisfaction to his colleagues and to the students.

In 1790 he was licensed to preach, and in this field his marked ability for oratory was so pronounced that he was invited to take charge of the church from which President Manning had resigned.

Maxcy was ordained in 1791, and on the same day was elected professor of divinity by the corporation.

Says Tristam Burgess of Maxcy:

His voice seemed not to have reached the deep tone of full age; but most of all to resemble that of those whom the Savior of the world said, "Of such is the kingdom of heaven." The eloquence of Maxcy was mental. You seemed to hear the soul of the man; and each one of the largest assembly, in the most extended place of worship, received the slightest impulse of his silver voice as if he stood at his very ear. So intensely would he enchain attention, that in the most thronged audience you heard nothing but him and the pulsations of your own heart. His utterance was not more perfect than his whole discourse was instructive and enchanting.

That same year (1791) President Manning was seized by an apoplectic fit and died within a few days. The most natural successor was Maxcy, and at the following commencement he was elected president *pro tempore*. As an instructor he was very successful, because his influence over his pupils was strengthened by his experience and reputation as a man of ability. He regarded his students as his sons, and in all his relations towards them endeavored to inculcate the principles of virtue and piety. He was thoroughly interested in all their concerns, and took great delight in bringing to them the results of his own experience. To those students who sought him for advice he was particularly cordial, and they felt that in him they had a true friend. Refined and dignified in manner, of brilliant conversational powers, and possessing the ability of adapting his instruction to the attainments of his students, he was very successful as a teacher. He had the power of grasping a subject as a whole and then presenting it attractively to the class. His discipline was described as "reasonable, firm, and uniform, and marked in its administration by kindness, frankness, and dignity." There was an absence of austerity in his manner, and he treated his pupils as young gentlemen. He always appealed to their understanding and conscience.

The few sermons preached while in the presidential chair were such as in no wise to detract from his reputation as an eloquent pulpit orator. Harvard bestowed upon him, when only 33, the degree of D. D. In 1797 he was formally elected president, his youth undoubtedly having delayed that honor. During the ten years in which he was at the head of the college, graduates were sent into all the professions, and acquired as favorable a reputation as had been gained for any other decade in the history of the university. In September, 1802, he sent in his resignation, assuring the corporation that nothing but necessity led him to take that step, and that his attachment to the college should ever be firm. The corporation accepted his resignation with regret, and expressed their pleasure in the thought that he would not withdraw from academic life. He accepted a call to the presidency of Union College, Schenectady, remaining there till 1804. In that year he accepted the presidency of South Carolina College. He died at Columbia, S. C., June 4, 1820.

PRESIDENT MESSER, 1802-1826.

This period in the history of the college immediately preceded that of Dr. Wayland. The latter, taking all things into consideration, was regarded by many as the most brilliant period of its history. Messer was connected with the university before he took the presidency, and had won, through public services of a professional nature, more than a local reputation. Dr. Wayland, by his celebrated sermon, awoke to find himself famous; he introduced a new system of education, experimentally, but successfully, and he had more than a local reputation through the merit of his text-books. President Messer was obliged to conduct the affairs of the college chiefly with what the students paid for tuition. It has been urged that the discipline under him was lax; but the personnel of the college was different, the students were older, and felt that they were preparing for what would be their life work, hence they needed little or no discipline. Under Dr. Wayland the students were younger, and to a greater extent the sons of wealthier parents, for the year 1827 was about the beginning of an era of greater wealth and a demand for more luxury. It has been urged that had the means been placed at the disposal of President Messer which Dr. Wayland had, by way of externals, the period would have been as brilliant. While there would be no detraction from all which the next administration deserved, yet Messer's should also receive all due honor.

PROFESSORSHIP OF ORATORY.

The first important event in this administration was the founding of the professorship of oratory by Nicholas Brown and the circumstances which lead to the change of name from Rhode Island College to Brown University.

In a letter written by John Brown, who was obliged to resign the position of treasurer, on account of declining health, towards the close, was added:

> Being located in the center of New England, and with one of the most liberal charters that has ever been granted, to warrant and secure a fair and generous equality to be extended to every religious sect, I do most sincerely recommend the promotion of its highest interests to every branch of the government of the college. And as the most beautiful and handsome mode of speaking was a principal object, to my certain knowledge, of the first friends of this college, I do wish that the honorable corporation may find means during their deliberations of this week to establish a professorship of English oratory, and that suitable funds for the purpose may be so placed that the annual income only can be touched for the salary pertaining to such a professorship.
>
> I am, gentlemen, with great regard, your obedient servant,
>
> JOHN BROWN.
>
> PROVIDENCE, *September 6, 1803.*

CHANGE OF NAME OF THE COLLEGE.

Till this time the name of the college was as provided by the charter. The charter also contained the provision that the trustees and fellows at any time thereafter might give such more particular name to the college, in honor of the greatest and most distinguished benefactor, or otherwise, as they should think proper.

In 1803 it was voted that the donation of $5,000, if made to this college within one year from the late commencement, shall entitle the donor to name the college.

The feelings of John Brown to the college were shown by the above letter, as well as by the faithful discharge of his official duties. That the same feelings were cherished by the son will be shown by this letter to the corporation.

> PROVIDENCE, *September 6, 1804.*
>
> GENTLEMEN: It is not unknown to you that I have long had an attachment to this institution, as the place where my deceased brother, Moses, and myself received our education. This attachment derives additional strength from the recollection that my late honored father was among the earliest and most zealous patrons of the college, and is confirmed by my regard for the cause of literature in general. Under these impressions I hereby make a donation of $5,000 to Rhode Island College, to remain in perpetuity as a fund for the establishment of a professorship of oratory and belles-lettres. The money will be paid next commencement, and is to be vested in such funds as the corporation shall direct for its augmentation to a sufficiency, in your judgment, to produce a competent annual salary for the within-mentioned professorship.
>
> I am, very respectfully, gentlemen, with my best wishes for the prosperity of the college, your obedient friend,
>
> NICHOLAS BROWN.

This fund accumulated from year to year till it more than doubled. In 1826 bank stock to the amount of $10,000 was purchased by the treasurer and constituted the special fund for this professorship.

In accordance with the gift for the foundation of this professorship by Nicholas Brown, September 6, 1804, it was voted that this college be called and known in all future time by the name of Brown University in Providence, in the State of Rhode Island and Providence Plantations.

UNIVERSITY GRAMMAR SCHOOL.

At this period this school was under the management of the college. In 1809 it was decided that a building for the school be erected on the college lands. A committee of three was chosen to procure subscriptions, and the sum of $1,452.86 was raised. The building was erected in 1810, and stands opposite the president's house. This school is described under the above title in the chapter devoted to academies.

HOPE COLLEGE.

The first mention of this building occurs under the date of September 6, 1821. The record concerned the appointment of a committee to consider the propriety of erecting another edifice. At an adjourned meeting held October 10, the committee was authorized to purchase a site and erect a suitable building.

The most interesting item is the report of the committee January 13, 1823:

The committee appointed in September, 1821, to procure a suitable piece of land and erect thereon a college edifice, beg leave to refer to the treasurer's report for the 3rd of September, 1822, for particulars of the lot purchased of Mr. Nathan Waterman. On this lot an elegant brick building of the following dimensions has been erected by Nicholas Brown, esq., the distinguished patron of the university: In length 120 feet, width 40 feet, 4 stories high, and containing 48 rooms. The object, therefore, is accomplished, and no part of the funds placed at the disposal of the committee by the corporation has been used toward said building. Mr. Brown, it is understood, will make a communication on the subject of the new college edifice at the meeting to be holden by adjournment in the university chapel on Monday, the 13th of January instant, to which communication the committee invite the attention of the corporation.

Respectfully submitted by the committee.

In the communication referred to, Mr. Brown said:

To the Corporation of Brown University :

It affords me great pleasure at this adjourned meeting of the corporation to state that the college edifice erected last season and located on the land purchased by the corporation of Mr. Nathan Waterman is completed.

Being warmly attached to the institution where I received my education, among whose founders and benefactors was my honored father, deceased, and believing that the dissemination of letters and knowledge is the great means of social happiness, I have caused this edifice to be erected wholly at my expense, and now present it to the corporation of Brown University, to be held with the other corporate property, according to their charter.

As it may be proper to give a name to the new edifice, I take leave to suggest to the corporation that of "Hope College."

I avail myself of this occasion to hope that heaven will bless and make it useful

BROWN UNIVERSITY — HOPE COLLEGE.

in the promotion of virtue, science, and literature, to those of the present and of future generations who may resort to this university for education. With respectful and affectionate regards to the individual members of the corporation,
I am their friend,

NICHOLAS BROWN.

This building is the fourth that has been built for the college and has been used as a dormitory. The records make no mention of its cost, but from various sources the expense was estimated at about $20,000.

Among the resolutions adopted by the corporation in accepting the gift of Hope College were two, as follows:

Resolved, That the members of the corporation entertain a very high sense of the liberality of this patron of science, in the gift of this new building, in addition to his former large donations to this university.

Resolved, That in compliance with the suggestion of the donor, the new edifice be denominated Hope College.

At the same meeting it was also voted that the old college edifice be named University Hall.

SKETCH OF PRESIDENT MESSER.

Rev. Asa Messer was born in Methuen, Mass., in 1769. He, too, was graduated from Rhode Island College in the class of 1790. He was chosen as tutor the next year, and held that position till 1796, when he was elected professor of the learned languages. He also held the professorship of mathematics and natural philosophy in 1799 and retained it till 1802. When the presidency became vacant by the resignation of President Maxcy in 1802, he was made president *pro tempore*. He became president in 1804 and retained this position till his resignation in 1826. Such is the outline of his work at his *alma mater*. To the duties of the manager of the college he brought an experience as pupil, tutor, and professor, so that he was conversant with its needs and shaped his policy accordingly.

In a critique of his administration allowance must be made for the conditions then obtaining. In the last few decades the march of progress has been very rapid, and because of this rapidity improvements had undue importance. They must not be so magnified as to mar the historical perspective. As has been said, he knew the needs and capabilities of the college.

In the first place, there could be said to exist no system of public schools. The law which had been passed establishing free schools in the State was inoperative, except in Providence. The acquirement of an education was expensive. Those who were wealthy preferred to send their sons to Harvard or Yale, the older, hence better endowed and equipped colleges. In the second place, the country was just entering upon the period which culminated in our second war with England. In Rhode Island this war was especially disastrous because disordering her commerce, which was then one of the chief sources of prosperity in the State. The demand of the day was for more clementary education. The country had not begun to realize the great possibilities in manufacture, in the applied arts, and in the sciences. The need was imperative for men fitted for the professions, hence the students who entered college desired a training in what was then the life work of the great body of professional men. At this period in the community there was not that wealth which endowed so liberally in a few years the institutions of learning. Then the tide of prosperity set in, because of the increased activity in manufactures and the application of the sciences. In view of these facts, the policy of the college had to be one of economy if it was to attract students. Those who resorted here were not able to afford an expensive education and, in fact, it was by self-sacrifice, not only on their own part, but by the members of their home circle that students could come at all. What then might have been the wishes of President Messer to place the university on a higher plane, with the means at his disposal, he could not accomplish.

How, then, did he manage during the twenty-four years of his presidency?

HIS POLICY.

Says Prof. Goddard, in a biographical sketch of Messer, in 1839:

During his administration the college continued to flourish. An increased number of pupils resorted thither, and at no antecedent or subsequent period of its history have the classes ever been so large.

Says a member of the class of 1823, regarding the characteristics of the students during Messer's administration:

The last half century will show them to you in every part of the land. In the churches, colleges, the schools, the halls of legislation, the courts of justice, in the practice of the healing art, and in all the departments of social industry, where science and skill are to be put in requisition, they have done, and are still doing, a noble work. All through our newly settled States and Territories they have been seen marching in the van of civilization, holding up the torch of science and religion, and doing their full share in supplying and working the intellectual, moral, and Christian forces, which alone can give health, strength, progress, and stability to the nation. Such results are a proud testimony to the wisdom and ability of Asa Messer as a college president and an educator of young men.

As a man he was popular; in his family relations he was charming; and he was held in esteem by his fellow-townsmen, for they elected him to offices of public trust.

For young men struggling to obtain a college education, and working in the chains of the *res angusta domi*, Dr. Messer had a heart of fatherly tenderness. Whenever he saw eager aspirations after knowledge, a high sense of duty and a resolute determination to prepare for an honorable and useful discharge of the responsibilities of life, there he was ever ready with the words of encouragement and the hand of help.

One more quotation from the same source will show how the college was regarded by those who were seeking an education:

There can be no doubt that the young men trained up under Dr. Messer were distinguished for habits of manly thought and self-reliant investigation, tempered with

REMINISCENCES OF PRESIDENT MESSER.

Said Dr. Sears, in a recent centennial discourse:

Of my old president I can not speak but with respect and affection. He had a vigorous and manly style of thought, and was a genial, pleasant teacher. In discipline, in his best days, he was adroit, having a keen insight into human nature, and touching at will, skillfully, all the chords of the student's heart. Rarely was he mistaken in the character of a young man, or in the motive to which he appealed, in order to influence him.

Foibles and weaknesses he treated with some degree of indulgence; but vice and willful wrong he treated with unsparing severity.

In government he followed no abstract principles, which so often mislead the theorist, but depended on his good sense in each case, giving considerable scope to views of expediency. The student who attempted to circumvent him was sure to be outwitted in the end. On account of his great shrewdness, he was sometimes called "the cunning president." One of the many anecdotes related of him is, that he kept in his room a bottle of picra for sick students, and that everyone who came to him to be excused from duty on account of headaches, found it necessary to swallow a dose before leaving him. * * * His individuality, both in body and mind, was strongly marked. He was altogether unpoetical in his nature. His language had no coloring of the fancy, but was naked, plain, and strong. His economy, which was proverbial, extended even to his words. His tendencies were rather to science than literature, and in the latter part of his life, as is often the case, more to practical wisdom and prudence than to either. * * *

His was not a mind to leave its own impress on that of his pupils. He had no imitators; he wished to have none. The many eminent men educated under him had no other resemblance to each other than freedom from authority. There is among them no uniform style of thought, resulting from its being run in the same mold. Even among the undergraduates, there was a personal independence of character and thought, and a manliness of deportment and self-respect, that gave a certain air of dignity to the two upper classes. Each man was expected to develop and retain his own individuality, without being schooled down to tameness, either by the faculty or by the collective will of his fellow-students. If he did right it was his own act; if he did wrong, he would scorn to say that it was because he did not dare to do right.

The following will show the esteem in which Dr. Messer was held by his co-laborers in his academic staff:

At a special meeting of the faculty of Brown University, held October 14, 1836, in the chapel of University Hall, President Wayland announced the departure from this life of Rev. Asa Messer, late president of said university, whereupon the following preamble and resolutions were unanimously adopted:

Whereas the Rev. Asa Messer, D. D. and LL. D., was for nearly forty years an instructor in this institution, and for twenty-four years its presiding officer, an expression of the sentiments of the existing faculty, upon the occasion of his unexpected and lamented death, is demanded by the respect which they individually and collectively entertain for the character of the deceased: Therefore,

Resolved, That the faculty of Brown University learn with deep regret that the Rev. Dr. Messer, an eminent son of this university, and for a long course of years

---

[1] Dr. Silas A. Crane, class of 1823. Brown University Under the Presidency of Asa Messer.

its presiding officer, is no more; that we are impressed with a strong conviction of his acknowledged merits as an instructor, of his vigorous intellect, and of his solid learning, and that we gratefully recognize his title to the best distinctions of the citizen, the man, and the Christian.

Dr. Messer received the degree of D. D. from his *alma mater* in 1806, and the same honor from Harvard in 1820. His administration could not be characterized as brilliant, yet it formed an important part in the history of Brown University.

President Wayland, 1826-1855.

Dr. Wayland was one of the presidents who was known not only at home but abroad, on account of his prominence as an educator. He was the son of godly parents, his father giving up a lucrative business to devote his entire attention to the ministry. His mother was a woman of piety and deep religious sentiments. Francis Wayland was born in New York, March 11, 1796. He early went to school, but his days there he considered as deprived of much that might have been for his mental improvement, for according to the ideas of education then, the lessons were but memory exercises.

The family moved to Albany, and at the age of 15 Wayland entered Union College. He describes his career at college as characterized by too much reading and too little study. Shortly after, he was called to a tutorship there. Graduating in July, 1813, he spent two years in the study of medicine with Dr. Eli Burritt, of Troy, after spending about six months with Dr. Hale, of the same place.

These years were most valuable, for Dr. Burritt, a genial and an able physician, delighted to unfold the treasures of his own mind to his enthusiastic pupil. Many rich experiences in his professional work and in a knowledge of men and things were acquired by the student. In 1816, in obedience to what he considered his duty, he ceased to devote himself to medicine and went to Andover, because the Baptists then had no theological seminary of their own. Moses Stuart held the chair of literature. With broad views and a most devout scholarship, Stuart opened up to Wayland and his fellows the stores of German philology and criticism. "Here at Andover," said Wayland, "I learned how to study and how to teach the Bible."

On leaving Andover a tutorship at Union was offered to him. Here he came to know Dr. Nott, its president, a man for whom his love and admiration deepened as the years went by. It was some time since Wayland had paid attention to the branches he was to teach; hence he devoted himself anew to their mastery. Although their teacher, he taught the students nothing by rote, but from his devotion to his studies brought new life to the class and thus inspired them with a love for the work.

The First Baptist church in Boston was without a pastor. Dr. Stillman had filled that position. Of him it was said: "He was probably the most popular pulpit orator of the day. He was a universal favorite." A friend of Wayland's suggested to the deacons of this church that they call him. It was done, and in 1821 he entered upon the pastorate which he retained till 1827. His pastorate was a trying one for him. He knew the call was not unanimous; he was conscious of his own deficiencies, unfitting him for anything like pulpit oratory; and he had a large place to fill in taking the position held by Dr. Stillman. The rich experience that his medical training had given him, and the broad knowledge that he had acquired as tutor, enabled him to preach powerful sermons. One bit of advice given to him he followed in his preaching, and it may have been the clue to the power he had with his audience. Said Dr. Welch to him: "Tell the people just what they tell you, and you will find that nothing will interest them so much."

Among the causes of his notoriety was a sermon preached before the annual meeting of the Boston Baptist Foreign Mission Society, October 26, 1823. The text was, "The field is the world," and the subject, "The moral dignity of the missionary enterprise." Such were the unfavorable circumstances, as he thought, of the preaching of this sermon that he said to a friend: "It was a complete failure. It fell perfectly dead." The sermon was requested for publication and various editions were quickly exhausted. Says his biographer:

In proportion to the population and the numbers then found in America, it is doubtful if its circulation has been exceeded by any American sermon, and certainly no other has held its place so permanently.

Dr. Wayland's ministry was successful; he was prominent in his own denomination, and from the distinguished merit of the sermon referred to, he had become prominent in the world of letters. On the resignation of Dr. Messer from the presidency of Brown in September, 1826, all eyes were turned to Wayland, and he was unanimously elected to the presidency, in December, 1826.

CHARACTERISTICS.

What, then, were the elements of success which he brought to the presidency? In the first place he loved the work. It was hard and exacting, how severe none knew but himself. His sense of duty and responsibility were deep and minute. "He recognized in every young man who entered the university a new trust imposed upon him, and held himself personally accountable to the student, to his parents, and to his God for the faithful fulfillment of so serious an obligation." In the second place his keen habits of thought and analysis enabled him quickly to comprehend and relegate to its proper generality each special case. He always sought to find the underlying general principle. His experience when studying medicine had given him an insight into scientific pursuits, and the opportunities for observation were varied, especially under the guidance of Dr. Burritt. In writing to a young man in after life Dr. Wayland said, "Neglect no opportunity of gaining useful information while visiting———. He is a great teacher in the art of fishing, managing a boat, etc." On another occasion, "Observe carefully the modes of thinking, and especially the points that are taken for granted. The things men take for granted without affirming are frequently of much greater importance than all that they affirm."

The life-long motto of the president was, "Whatever is worth doing at all is worth doing well," and he was also in the habit of saying to his friends, "Nothing can stand before days' works." Perhaps no paragraph could better state his character than the advice he gave to a young friend:

> Let me urge upon you, if you wish to be respected, to be thoroughly master of your studies. I would sit up till midnight rather than not know them. Never think "This will do," unless it be done as well as you can possibly do it. You will thus acquire the habit of using your faculties to the best advantage, and you will double your intellectual powers in a single year. The true way to increase our talents is to employ them to the utmost.

The following sketch of his manner and power in addressing the students is stated by Prof. Chace in his commemorative discourse:

> As the students then, with few exceptions, lived within the college buildings and took their meals in Commons Hall, they constituted much more than at present, a community by themselves. They were more readily swayed by common impulses, and more susceptible of common emotions. When gathered in chapel they formed a unique but remarkably homogeneous audience. President Wayland was at that time at the very culmination of his powers, both physical and intellectual. His massive and stalwart frame, not yet filled and rounded by the accretions of later years, his strongly marked features, having still the sharp outlines and severe grace of their first chiseling, his peerless eye, sending forth from beneath that olympian brow its lordly or its penetrating glances, he seemed, as he stood on the stage in that old chapel, the incarnation of majesty and power. He was raised but a few feet above his audience, and so near to them that those most remote could see the play of every feature. He commenced speaking. It was not instruction; it was not argument; it was not exhortation. It was a mixture of wit and humor, of ridicule, sarcasm, pathos, and fun; of passionate remonstrance, earnest appeal and solemn warning, poured forth not at random, but with a knowledge of the laws of emotion to which Lord Kames himself could have added nothing. The effect was indescribable. No Athenian audience ever hung more tumultuously on the lips of the divine Demosthenes. That little chapel heaved and swelled with the intensity of the pent-up forces. The billows of passion rose and fell like the waves of a tempestuous sea. At one moment all were burning with indignation; the next they were melted to tears. Now every one was convulsed with laughter, and now as solemn as if the revelations of doom were just opening upon them. Emotions the most diverse followed one another in quick succession. Admiration, resentment, awe, and worship in turn swelled every bosom. At length the storm spent itself. The ground had been softened and fertilized, and the whole air purified.

DR. WAYLAND IN THE CLASS ROOM.

The personality of a teacher is a strong characteristic in determining his success. Dr. Wayland in the class room was a manifestation of power. This description is by one of his pupils:

> Dr. Wayland's recitation room was the goal toward which every student turned his eye. As the distance lessened his eagerness increased. When he had at last

passed through the preliminary years his joy was full, because he would now be under the "old doctor." This silent influence, this unconscious tuition, was of unspeakable value. Although not directly unfolding any science or evolving any principle it imparted inspiration. The president threw over his pupils the spell of his own genius, and many of them still feel the enchantment, although the mighty spirit which imparted it has been withdrawn.

At the time to which I refer his recitation room was on the first floor of the middle hall of Hope College and in the rear of his own study. It had been a dormitory, but afterwards furnished with benches, and what served for writing desks, narrow pine boards upheld by pine uprights. We were obliged to use these with great care lest we should be left without any support for our papers and arms during the severe trials of skill in handling our pencils. The entire furniture of the room did not exceed $10 in value.

Entering by a door connecting the recitation room with his study he was in his chair at the moment, and he required the same promptness of each pupil. A second or third instance of tardiness was a dangerous experiment. The form of penalty could never be anticipated. Sometimes it was a look not likely to be soon forgotten; sometimes there was a painful pause; if the recitation had commenced sometimes the delinquent was formally introduced to the class.

All being present, and subsiding instantly into silence, the work began. He had no table, but sat with his manuscript for the lecture of the hour resting upon his knee. At this period none of his text-books had been published. The members of the class in succession recited the lecture of the preceding day, or perhaps one still farther back in the series. The recitation proceeded in this quiet manner until the lecture or lectures had been recalled to the minds of the pupils. Occasionally a question was asked by teacher or student until everything obscure or ambiguous had been not only cleared up, but made as definite as language could render it. At the same time no irrelevant discussion was permitted, no argument for the sake of argument was encouraged. The class and instructor were there for a definite purpose, and that purpose could not be thwarted by any art or subtlety, meanwhile, as all his pupils will readily remember, a silver pencil case passed from end to end between his thumb and finger. The compressed lips were moved slightly, but nervously. The small dark eye, through which, even in repose, his whole nature spoke, was resting steadily, but kindly, upon each student as he rose and recited.

This exercise concluded, there was a rustling all around the room; papers were adjusted and preparation made for writing. The president's manuscript was opened and the well known a-hem was the signal for all to be ready and for the work of the hour to begin. He read slowly and the class copied, each member following his own method, some using shorthand, others abbreviating words, or omitting some altogether. All were intent to catch the thought, at any rate, and the exact phraseology, if possible. The lecture was written out in full by the students at their rooms. What one failed to catch he gathered from another and thus by "comparing notes" a correct copy was secured.

These lectures seemed to us more wonderful than anything we had ever heard. They carried all the conviction of a demonstration. To have believed otherwise would have seemed absurd. Some of us at a later day found reason to modify the views there received and accepted. But at the time the conviction was complete.

His definitions were clear, simple, and easily remembered. His analysis of any obscure but important part was exhaustive, omitting no essential element. His progress through either of his favorite sciences was that of a prince through his own dominions.

At intervals, not regular in their recurrence, yet sure to occur somewhere, he suspended his reading for a few minutes and, waiting for a short time until each member of the class could complete his notes and give his attention, he would relate some incident or anecdote strikingly illustrating the point last made. In this department he was always most happy. The confirmation imparted to the argument was often unexpected and even irresistible. These anecdotes were drawn from any source that offered the richest supply; from history, from romance, from poetry, from common unrecorded every-day life. Often they were mirthful, sometimes ludicrous. Frequently statistics would be given, conclusively verifying the position which had been assumed. Illustrations, anecdotes, and statistics came at his bidding and always did capital service. They were "as arrows in the hands of the mighty."

Hands and arms having been rested, the reading was resumed and the lecture advanced to the stroke of the bell. It was concluded as promptly as it commenced, closing abruptly, even in the middle of an argument or a paragraph. Those were short hours. We wondered whither the sixty minutes had flown and how it was that we had taken no note of their flight. Half in doubt of the correctness of the bell, we left the recitation room.

Whether in these exercises Dr. Wayland stirred up the intellect of his pupils, it was not difficult even for a stranger to determine. As they issued from the lecture room, and went by twos and threes to their own apartments, the subjects which had just been discussed became the theme of most earnest conversation. Nor did the momentum thus acquired expend itself during the next twenty-four hours. The mental machinery was still in motion, when, on the following day, the class was again summoned to that unpretending room.

DISCIPLINE.

Not only must the president of a college be a teacher, but he must be an administrator. As he provides for the discipline of a college, will depend the success or failure of his administration. The methods which Dr. Wayland followed are best told in his own words.

With respect to the discipline of a college, it is, perhaps, proper that I should give my experience. I may say that my views on this subject are very simple. So far as I know, it has been generally supposed that the head of a college can only succeed by understanding the peculiar temperament, habits, disposition, etc., of every pupil, and, on the basis of this knowledge, making out a distinct mode of treatment for each undergraduate. In strict accordance with this theory, parents without number, when entering their sons in college, have come to me, and at great length have informed me of the peculiarities of their children, stating that their dispositions were excellent if they were only governed in some particular manner. I always listened with due attention to such statements, but paid to them no regard whatever. Indeed, I very soon learned that these peculiar young men were in fact, in almost every case, spoiled children, with whom I was likely to have more than the usual amount of trouble.

It seemed to me that such a view of the proper method of governing a public institution for instruction would greatly impair, if it did not entirely destroy, the value of any college in which it should prevail. If it were the business of instructors to study the character of every pupil, and in each instance to modify the course of discipline to suit the peculiarities of every individual, sound judgment would, from the very nature of the case, be impossible. A college would then fail in one of its most important designs, namely, as an intermediate place between the family and society, to prepare the student for entrance upon the practical duties of life. I came, therefore, to the conclusion that the laws of a college should be simple, just, kind, and of such a character that they could be shown to be right and salutary, both to parents and pupils. These laws, having been established, were to be rightly observed, and, by making every young man feel that he must be accountable for his own actions, prepare him for becoming a member of society, where this rule is to be enforced under more severe penalties. The more peculiar a young man is, and the more his peculiarties have been suffered to gain strength, the more important it is that he should be subjected to the same restraints as his fellows, without making any allowance for his eccentricities. If a young man be rude, arrogant, passionate, untruthful, indolent, unpunctual, it is far better, after one admonition, that no allowance whatever be made for these evil habits, than that they should ripen into confirmed biases, which a whole lifetime might be insufficient to correct.

It was therefore my aim to have no laws which could not be shown to be perfectly reasonable, and then to execute those laws with all possible strictness and impartiality. Of course, in saying this I assume that it will be understood that the government of impulsive, thoughtless young men is different from the government of adults. It must, of necessity, be kind, conciliatory, persuasive, or, in a word, parental. Penalty must be visited only after other means of restraint and correction have been tried in vain. But it must be distinctly understood that when these laws have proved ineffectual, punishment will inevitably come, and come on all alike, without the shadow of partiality.

In the government of a college, every case becomes a precedent; and if the precedent be a bad one, it will never be forgotten, but will be pleaded without fail, as though it established a law. I always, therefore, considered it a matter of prime importance to decide every new case correctly. It was my habit to take time for deliberation, to examine each case in all its bearings, and to see what would be the result of a decision if generally adopted as a rule. I endeavored to ascertain the principles on which a decision should be founded. I appreciated the fact that a case settled on true principles would harmonize with every other case that might subsequently occur, whether nearly or remotely connected with the one before me. The laws of college, and the results of violating them, became thus perfectly well known. When the younger students were disposed to combine in perpetuating some violation of law, their seniors would tell them distinctly what would be the inevitable consequence, and their predictions rarely failed of fulfillment. The principles which governed in such cases were well understood, and it was known that by these principles all cases of discipline were to be decided.

SERVICES FOR THE COLLEGE.

No two persons carry away just the same impression from seeing a beautiful painting, nor do they use the same thoughts in attempting its description. Perhaps another phase of what Dr. Wayland did for Brown may be seen from the graphic delineation given by Prof. Diman:

Yet who, after all, that knew Dr. Wayland, will be likely to accept any biography of him as satisfactory? No analysis of his intellectual qualities, no summary of his personal characteristics could set him forth. What power in his very presence, defying all description, as the most speaking faces defy the art of the photographer. What reserved force, sleeping in silent depths till stirred by great occasion. Such as know him only from his writings have gained no adequate impression of the man. There are works that seem vitalized with a writer's personality. In the vascular sentences of the immortal Essais we clasp hands across the chasm of three centuries, with the owner of that quaint tower that still looks down the valley of the Dordogne; and in the pensive periods of the Sketch Book we almost catch the beat of Irving's heart. But what suggestion of flesh and blood was ever associated with a text-book of moral science or of political economy? Who would infer the uproarious fun of Luther from his Commentary on the Epistle to the Galatians, or trace in the pages of The Wealth of Nations the winsome traits of Adam Smith? Not even in his printed sermons is Dr. Wayland presented with entire accuracy, for, much as he commended an "unlearned ministry" he somehow himself selected for publication his more ornate and elaborate productions. He appears in some of these as he used to appear, arrayed in cap and gown, in the stately ceremonial of commencement day, or, as he will appear to posterity, in the stiff full-length portrait, hanging in Rhode Island Hall, which, as an achievement of high art in wood, is only equaled by a work of the same artist, the picture of Mr. Webster in his reply to Hayne, that usurps so undue a share of Faneuil Hall. How little does all this resemble the image so vividly recalled as we turn the pages of these volumes. That little, ill-lighted chapel, long since numbered among the things that were, with its wide gallery, its narrow dais, its benches carved all over with the images and superscriptions of successive generations, in painful compliance with the monkish maxim, that to labor is to pray. How distinct, even now, sounds that heavy tread along the narrow hall, with what emphasis that burly form bursts through the door and up the steps, with what terrific frown that brow at once is clouded as impatient sophomores beat, with their heels, an unseemly march. With what utter disregard of conventional proprieties, yet with what genuine and awful sense of divine sanctities, the voice rolls out the strains of Hebrew David, and anon melts in humble, fervent prayer. Never did Dr. Wayland seem so grand, one might almost say inspired, as in those unbidden gushes of emotion that would sometimes convulsively shake his great frame and choke his utterance. The finest paragraph in his missionary sermon would not compare for eloquence with some of those pungent appeals that at times electrified the students at their Wednesday evening prayer meeting. How the chapel would be hushed with the stillness of death itself, as, in tremulous accents and voice sinking to a whisper, he would dwell on the dread responsibilities of the soul. There was never any cant of stereotyped exhortation, never any attempt to rouse a superficial emotion, but always direct appeal to conscience and to all the highest instincts of youthful hearts. In this most difficult task of dealing with young men at the crisis of their spiritual history, Dr. Wayland was unsurpassed.

How wise and tender his counsels at such a time! How many who have timidly stolen to his study door, their souls burdened with strange thoughts, and bewildered with unaccustomed questionings, remember with what instant appreciation of their errand the green shade was lifted from the eye, the volume thrown aside, and with what genuine, hearty interest that whole countenance would beam. At such an interview he would often read the parable of the returning prodigal; and who that heard can ever forget the pathos with which he would dwell upon the words, "But when he was yet a great way off, his father saw him, and had compassion, and ran, and fell on his neck, and kissed him." These were the moments when the springs of his nature were revealed.

"It is not so much what is said, as the way in which it is said." Never was the truth of an aphorism more patent than when a description is attempted of Dr. Wayland's method of conducting a recitation. But the picture would be incomplete without that detail. The following reminiscence is by Rev. Dr. Silas Bailey, who entered Brown in 1830:

In a résumé of what he did for the university, his first service was reorganization in discipline and instruction. A new era had opened and its demands were different from those of the preceding period. The need of education then had been for what was elementary. The country now was feeling the mighty possibilities that were inherent in itself and was developing them. The educational complexion had changed, and there was a call for what is now termed "practical education." Dr. Wayland saw the drift and met it, and to him is due the credit of inaugurating the new system at Brown, and of disseminating his ideas as an instructor to the country. In the class room he did away with the use of text-books. His theory was that the instructor should himself know what he was to teach, and should draw out the pupil so that he could state in a thorough manner what had become a part of his own knowledge. The method was analytic; that method which was used so masterly by the president, and which since his day has been characteristic of the students of Brown.

Judge Story, when professor at the Cambridge Law School, was accustomed to say that he could distinguish a graduate from Brown University by his power of seizing upon the essential points of a case and freeing it from all extraneous matter.

The value of his moral solicitude for the student was great. He was in the habit of addressing each as "my son," and impressing upon him his own personality. In an estimate of what he did for the individual members of Brown, says Prof. Chace: "We should look rather to the characters he molded, and to the moral and religious forces he set in action. These, as well as the productions of his pen, still live and will continue to live. Where in all the land can be found a place in which to-day he is not working, directly or indirectly, through those whose minds he formed and inspired. Nor will his influence terminate with the lives of those who were its immediate recipients. Moral forces never die. By a law of their nature they perpetuate and extend and multiply themselves indefinitely."

He constantly practiced what he preached, and the students knew that when a decision was given by him it had been carefully examined on all sides.

As a writer of text-books he placed within the reach of the students what they could use for themselves. His chief work, because more universally accepted, and because of its merit, was his Moral Philosophy. This was an exposé of a system of morals not culled from other writers and tinged with their views, but as it had filtered through his own mind and been subjected to his searching and critical analysis. His Intellectual Philosophy and Political Economy were of value to his own students, and, like his Moral Philosophy, were used by other institutions. The library received under him careful attention, and he fostered and developed its life. The scientific resources of the college were placed on a firm basis.

PUBLIC SERVICES.

Dr. Wayland labored not alone for the college, although that was ever first in his thoughts, but was always alive to what he could do for the community. He was the first citizen in the State, and the university was the center from which emanated those impulses that guided and maintained a high tone in the community. True, the city was not so large, and the desperate struggle for wealth had not set in, but a man of narrower mind could have caused the position of the college as a center to be much less.

The public charities found in him a ready helper, and with many he had an official connection. Through his aid as an inspector the State prison became a reformatory and not a place where criminals were confined.

During a large part of the last twenty years of his life he conducted every week a Bible class composed of convicts. The spectacle presented was most impressive— one which the angels might desire to look upon—as with heart full of love to God and man, and thought intent on serving one and doing good to the other, he took his way on the quiet Sabbath morning toward yonder prison, to seek there the outcasts from society, the children of shame and sin and crime, to gather them around him and tell to them in language of indescribable simplicity and tenderness of a Savior who loves them and who has died for them; of an atonement so large and so free that each one of them, however guilty, may have pardon and cleansing; to lift them by his broad, overflowing sympathies from their sense of forsakenness and isolation;

to kindle repentings within them; to awaken anew their moral affections, and to restore their broken relations to humanity, to God, and to heaven. He may have done many things of which the world will think more and longer, but his great life offers nothing surpassing in moral grandeur these almost divine labors.[1]

For his fellow-townsmen he was always ready to address them in words of cheer or of admonition and warning. From all the tributes to the service of the man in times of public need, no better selection could be made than from the scholarly and classic words of Prof. Chace:

A few months before his death an occasion arose for a touching exhibition of the respect in which he was held by the whole community. The country had in an instant been plunged from the height of joy into the deepest mourning. Its honored and beloved Chief Magistrate, at the moment when he was most honored and beloved, had fallen by parricidal hands. The greatness of the loss, the enormity of the crime, the terrible suddenness of the blow bewildered thought and paralyzed speech. It seemed as if Providence, which had just vouchsafed so great blessings, was, from some inscrutable cause, withdrawing its protective care. In this hour of darkness to whom should the citizens go but to him who had so often instructed and guided them? As evening draws on they gather from all quarters with one common impulse to turn their steps eastward. Beneath a weeping sky the long dark column winds its way over the hill into the valley. As it moves onward the wailings of the dirge and the measured tread are the only sounds which fall upon the still air. Having reached the residence of President Wayland, it pours itself in a dense throng around a slightly raised platform in front of it. Presently he appears, to address for the last time, as it proves, his assembled fellow-citizens. It is the same noble presence which many there had in years long gone by gazed upon with such pride and admiration from seats in the old chapel. It is the same voice whose eloquence then so inflamed them, and stirred their young bosoms to such a tumult of passion. The speaker is the same, the audience is the same. But how changed both, and how altered the circumstances! That hair playing in the breeze has been whitened by the snows of seventy winters. That venerable form is pressed by their accumulated weight.

The glorious intellectual power which sat upon those features is veiled beneath the softer lines of moral grace and beauty. It is not now the Athenian orator, but one of the old prophets, from whose touched lips flow forth the teachings of inspired wisdom. The dead first claims his thought. He recounts most appreciatively his great services and dwells with loving eulogy upon his unswerving patriotism and his high civic virtues. Next, the duties of the living and the lessons of the hour occupy attention. Then come words of devout thanksgiving, of holy trust, of sublime faith, uttered as he only ever uttered them. They fall upon that waiting assembly like a blessed benediction, assuaging grief, dispelling gloom, and kindling worship in every bosom. God is no longer at a distance, but all around and within them. They go away strengthened and comforted.

THE NEW SYSTEM.

Wayland had come before the public as an advocate of what was called the "New System in Education."[2] In a report which was pre-

---

[1] The Virtues and Services of Francis Wayland, by George I. Chace, p. 35.

[2] The influence of Thomas Jefferson's ideas of university education may perhaps be traced in Dr. Wayland's report.—ED.

sented to the corporation he embodied his ideas. As this system made a change in educational methods, an abstract of the paper is presented:

The present condition of the university can not be well understood without considering its relation to collegiate education in this country, nor can the present condition of collegiate education in this country be understood without referring to its past history and its relation to university education in Great Britain, from which it originated. The subjects, therefore, to which the attention of the corporation will be directed in the present report are the following:

1. The system of university education in Great Britain.
2. The progress and present state of university education in this country.
3. The present condition of this university.
4. The measures which the committee recommend for the purpose of enlarging the usefulness of the institution.
5. The subject of collegiate degrees: Nos. 1 and 2 were a review of these subjects. Toward the end of 2 it was shown that for the last thirty years the New England colleges could not support themselves. The demand for the article produced in the colleges was falling off, not from the want of wealth, or intelligence, or enterprise in the community, but simply because a smaller number of the community desired it.

In this dilemma two courses were again open before the colleges. The first was to adapt the article produced, to the wants of the community. The other course was to appeal to the charity of the public, and thus provide the funds by which the present system might be sustained. Have the efforts that have been made in this direction accomplished the object intended? The objects designed to be accomplished by endowment for the reduction of tuition and for furnishing it gratuitously to our colleges have been, we suppose, the following:

First. To increase the number of educated men in the whole community.

Second. To raise the standard of professional learning, and thus increase its intellectual power.

Third. To increase the number of ministers of the gospel.

From a review of the field our present system of collegiate education is not accomplishing the purposes intended. We are, therefore, forced to adopt the supposition that our colleges are not filled because we do not furnish the education desired by the people. We have instructed them upon the idea that they are to be schools of preparation for the professions.

The third point was a review of the financial situation of the college and of the impending crisis. If the institution was to be maintained some means must be adopted for its relief. Two methods present themselves.

The first is to continue it upon its present system, retaining the four years' course, considering the college as a mere preparatory school for the professions of law, medicine, and divinity, and digesting the various branches of instruction in conformity with this idea.

A second method of relieving the institution from its present embarrassments has been proposed, suggested from the view your committee has been led to take by the present condition of collegiate education in New England.

Were an institution established with the intention of adapting its construction to the wants of the whole community, its arrangements would be in harmony with the following principles:

I. The present system of adjusting collegiate study to a fixed term of four years, or to any other term, must be abandoned, and every student be allowed, within limits to be determined by statute, to carry on at the same time a greater or less number of courses, as he may choose.

II. The time allotted to each particular course of instruction would be determined by the nature of the course itself and not by its supposed relation to the wants of any particular profession.

III. The various courses should be so arranged that in so far as it is practicable every student might study what he chose, all that he chose, and nothing but what he chose. The faculty, however, at the request of a parent or guardian, should have authority to assign to any student such courses they might deem for his advantage.

IV. Every course of instruction, after it has been commenced, should be continued without interruption until it has been completed.

V. In addition to the present courses of instruction, such should be established as the wants of the various classes of the community may require.

VI. Every student attending a particular course should be at liberty to attend any other that he may desire.

VII. It should be required that no student be admitted as a candidate for a degree unless he has honorably sustained his examination in such studies as may be ordained by the corporation; that no student be under any obligation to proceed to a degree unless he choose to do so.

VIII. Every student should be entitled to a certificate of such proficiency as he may have made in every course that he has pursued.

The courses of instruction to be pursued in this institution might be as follows:

I. A course in Latin, occupying two years.
II. A course in Greek, two years.
III. A course in three modern languages.
IV. A course in pure mathematics, two years.
V. A course in mechanics, optics, and astronomy, either with or without mathematical demonstrations, one and one-half years.
VI. A course in chemistry, physiology, and geology, one and one-half years.
VII. A course in the English language and rhetoric, one year.
VIII. A course in moral and intellectual philosophy, one year.
IX. A course in political economy, one term.
X. A course in history, one term.
XI. A course in the science of teaching.
XII. A course on the principles of agriculture.
XIII. A course on the application of chemistry to the arts.
XIV. A course on the application of science to the arts.
XV. A course in the science of law.

By extending its advantages to every class in the community the number of pupils would be increased for the following reasons:

I. The course of instruction will, it is hoped, present a better preparation for the learned professions than that pursued at present. There is no reason, therefore, why this class of persons should be diminished.

II. Opportunity would be afforded to those who wished to pursue a more general course of professional education to remain in college profitably for five or six years instead of four, as at present.

III. Many young men who intend to enter the professions are unwilling or unable to spend four years in the preparatory studies of college. They would, however, cheerfully spend one or two years in such study if they were allowed to select such branches of science as they chose. This class would probably form an important addition to our numbers, and we would thus, in some degree, improve the education of a large portion of all the professions.

IV. If we except the ancient languages, there are but few of the studies now pursued in college which, if well taught, would not be attractive to young men preparing for any of the active departments of life. If these several courses were so arranged as to be easily accessible to intelligent young men of all classes, it may reasonably be expected that many will desire to spend a term, a year, or two years under our instruction.

V. It is not probable that the courses of instruction in agriculture or chemistry, or science applied to the arts, will, of necessity, occupy all the time of the student.

BROWN UNIVERSITY—MANNING HALL.

Many of these persons will desire to avail themselves of the advantages so easily placed in their power. Another source of demand for the courses in general science would thus be created.

If reasons need be offered for attempting the change in our collegiate system that has been indicated, the following will readily suggest themselves:

I. It is just. There are in this country 120 colleges, 42 theological seminaries, and 47 law schools, and we have not a single institution designed to furnish the agriculturist, the manufacturer, the mechanic, or the merchant with the education that will prepare him for what his life is to be devoted to.

II. It is expedient. Civilization is advancing, and it can only advance in the line of useful arts. It is, therefore, of the greatest national importance to spread broadcast over the community that knowledge by which alone the useful arts can be multiplied and perfected.

III. It is necessary. Anyone who will observe the progress which, within the last thirty years, has been made by the productive classes of society in power, wealth, and influence, must be convinced that a system of education practically restricted to a class vastly smaller and rapidly decreasing in influence can not possibly continue.

The fourth topic discussed the history of degrees, and a comparative view of them as in use here and in England was presented. The fear was expressed that the amount of study on the classics would be diminished. To this it was replied if, by placing Latin and Greek upon their own merits, they are unable to retain their present place in the education of civilized and Christianized man, then let them give place to something better. They have by right no preeminence over other studies, and it is absurd to claim it for them.

In view of these facts and arguments, the committee have arrived at the following conclusions:

I. This college can not, under any circumstances, be long sustained without large addition to its funds.

II. In the present condition of collegiate education in New England it is not probable that addition to its funds would increase the number of its students, unless large provisions were also made for gratuitous tuition.

III. Such funds might attract students from other colleges, but would do little either to increase the aggregate number of educated men or to extend the advantages of education to those classes of the community which do not now enjoy them.

IV. There is reason to hope that the same amount of funds which would be necessary to sustain the college under the present system might, if the system were modified in the manner above suggested, add greatly to the number of students and at the same time confer inestimable advantages on every class of society.

This report was adopted and the sum of $125,000 raised. This pamphlet created no little excitement in academic circles, and was criticised favorably and unfavorably. Suffice it to say, it marked the dawning of a new era in education. The system was never adopted in its entirety as devised by the author; but sufficiently so to demonstrate its success at that time, although eventually it was modified.

MANNING HALL.

This, the third building of the university, was the gift of Nicholas Brown, who gave it the name, Manning Hall, in honor of the first president. The ground floor was at first used for the library, and the chapel was in the upper portion. In the chapel is a memorial tablet to Nicholas Brown and to those who fell in the civil war. The building possesses some interest from the fact that it is a model of the temple of Diana—Propylea in Eleusis—but just twice the size. When the new building was erected for the library, the books were removed from Manning Hall, and the room used for recitations. It now contains the collection of casts.

RHODE ISLAND HALL.

The university had been in need of a building for lecture rooms and for the reception of geological and physiological specimens. In 1836 the corporation appointed a committee to devise means for erecting such a building. The history of Rhode Island Hall will be given in the following extract from the president's annual report to the faculty in 1839:

Nearly two years since the president of the university received a letter from a lady interested in the prosperity of the institution, generously offering the sum of $500, to be appointed to the increase of the means of instruction in physical science, provided that the additional sum of $1,500 should, within a specified time, be subscribed towards the same object. An effort was made to raise the requisite sum, but it unfortunately failed. The lady then expressed her willingness to contribute the the same amount in aid of any other effort which might be made to promote the interests of learning in the university.

At the very time when this subject was in agitation, several benevolent gentlemen in Providence privately expressed to some members of the corporation a willingness to unite in any attempt that might be thought important to promote the prosperity of the institution. Soon after the last commencement (1838) these gentlemen met at the house of the president, and the sum of $2,500 (including the offer before mentioned) was subscribed towards the erection of an additional building to be devoted to the purposes of physical science. After considerable effort had been made, and it seemed impossible to raise the subscription to the required amount, the treasurer of the university received from the munificent benefactor of this institution—the Hon. Nicholas Brown—a letter, of which the following is a copy:

PROVIDENCE, *March 18, 1839.*

MOSES BROWN IVES, Esq.,
Treasurer of Brown University:

DEAR SIR: In common with a number of the friends of Brown University, I desire the erection of a suitable mansion house for the president, and likewise of another college edifice for the accommodation of the departments of natural philosophy, chemistry, mineralogy, geology, and natural history. As it is highly important that these buildings, so necessary to the welfare of the institution, should be erected without delay, I hereby tender to the acceptance of the corporation two lots of land on Waterman street as a site for the president's house and the lot of land called the "Hopkins estate," on George street, as a site for the college edifice; and I hereby pledge myself for the sum of $10,000, viz, $7,000 for the president's house and $3,000 toward the erection of the college edifice, the suitable improvement of the adjacent grounds, and the increase of the permanent means of instruction in the departments of chemistry, mineralogy, etc., provided an equal amount be subscribed by the friends of the university before the 1st of May next.

I am, with affectionate regards, and great personal respect for all the friends and patrons of the university, respectfully,

NICHOLAS BROWN.

The additional sum of $10,890 was raised, and Rhode Island Hall was dedicated September 4, 1840, Prof. William G. Goddard having written the address. On account of his sudden illness he was prevented from reading it.

In 1855 Dr. Wayland tendered his resignation, for he felt that his health would not permit him to carry on the responsibilities of the office. Regretfully this was accepted. During his retirement he pursued his literary duties, and in 1857 he resumed pastoral duties for a year. He never ceased to identify himself with every good word and work. His death occurred at his home in Providence, September 30, 1865.[1]

UNIVERSITY EXTENSION.

In late years much has been said and accomplished with reference to university extension, or an attempt to bring the university, or higher education, down to the people. The movement, when fairly tried, has met with success. Reference has been made to an earlier attempt, in 1785, by Prof. Waterhouse, who gave a course of lectures in the State house. In 1853 there was another course, for the professor of chemistry wished, in accord with the design of the new system, to make his department of some practical benefit to the artisans and mechanics in the city. The number of men engaged in the jewelry trade gave him the idea for his course, which he announced as "The chemistry of the precious metals," and consisted of eight lectures. They were made just as practical as possible, and their success may be inferred from the fact that an audience of nearly 335 assembled. Said one: "I see now why it is that I have so often failed. I have been doing, or trying to do, these things all my life without ever knowing why." Said another: "If I had known these things years ago, it would have saved me thousands of dollars."

In recent years lectures have been given under university auspices from time to time, and in 1890 was formed The Historical and Political Economy Association, which brought the university to the people, through the medium of lectures.

PRESIDENT SEARS, 1855-1867.

President Wayland resigned the presidency in 1855, and the corporation, by a unanimous vote, elected the Rev. Barnas Sears to be his successor. Wayland by his withdrawal had made a large place vacant, and the position demanded a man of ability. At the time of his acceptance Dr. Sears had been serving as secretary of the Massachusetts Board of Education, to which office he had been elected upon the res-

---

[1] Dr. Wayland is the author of that characteristic saying quoted with evident approval by ex-President A. D. White, "A college president's time is nibbled away by ducks." President Edward Everett, on learning that Fisher Ames had once declined the presidency of Harvard College, said to Jared Sparks, "Fisher Ames is a wise man."—ED.

ignation of Horace Mann in 1848. Sears was prominent as an educator and had filled all the positions of trust with such fidelity and efficiency that he was the choice of the corporation for the presidency of the college. His labor was honorable not only to his *alma mater*, but also to the nation, to whom he had rendered devoted and efficient service in his wise administration of a great philanthropy, of which he was the general agent.

BIOGRAPHY.

Barnas Sears was born in Sandisfield, Mass., 1802. His father was a farmer and his mother a woman of piety. As a boy Barnas was said to be bright and full of fun. When he reached the age of 15 he asked his father for his time, in order that he might support himself. At this time an uncle of his told the father that he might as well let the boy go, as he was nothing but a book boy anyhow, and never seemed to care about work. The boy was a lover of books, and his eager desire for a liberal education was encouraged and stimulated by his mother. So eager was he in the pursuit of knowledge that it is said he would spend the noonings in reading, and would sometimes encroach on the work hours. The crisis of his life dated from his thirteenth year, when he united with the church. It was then that he decided to consecrate himself to the Christian ministry, and his later effort at self-support was to secure the means for the fulfillment of his life's purpose. By laboring on the farm in the summer and teaching school in the winter he accumulated the means for his collegiate education. He entered Brown, graduating in the class of 1825. He said while in college that it was his ambition at the outset of his college career to stand at the head of his class, but subsequently he preferred a broader scholarship without "cramming," and therefore he devoted himself to a wider range of study than that which was prescribed in the ordinary curriculum.

The following statement which he made to Prof. Stearns will illustrate his thoroughness. He told him that he once failed to locate an event which happened in Constantinople. In consequence he secured all the maps and plans he could find concerning the city, and made himself so familiar with its lanes and streets that he believed were he to visit it he would be as much at home as in the city of Boston. A favorite maxim of his was, "Whatever is worth doing at all is worth doing well."

After the completion of his course at Brown he entered the Theological Seminary at Newton, graduating with the class of 1828. He took the pastorate of a Baptist church in Hartford, but in consequence of ill health was obliged to leave after two years. From there he went to the professorship of ancient languages in Hamilton Literary and Theological Institution, now Colgate University. At his suggestion a change was made in the course of study in theology, and he was transferred to the chair of Biblical theology. Ill health and the fact

BROWN UNIVERSITY — RHODE ISLAND HALL.

that no class was ready for instruction in the new department enabled him to study in Germany for a season.

From Halle he went to Leipsic and came under the influence of Winer, Rosenmüller, and Hermann, "stimulated," as he says, "by their genius and learning." Here we find the old love for classical studies coming to the front. "I am drinking," he says, "at the fountain of Greek and Roman literature, and could easily make this the pursuit of my life. English is becoming a dead language to me and Latin a living one." From Leipsic he went to Berlin. Here, to use his own language, he came into "more or less relationship with Müller (with whom no living philologist can dispute the palm); Bopp, the founder and richest ornament of the Sanskrit school of comparative philology; Böckh, the greatest living master of Grecian antiquity; Bekker, the greatest editor of the Greek classics from manuscript authorities; Zumpt, the Latin grammarian; Grimm, the greatest German lexicographer and antiquary; Charles Ritter, the prince of geographers; Ranke, the historian, with no rival but Guizot; Neander, the reformer and almost the creator of philosophical church history; and Tieck, the poet, until recently the pride of the court of Dresden."[1] In these three universities, Halle, Leipsic, and Berlin, he laid the foundations and marked the boundaries of the department of Biblical theology in Hamilton.

Sears had gone to Germany at a time when few, especially in the department of Biblical criticism, had been able so to do; but he felt the need of a fresh study of the Hebrew and Greek, with all the side lights. He himself was unwilling "to rest until a conscious mastery of the scholarship and advanced thought of Germany had rendered him master of the situation as a helper, interpreter, and leader of the advancing thought of his own country." Returning to this country he was called to Newton, but he felt that Hamilton had the prior claim, although before the year closed he accepted the call to Newton, and was there till 1848.

While at Newton, in a report to the trustees, he said: "The leading objects of the teachers have been: (1) To create a deep interest in the work; (2) to point out the extent and connections of the subject of inquiry, together with the method to be pursued, and the means to be employed; (3) to have the results of such investigations and reflections presented, first by the student, then by the class, and lastly by the teachers, in free but not polemic discussions; to have the fundamental doctrines, collateral topics in any branch of study, the most important works, ancient and modern, on theology, the best chapters and treatises on particular topics made the subject of analysis, critiques, translations, etc., to be read before the class and followed by oral discussions. Neither the examination of text-books nor formal lectures have been adopted."

Such were his methods while at the seminary.

---

[1] Prof. O. S. Stearns. Baptist Quarterly Review, 1883. No. 17.

PUBLIC SERVICES.

When Dr. Sears assumed the presidency of Brown he had gained a practical insight into educational matters, inasmuch as he had succeeded Horace Mann as the secretary of the Massachusetts Board of Education. Previous to that he had taught at Madison University and also at Newton. The time spent in foreign study was used most advantageously, as may be seen from his letter quoted above. The success which he had acquired by his management of the Board of Education may be seen from the remarks made by Mr. Boutwell:

> When the intellectual powers of Dr. Sears were in their fullness, when his scholarship was recognized generally by learned men and by universities, when his capacity for useful public services had been decided and justified by experience, he accepted the office of secretary of the Massachusetts Board of Education. His predecessor—his only predecessor—was Horace Mann, that eminent leader of public opinion, the reformer of the methods and the results of education, who had impressed his ideas upon the people and woven his policy into the institutions of the State before his career had been a career of adversity, in which, indeed, he had triumphed. But there lingered in the minds of many the belief that the changes which he had introduced and the reforms which he had established would in no distant day be overthrown. The State in Dr. Sears secured an exponent, an advocate, and a most temperate defender of the reforms which Horace Mann had introduced. There was no step backward, but he presented always a genial and attractive side to every subject to the public. In the normal schools, in the teachers' institutes, in the county associations, he brought into the public service eminent men and distinguished teachers, of whom I may mention Prof. Felton, Prof. Agassiz, Lowell Mason, and others; and thus were the youth and the children of the State brought under the influence of persons who gave them high ideas of life and the best practical illustration of the art of teaching. What had been regarded in Mr. Mann's time by many as experimental became under Dr. Sears an established and recognized institution of the State. Our system of education—schools for all the people and sustained by the people—was placed upon a foundation as immovable as the foundation of the State itself.[1]

PEABODY TRUST FUND.

From these experiences, that were rich in developing and rounding his scholarly mind, he took the presidency of Brown University. He was at its head till 1867. In order to understand what a rare man he was, and what an institution would gain with him at its head, his career from 1867 will be sketched. It is apropos of his presidency, because he was called away from the very midst of his duties at the university, and was able at once to assume the duties of his new position, which was that of general agent of the Peabody Trust Fund, for promotion of education in the more destitute portions of the Southern and Southwestern States. Mr. Peabody had told his intention to Robert C. Winthrop and that gentleman knew his wishes. The board which he had chosen to care for the trust, was organized in February, 1867, but was at a loss as to how the trust should be executed. Mr. Winthrop met Dr. Sears the next month in Boston, and told him the perplexities

---

[1] Remarks by Hon. George S. Boutwell on the death of Dr. Sears

and embarrassments which were weighing upon him, for Mr. Peabody had wished him to direct the primary action of the board. He asked Dr. Sears if he would give him the benefit of his advice and judgment on the whole matter. Dr. Sears consented and wrote him a letter, which contained in suggestion the very policy which was adopted in the execution of the trust. He also promised that he would meet with the board for aid and counsel if his help should be needed. The board did need him and he met with it in March at the adjourned meeting. He was unanimously chosen as its general agent, but did not accept till the 9th of April. He served in this capacity for thirteen years, till his death, in 1880, at Saratoga.

The administration of this trust of $2,000,000 was difficult and delicate. The South was in that condition in which a country is left after the conclusion of a civil war; there was no precedent which could be followed in the execution of the trust; and such a course of conduct must be followed that should prove advantageous for the future. In the words of Mr. Winthrop, in reference to the letter of suggestion which Dr. Sears wrote him—

> This letter, so hastily written, has indeed proved to be a perfect chart of our course, as the writer of it has proved to have been a perfect pilot.

The relations existing between Dr. Sears and Mr. Winthrop were close, and the choice of Dr. Sears was a wise one. How wise was his management, the following extract from Mr. Peabody's own words will indicate:

> I must not omit to congratulate you, and all who have at heart the best interests of this educational enterprise, upon your obtaining the highly valuable services of Dr. Sears as your general agent—services valuable not merely in the organization of schools and of a system of public education, but in the good effect which his conciliatory and sympathizing course has had, wherever he has met or become associated with the communities of the South, in social or business relations.[1]

The general esteem in which Dr. Sears was held, as agent of the Peabody Fund, was voiced by Mr. Winthrop when he addressed the board at its meeting in February, 1881, the year following the death of Dr. Sears:

> * * * But he did not conclude that letter without recalling the words of encouragement addressed to him by Mr. Peabody when they parted for the last time: "Your name will be remembered in connection with mine." And so it will be. It is not too much for me to say, and I am sure you will all agree with me, that whenever and wherever the name of George Peabody shall be remembered and honored as the munificent founder of this great trust for Southern education—the earliest signal manifestation of a spirit of reconciliation toward those from whom we have been so unhappily alienated—the name of Dr. Barnas Sears will be recalled and honored also, as the original organizer and devoted administrator of the trust for the first thirteen years of its existence—the years which have determined its policy and insured its success.[2]

---

[1] Peabody Educational Fund. Proceedings, Vol. II, p. 314.
[2] Hon. Robert C. Winthrop in Peabody Educational Fund. Proceedings, Vol. II, p. 320.

RECOLLECTIONS OF DR. SEARS.

The public services of Dr. Sears just preceding and subsequent to his presidency of the college have been cited to show the generous equipment of the man who was to preside over the academic councils of the university. His genius was excelled only by his modesty. Said one who knew him well at this period:

> He was one of the most unassuming men I ever saw. The charms of his conversation I shall never forget.

The students respected and loved Dr. Sears. It was his practice to put the young men on their honor, and he also abolished many of the minor penalties of college discipline. He wished his pupils to feel that they could confide in him and that they would allow him to aid them. But while his discipline was paternal, he could also be severe if the occasion warranted it, and the student who incurred his righteous indignation found him strict and stern. He was able to arouse in his pupils a desire to know the truth and to set before them lofty ideals, whereby they could make better their own and the lives of their fellows. Said one of his students:

> If I have made any attainments in study or done any good work for the church of Christ it has been largely due to the influence of Dr. Sears. I have always cherished a filial reverence for the great teacher who inspired me, and a genuine love for the large-hearted Christian, who has been to me an ideal manhood.

The best impression of his class-room manner is obtained from this reminiscence by J. B. G. Pidge, of Philadelphia:

> There will be no sincerer mourners for Dr. Sears than the graduates of Brown under his presidency from 1855-1867. They will feel such sorrow at his loss as is only experienced at the death of a dear friend. They will recall him as the well-beloved president, the inspiring teacher, the broad and generous scholar. Whatever other testimonies his memory may receive, the students of Brown during those years will pay the tribute of love. For Dr. Sears was, above all, perhaps, a "loved" president. The students in his classes were led, not driven. Perhaps on this account lazy and dull students made but little progress under him, and those who only learned what they must came forth from his instructions with a smaller amount of actual information than they were in the habit of carrying away from a course of study. But even such students came forth with minds broadened with contact with scholarship so complete and well rounded, and if he did not succeed in enticing them to a love of good learning he made them feel the immense superiority of true scholarship and culture, the culture and scholarship which embrace both heart and mind, to that education which makes a man merely a walking text-book.
>
> It was doubtless an easy task for the indolent to pass through the studies of Dr. Sears's course, for he was not a severe disciplinarian, and those who had been in mortal dread of the recitation room felt that they had at last reached a haven of rest. The little book in which the professor was wont to mark the value of a student's recitation was no longer seen. It was a tradition in the college that Dr. Sears did all the marking of his classes at the end of the term. But, however that might be, the students were well aware that their recitations were estimated not by any accidental qualities which they might possess, but by their general character. He knew that he should not receive any special credit for some sudden brilliancy nor any discredit for some momentary deficiency. Dr. Sears acted on the principle that learning should be sought for its own sake; and, therefore, he kept entirely in

the background every other incentive. The student who could not be stimulated by the mere love of learning had, therefore, an easy time of it and brought away but small results. But for those who could be led by such an incentive the introduction to Dr. Sears's classes marked an epoch in their mental development. The recitation room lost the feverish interest it had possessed as a place where each day the student's measurement was taken and recorded, and became a place of purest enjoyment. Study was made easy for the bright as well as for the dull student, but it was made easy for the former because it was rendered so attractive. He began to see the difference between culture and learning, and he grew to take broader ideas of what education should be.

The hours at the feet of Dr. Sears sifted men as they had not been sifted before. No mere parrot-like recitations would now suffice—such scholarship was at a discount. It was no longer mere fluency of tongue and readiness of memory, nor on the other hand any pretensions and profound egotism that stepped to the front, but the true scholar who loved learning, but also enduring labor as a necessary means to its acquisition. And I am convinced that the influence of that recitation room has been a larger one than we ever dreamed it could become. Dr. Sears cared so little to impress his own ideas upon us that he used to say he cared not whether we remembered what he taught or not, so that we only learned to think for ourselves. Few of his students, perhaps, will be able to remember his views of disputed points in philosophy, for he never made them prominent; but they can never forget the general tenor of his instructions, which sought to imbue them with a love of truth and goodness, and made the good life appear the only true life.

His task was a difficult one, in that he was called to be the successor of Dr. Wayland, who for twenty-five years had served the university. But by his devotion to the cause of religion and education he soon won the confidence of the friends of Brown. Regarding his connection with the faculty Prof. Lincoln said:

Of all the administrators of the affairs of the college no one was more highly esteemed and more truly loved during all the time of his administration than President Sears. I remember how he awakened our admiration by the stores of knowledge which he had always ready at either hand, how he impressed all with profound respect for religion and love of God. I am sure that all his pupils, whether in the class room where he taught them or in the chapel where he preached to them, were impressed by the soundness of his judgments, and I think he bound them to him by the sincerity and unaffected interest which he always showed for their personal welfare.

SCHOLARSHIPS.

In the days of Manning a scheme had been devised by him whereby worthy young men could be aided in securing an education when they had not sufficient means of their own. Manning's views are embodied in a letter which he wrote in 1783 to Dr. Stennett, of London:

Several pious youths, who promised fair for the ministry, having picked up some grammar learning, have applied to me to know whether anyway can open for their assistance in getting an education. This has led me to think of a plan to assist such, and I have sketched out the following: That the Rev. Messrs. Samuel Stillman, Gardner Thurston, Isaac Backus, John Gano, Hezekiah Smith, with the president, be a standing committee of the corporation, and in case of the demise of any of them their number to be filled up from time to time by themselves, who, or the major part of them, shall examine or approve of such as shall be candidates to receive the assistance which may be proffered to worthy characters in that way, and to say in what proportions it shall be dealt out to them. It will be easy to procure a vote of the corporation to invest this committee with all necessary powers to discharge this trust, and I have fixed upon men whose doctrinal and practical principles, as well as their character in this country, will entitle them to the highest confidence of benefactors to this fund. I was long convinced that a plan of this kind would be vastly serviceable and proposed it to some of my friends, whose only objection against it was its interference with endowing the college, which was an object of the greatest importance; but I am of opinion that many would be induced to give for this purpose who would not on any other consideration. Should a donation be offered, and these persons be mentioned for the trust in this way I have suggested, by some gentleman out of the corporation, I am convinced that it would immediately take, and that something considerable could soon be raised, which would be of standing benefit to our churches and more widely disseminate the knowledge of truth. Such has been the feeling through New England in favor of a college education that our pious illiterate ministers are greatly circumscribed in their sphere of usefulness, of which many of them are sufficiently sensible, and heartily wish their successors may be enabled to obviate this objection. A great and effectual door is opened for the labors of Baptist ministers throughout our vast, extended frontiers, and many new churches have been lately constituted in that howling wilderness; and indeed the labors of our society seem there generally preferred.

Nothing was accomplished at this time, because there was no provision made by which funds could be secured for that purpose. It was problematical what Dr. Stennett would have done had he lived, for he died nearly three months before this letter was sent. The letter, however, indicated Manning's sentiments on the matter.

During the presidency of Dr. Sears a system of scholarships was founded upon a basis very similar to that suggested by Manning, except that they were open to young men of any denomination. President Sears considered this foundation as one of the most important acts in his administration. He said:

The contributions for scholarships and for general purposes made by the business men of Providence and vicinity during the past year are received, not only as an evidence of interest in the success of the college, but as a pledge of future support from the people themselves, as well as from a few distinguished patrons. That between 25 and 30 individuals could be found, most of whom had never before been in any way identified with the college, to contribute $1,000 apiece to supply its wants and increase its influence is one of the most pleasing and encouraging signs of the times. This is not, indeed, the first time that the people of Providence have shown their liberality as patrons of learning, but never before have contributions fixed at this standard come from so many individuals.

A fund had been left by Nicholas Brown and the corporation voted in 1858 to devote it to the purpose of aiding deserving young men in obtaining their education while members of the university. This gave 11 scholarships, at $1,000 each. In addition to those there were 36 others, at $1,000 each.

The university has now about 100 scholarships. Sixty-four of them are of $1,000 each. The income of these is given, under the direction of a committee appointed by the corporation, to meritorious students who may need pecuniary assistance; but a scholarship is forfeited if the candidate incurs college censure, or fails to secure at least 75 per cent of the maximum marking. The $1,000 scholarships are as follows, each, unless otherwise indicated, bearing the name of its founder:

The eleven Nicholas Brown Scholarships.
The four University Scholarships.
The President's (Sears) Scholarship.
The six Alva Woods Scholarships.
The James H. Duncan Scholarship.
The Isaac Davis Scholarship.
The Arnold Whipple Scholarship, founded by Mrs. Arnold Whipple.
The Ephraim Wheaton Scholarship, founded by James Wheaton.
The Joseph Brown Scholarship, founded by Mrs. E. B. Rogers.
The Gardner Colby Scholarship.
The James Y. Smith Scholarship.
The two S. S. Bradford Scholarships.
The Frances R. Arnold Scholarship.
The Cornelia E. Green Scholarship.
The Crocker Scholarship, founded by Robert H. and Thomas P. Ives, trustee.
The Clark Scholarship, also founded by the Messrs. Ives.
The Albert Day Scholarship.
The Henry P. Kent Scholarship.
The Romeo Elton Scholarship.
The five Annie E. Waters Scholarships.
The L. Fairbrother Scholarship, founded by Mrs. L. Fairbrother.
The George Lawton Scholarship.
The John P. Crozer Scholarship, founded by Mrs. Margaret Bucknell.
The Horatio N. Slater Scholarship.
The Earl P. Mason Scholarship.
The Newport Scholarship, founded by William Sanford Rogers.
The Alexis Caswell Scholarship.
The George K. and H. A. Pevear Scholarship.
The Joseph C. Hartshorn Scholarship I.
The Rogers High School Scholarship, founded by William Sanford Rogers.
The James Wheaton Scholarship.
The Charles Thurber Scholarship.
The Pardon Miller Scholarship, founded by Mrs. Ann E. Miller.
The Hezekiah S. Chase Scholarship.
The William Bucknell Scholarship.
The Austin Merrick Scholarship, founded by Mrs. Olive E. Merrick.
The three (Henry) Jackson Scholarships.
The Mumford Scholarship, founded by Mrs. Louisa D. Mumford.
The Henry Clifford Knight Scholarship, founded by Miss Amelia S. Knight, in memory of her brother, a member of the class of 1875.
The Thurston Scholarship, founded by Hon. Benjamin F. Thurston.
The Rufus Babcock Scholarship, founded by Mrs. Caroline Vassar

Babcock Jones, in memory of her father, Rev. Rufus Babcock, D. D., of the class of 1821.

Besides the above scholarships there are others, the assignment of which is made subject to special provisions. These are as follows:

The Bartlett Scholarship, of $4,000, founded by Mrs. Elizabeth Slater Bartlett, the income to be "devoted to the support of one or more students needing pecuniary aid and giving promise by studious aims and by character and scholarship of rising to distinction and usefulness."

The Glover Scholarships, of $5,000, founded by Henry R. Glover, "in memory of his father, Samuel Glover, a graduate of the college, of the class of 1808, and of his brother, Samuel Glover, jr., of the class of 1839." Assignment is made upon the basis of character and attainments.

The Scholarship of the Class of 1838, of $3,800, founded by members of the class of 1838, and also assigned upon the basis of character and scholarship.

The Philadelphia Alumni Scholarship, of $1,500, founded by the "Philadelphia Alumni Association of Brown University."

The Joseph Charles Hartshorn Scholarship II, of $2,000, founded by the gentleman whose name it bears.

The George J. Sherman Scholarships I and II, of $1,000 each, founded by the gentleman whose name they bear.

The Scholarships of the Department of Agriculture. By resolutions of the general assembly of the State of Rhode Island the national grant "for the benefit of agriculture and the mechanic arts" was given to Brown University; and the fund of $50,000 which has accrued from this grant is, by agreement on the part of the university, devoted to the education of scholars, each at the rate of $75 per annum, to the extent of the entire annual income. Appointments to these scholarships are made, on the nomination of the general assembly, by the governor and secretary of state, in conjunction with the president of the university.

The "aid fund" is a fund of several thousand dollars, the income of which is applied, either by loan or by gift, to the assistance of deserving young men of limited means.

EXEMPTION FROM TAXATION.

And furthermore, for the greater encouragement of this seminary of learning, and that the same may be amply endowed and enfranchised with the same privileges, dignities, and immunities enjoyed by the American colleges and European universities, we do grant, enact, ordain, and declare, and it is hereby granted, enacted, ordained, and declared, that the college estate, the estates, persons, and families of the president and professors, for the time being, lying and being within the colony, with the persons of the tutors and students, during their residence at the college, shall be freed and exempted from all taxes, serving on juries, and menial services.

Such were the provisions of the charter with regard to exemption from taxation. During the commencement of the war period this subject of taxation was made a matter of discussion, but was so settled as to preserve cordial the relations between the university and the city. This was not, however, the first time that this subject had aroused discussion. As early as 1772, by the town meeting, "all taxes" were construed as applying to the taxes that were due the colony, and the annual town tax was assessed and levied on the estates of the president and the professors. For two years this practice was followed, but in 1774 the assessors omitted to assess them on the ground that they were exempted by the charter. This provoked a newspaper discussion which was so animated that it was suggested a special town meeting be called, but wiser counsel prevailed. The following document, found in the archives of the university, will show the feeling in the college on the subject:

In order to give satisfaction to the town of Providence, we whose names are underwritten do declare and make known that it is our real sentiment that the college estate within the town (the edifice itself, president's house and garden, and the land appropriated to the use of a yard to the college excepted), together with the person and estates of the president and professors, are in law and justice bound to pay their equal proportion of the town rates. Therefore, we do publicly and solemnly promise, under the freemen of the town now in town meeting assembled, that we will both in our public and private assemblies exert ourselves to the utmost of our abilities to cause for the future all taxes that shall be levied on the person and estates aforesaid by this town to be punctually paid. In witness whereof we have hereunto set our hands, in Providence, this 19th day of April, A. D. 1774.

The discussion was revived during the period of the "late unpleasantness" and conducted with calmness on each side. The president, with an eye to the future good of the college, argued that the wealthy professors were the ones who would receive the greater advantage from such exemption, and not those who had but little property to be taxed. Then, too, in our form of government, for an institution of learning to flourish it must have the good will of the people. On the other hand, he held that the general assembly had never made any appropriation for the college, which had been of great benefit to the State, hence any interference with the chartered rights would be unjust.

In 1862, after various preliminary steps, the following act was passed:

Whereas in times of public danger all persons ought to bear their share of the public burdens in proportion to their ability, and this general assembly have full confidence in the patriotism of the said president and professors and in their willingness to bear their proper share of the taxation necessary for the preservation of one Union and Constitution: Therefore,

It is enacted by the general assembly as follows: So much of the act entitled "An act for the establishment of a college or university within this colony," passed at the February session, A. D. 1764, as exempts the estates, persons, and families of the president and professors of said institution, now known as Brown University, from taxation, is hereby repealed.

In the house there was a spirited debate on this act, and it was voted to refer the matter to the committee on the judiciary, with instructions that the subject be presented to the corporation of the university. The final act, as below given, will indicate the next succeeding steps and the compromise which was adopted.

The corporation referred to the fact that the legislature proposed to free from taxation property under the value of $10,000, belonging to the academic staff; that the institution had been created to promote liberal education, and had been maintained solely by private benefactions; that the greatest good could be accomplished by maintenance of cordial relations between the university and the State, and that the action of the assembly was based on the event of the assent of the corporation. In accordance with these statements the following resolution was passed by the corporation:

> It is hereby voted and declared by the corporation of Brown University that, being authorized by the president and professors of said university, this corporation does, in behalf of the president and professors and in behalf of said corporation, consent to said act passed by the general assembly of the State of Rhode Island at its present session as aforesaid.

This compromise effected an amicable settlement of this vexed question, and was considered by each side to be fair. It did much to remove any prejudice which was beginning to arise on the part of the people against the college.

AGRICULTURAL LANDS.

In 1862 the college funds were increased to the extent of $50,000 through the acceptance of the agricultural lands, as they were called. These were lands of which the income was to be devoted to "Endowment, support, and maintenance of at least one college, where the leading object shall be, without excluding other scientific and classical studies, and including military tactics, to teach such branches of learning as are related to agriculture and the mechanic arts, in such manner as the legislatures of the States may respectively prescribe, in order to promote the liberal and practical education of the industrial classes in the several pursuits and professions of life."

The State legislature made the proper application, and the proportionate number, 120,000 acres (30,000 acres for each Senator and Representative in Congress from the State in question), fell to Rhode Island. They were transferred to Brown University by the legislature, upon the agreement of the corporation to fulfill certain particulars, among which were the following: To provide a college or department in the university where the branches of learning relating to agriculture and mechanic arts could be taught. Also to educate scholars, each at the rate of $100 per annum, to the extent of the entire annual income from said proceeds, subject to the proviso as aforesaid; the governor and secretary of state to have the right on or before commencement day of each year, and in conjunction with the president of the university, to nominate candidates for vacancies occurring in said college or department.

The sale of these lands brought into the treasury of the university the sum of $50,000.

In the report of President Andrews, to the corporation for 1890, there appears the following sentiment regarding the agricultural fund:

> The attention of the corporation is invited to the agricultural fund of $50,000, which originated from the sale of the land scrip donated to the State of Rhode Island by act of Congress, July 2, 1862, and to Brown University by an act of the Rhode Island general assembly in January, 1863. Although decisions by the highest courts in the land are to the effect that this money actually belongs to us and not to the State, yet now that Rhode Island has its own college devoted to agricultural studies, it seems to me both just and wise to let the State, whence we derived it, receive it back. Being applied in the way of scholarships, it affords no sustenance to our teaching staff—the reverse, rather, since it is ours only on condition that we maintain a course in agriculture, which would otherwise, however desirable, not be strictly necessary. Much as this fund has enlarged our ability to aid students, we shall manage to get on without it; while the relinquishment of it can not but affect favorably the name and influence of the University throughout this State. Should the gift be refunded, it might be well to stipulate that all the worthy men upon the foundation at the time remain its beneficiaries till their graduation.

Such being the opinion of the president, a committee was chosen to consider the question, and report to the corporation at its meeting in September, 1890.

The committee on the return of the agricultural fund reported that while the university was under certain obligations to the State, it had not come under any obligation to the United States by the acceptance of the sum, which would make it improper to return it to the State without the National Government's consent. The committee therefore thinks it will be the part of wisdom and good policy for the corporation to make the return providing it can be made on such terms as will be proper and satisfactory and as will relieve the corporation from further duties and obligations in the matter.

CHEMICAL LABORATORY.

As the college had been adding to the facilities in the departments of the arts and sciences, a laboratory for chemistry was needed. In 1862 a building for such a purpose was erected, through the instrumentality of Nathaniel P. Hill, who obtained subscriptions to the amount of $14,250. The credit of the plans without and the arrangements within are due to Prof. Hill. He had visited some of the best laboratories in the State and had given much attention to the department of science. The building was well adapted for its uses and has served as a model for other institutions which have been seeking one of a similar nature.

PROFESSOR DUNN.

During the latter part of this period occurred the death of Prof. Dunn, who, for the last sixteen years, had occupied the chair of rhetoric and English literature. Prof. Diman, in a discourse which he delivered on Prof. Dunn, called him a Christian scholar. Too often chief importance is attached to what is taught rather than to the ability and influence of the teacher. Such was the opinion of Prof. Diman, who said of him,

> I am inclined to estimate his success and usefulness as an instructor, yet I am not sure that, after all, one of the chief advantages which his pupils derived from contact with him was the inestimable privilege of being so long and so familiarly associated with such a polished gentleman.

It is fitting, therefore, that in the history of the university he loved so well particular tribute should be paid to him. He was graduated from Brown at the age of little more than 18, and secured the highest honors of the class. For the two years succeeding 1844 he gave instruction in French at the university. Three years were devoted to study at the theological seminary at Princeton, where he excelled as a Hebrew scholar. In 1848 he had a parish in Camden, and from there, in 1851, received a call to the professorship of rhetoric and English literature at Brown. To this position he brought an ability in the languages and a love for his work. He was a man of great conscientiousness; hence in making such a change from the pulpit to a professorship he was influenced by the most serious convictions.

> Prof. Dunn did not embrace a literary career as a mere refuge from irksome obligations. He relinquished the ministry with profound regret, and often looked back upon it with longing eyes. It was evident to all that he did not enter upon his new position enamored of that lettered ease, which, with too many, is the chief recommendation of a literary life. Still less did he look upon it as a mere support, to be laid aside when some more lucrative employment should present itself.

The unconscious influence of a man like him upon the students was impressive, how impressive they never knew till, without the spell of its quiet and calm, they could reflect and then feel its loss.

> He was not one of those supreme natures that grasp and hold; he rather by his genial and subtle contact unconsciously insinuated into others something of his own refinement, so that perhaps he really shaped them most when they seemed least subject to his sway.

Perhaps no better outline of the man, or marked characteristic of Prof. Dunn, could be given than in the words again of Diman:

> Disposition as well as duty made him a purely academic man. Simple in his habits, and with no expensive tastes save a pardonable craving for the best editions of the best authors, he was satisfied with his moderate stipend, and no outside interests ever chilled his zeal in his proper work. With this work nothing was ever allowed to interfere. Early and late it filled his thoughts. It pursued him in the seasons set apart for rest and relaxation, and often called him back in the heat of summer, and when his colleagues were yet oblivious of all college cares, to direct, through weary days and sleepless nights, the laborious preparations for commencement. It was characteristic of the man that he left full directions for the day which he did not live to witness.

Of books his favorite was Bacon's Essays. On Sunday he would read the Christian Year, and always the Collect. Thackeray had for him a peculiar charm, and when tired, he would find amusement in the mirth-provoking pages of Pickwick. He was a man of simple, unaffected faith. "He entered the kingdom of Heaven as a little child, and the simple unquestioning faith of childhood he never lost." In a man of scholarly attainment it is always a pleasure to note a broad outlook and a catholicity of view. "As his experience became richer, his sympathies became more enlarged. The longer he lived the less he regarded what is outward and accidental, the more what is inward and essential."

In concluding the sketch of the life of Prof. Dunn, we may quote the eulogy paid to cultured scholarship so characteristic of him:

But the culture of Prof. Dunn, whether displayed in his conversation or in his style, derived its peculiar charm from its inseparable connection with himself. It was not, as with so many, a mere external varnish; it permeated the whole man. To this was due its delightful simplicity and its constant growth. Because it was so vital it was so assimilative. With his unusual versatility of talent he might have become a superficial, showy scholar; but no man was over farther from mere display of parts. The impression of learning that he made was never disproportioned to his solid acquisitions. On subjects respecting which he was but moderately informed, he rarely ventured an opinion. When he spoke it was of things that he understood and his judgment was almost without appeal. His easy mastery of all matters that he allowed himself to handle, the rapid flow of his ideas, the variety and pertinence of his illustrations, were proofs of a full mind and of a culture intrinsic and unaffected. In this respect Prof. Dunn realized a type of scholarship but seldom witnessed in this country. He resembled rather the fine products of the English universities, those ancient seats whose centuries of traditional refinement soften the very air that sighs through their dreamy quadrangles. With us scholarship is valued in proportion as it is directly practical. It must concern itself with living interests to win the respect of men. We need a serener social life, a fuller emancipation from material interests, to make culture loved for its own sake. But if, as Matthew Arnold claims, sweetness and light compose the highest culture, this child of our training would not have lacked admission to the inner circles of English academic life. To borrow another phrase from the scholar I have just quoted, Prof. Dunn had the "note of urbanity." How easily would he have mingled with the fellows of an Oxford college; how congenial to his nature that still air of study; how nimbly would his wit have played in the encounters of the common room.

The faculty in their minutes expressed a profound sense of the loss which they sustained in the deprivation of his strength and usefulness, and paid a tribute to his fidelity, scholarship, and character.

Reviewing the administration of Dr. Sears, we have seen that the first decade extended through the financial crisis of 1857 and the civil war; yet there was progress. A laboratory for chemistry had been built by liberal citizens of Providence; a system of scholarships had been established; the relation between the State and the municipality had been made cordial by wise concessions regarding the matter of taxation; a debt of $25,000 had been met and additions had been made to the college funds. The new system had been modified, so that the three years' course for the degree of bachelor of arts had been abandoned, and the degree was now bestowed at the end of a four years' course. The increased opportunities for a practical education were still afforded.

PRESIDENT CASWELL, 1868-1872.

Dr. Alexis Caswell succeeded Dr. Sears, who had been appointed agent of the board of trustees of the Peabody Educational Fund. He was elected to the presidency in February, 1868, and in the same month assumed the duties of the office. The years of his presidency were characterized by no special addition to the equipment, but were rich in the personality which Dr. Caswell brought to the spiritual and intellectual prosperity of the college. He had been long identified with the college before he was called to the position of president, and had been associated with Wayland, who had accomplished so much for the cause of higher education, so that Dr. Caswell was thoroughly conversant with the personnel of the college.

Dr. Caswell was born of parents of Puritan stock, and from them inherited the sterling qualities of that race; but these traits were softened by his genial and sunny disposition. He was one to attract and hold men by the charm of his manner. Some of his life-long friendships were made while a student by the power which he seemed to possess of drawing to him those who were congenial.

His youthful training was such as to develop a character of sturdy and manly independence. His father was a New England farmer. He was kept at school during the winter, and in the winter evenings, when the children would gather about the fire, the father would quiz them on what they were learning at school and would also set them problems in mathematics.

By such methods his intellectual progress was stimulated, and his ambition was aroused for more advanced study.

He was obliged to walk a distance of 5 miles each day to and from school, and there is no doubt but that this intercourse with the various phases of nature in his daily walks aroused in him that interest which he afterwards developed in the sciences.

He was prepared for college at Taunton and entered the university in 1818. He graduated with the highest honors of the class. At college he had the reputation of being one of the best athletes, and was remembered for his social qualities. But while very fond of all intercourse with his fellows he did not allow such fondness to interfere with the purpose for which he had come to college, nor did his popularity ever bring any tarnish upon his good name.

It was his determination to study for the ministry, but he accepted an appointment to a tutorship in the Columbian College, Washington, D. C. He went there in 1823, and received the appointment of professor in 1825, so acceptably did he fulfill the duties of his position. He held the professorship of ancient languages. In 1827, having resigned this professorship, he returned to New England; but in the fall, in company with Prof. Chace he went to Halifax to assist in the formation of a Baptist church. As a result of this trip he was ordained pastor of the church which had just been formed. His ministry here continued from month to month; but in 1828 he had a call to the First Baptist Church in Providence. Very soon after he returned to Providence he was offered the professorship of mathematics and natural philosophy in Brown University. This offer he accepted. He was a member of the academic staff of the college till 1863, when he resigned the position. In 1850 the chair which he held was changed to that of mathematics and astronomy, and it was to this latter branch of the sciences that he seemed to find himself most strongly drawn. Not only did he conduct the instruction in these branches at the university, but he delivered a course of lectures in astronomy at the Smithsonian Institution. His rank as a scientist made him a member of the American Academy of Arts and Sciences, and on the establishment of the National Academy of Sciences by Congress in 1863, he was selected by the Government as one of the 50 men of science in the United States to be the corporators.

THE MAN AND TEACHER.

Prof. Caswell was an earnest and laborious searcher for truth, and in the honors that were paid him as a scientist may be seen the appreciation of his success. The following reminiscence which was presented in the commemorative discourse will sketch a picture of him as a teacher and as a man:

Prof. Caswell's power of communicating knowledge as a teacher was not fully equal to his faculty of acquiring it as a student and a scholar. He made the impression upon his classes as being a professor in his sciences, able and learned, and imparting his abundant and well-ordered knowledge with ready speech and ample illustration; but he did not so much excel as a teacher in stimulating the minds of his pupils and in molding their intellectual character. If my revered instructor were listening to me now—and I confess I have all the while the thought that, though invisible, he is yet one of my hearers—I think he would not chide me for saying that he did not always hold us to so strict an account for the vigorous action of our minds upon our tasks; and that sometimes, in his own thorough interest in his subjects, he would be drawn away by a certain class of questions into excursions of remark somewhat remote from the educating province of the hour; but certainly we should all say that these excursions were always interesting and useful, though perhaps most enjoyed by men in the class who were least ambitious of opportunities to recite. But how ready he always was with ability and resources to meet the real wants of pupils who were willing and resolved to learn; and how patient and considerate with those whom nature had not blessed with mathematical endowments. And I think that he showed his good sense as well as his kindness in treating with indulgence such men in the class as had to study the mathematics, even in spite of nature and their stars.

Those ingenious devices and inventions in the class room, which, among students, belonged to the "idols of their tribe," never seemed to disturb Prof. Caswell. He saw and knew them, and often when their authors were least aware of it, but he did not always visit them with animadversion; as Tacitus says of Agricola, *omnia scire, non omnia exsequi;* often he disposed of them with a judicious pleasantry, which was generally quite efficient; but in more serious cases, the look of that benignant eye and troubled face, resting upon the offender, was a severer censure than the gravest lecture from a man of more austere nature. He could rebuke, however, if need be, and that with severity, too, but it was a rebuke that came from the heart; you felt that it was made in the interest of truth; it stirred u> hard feeling, and left no stinging remembrance, as when one is pierced by an arrow of censure which has been tipped with satire; in short, it was a moral rebuke, and wrought its wholesome moral effect. Indeed, in the class room and in all the interior discipline of college, a large part of which devolved upon him, a chief source of his success was in his fine personal character. You never felt as a student that he held only official relations to you; he never met you with professional stateliness or reserve; the man in him was far more and better than the mere professor, the man of large heart, of generous sympathies and warm affections; as you came into his lecture room or study, you felt that you were in the air of a genial humanity, in a friendly, humane presence, that inspired your confidence and awakened your love. An unspeakable blessing it is for a young man in his college days to have such a teacher ever moving before him and near him, and insensibly instilling into his developing nature and life the fine virtues of a true character; whose words of counsel and warning, of admonition and encouragement, are not drawn out from a sense of official duty, but flow forth spontaneously from a living fountain of goodness and kindness of heart. I can recall an instance of his personal influence; how he quite won the heart of a student, who, in his first college term was summoned home by the tidings of his father's sudden illness, and reached the door where he had gone out only two months before with that father's blessing upon his head, now only to join the procession that was bearing him to the grave. When that youth came back to college, the first great grief of his life heavy on his heart, Prof. Caswell came directly to see him at his room, which was next to his own, and spoke to him in those low tones of his such comforting words the fatherless boy felt rising in him the hope that he had a teacher near by him who might be his paternal friend; and such I have reason to know he was and has been through a long series of subsequent years; and in turn there has been cherished for him in a grateful heart, a reverent filial love.

PROFESSIONAL SERVICES.

It is ever true that men of liberal education are interested in more than merely concerns their round of professional duties. They touch men at many points, and they honor the college by using the culture and knowledge there obtained for their fellow men who are outside the academic walls. Quoting again from the commemorative discourse:

But Dr. Caswell was more than an academic man; within no seclusion of learned study could such a nature and character as his have been content to dwell. He was born for companionship with his kind; he loved the light and air of the world of human life, and his sympathies ran forth and touched it with living contact on every side. He belonged to this community no less than to the university; and he watched and followed, as with a personal concern, its fortunes and affairs. There is hardly an institution among us, established for the promotion of general intelligence, or for the relief of suffering and want, or for the moral and religious elevation of the people, in which he has not borne a leading part, either in its origin or in its after history. He was one of the pioneers, in counsel and labor, in the establishment of our system of public instruction, and was, for many years, a member of the school committee. He was one of the earliest friends of the Providence Athenæum, and for eight years was one of the board of directors, and for eight years more was vice-president of the institution. He was one of the original trustees of the Rhode Island Hospital, and a member of the building committee.

It was under his auspices that the present Alumni Association was formed; and he was unanimously elected as its first president. As president of the college, he proved himself to be fitted to administer its affairs, in a somewhat peculiar crisis of its history, to unite more closely its friends, and to set it forward in a new career of prosperity. Under his presidency, its resources were enlarged and new departments of study were organized and provided with the means of instruction. The Museum of Natural History, which is becoming a valuable interest of the university, owes its origin and establishment to his well-ordered plans and efforts. He administered the presidential office in a spirit of manly independence, and stood firmly, at whatever cost of personal convenience and personal interest, to the responsibilities which devolved upon him. To dwell upon the manner in which he conducted the discipline of the college would only be to illustrate, from a higher point of view, what I have already said of his career as a professor.

In 1863 he resigned his professorship, but in 1868 he was called again to the academic circle as its chief, the presidency being vacant on account of the resignation of Dr. Sears. As he had been connected with the faculty for nearly thirty-six years, and had sustained very intimate relations with the two preceding presidents, Wayland and Sears, he was admirably fitted to direct the college.

Said one of the faculty:

To dwell upon the manner in which he conducted the discipline of the college would only be to illustrate, from a higher point of view, what I have already said of his career as a professor. In his intercourse with the students, he so tempered his official dignity with the courtesy and kindness of a friend, silently drawing all into a reciprocal relation of Christian gentlemen, that he was universally esteemed and loved.

CLOSING DAYS.

Caswell acted as president till 1872. His resignation took effect in June, at the close of the academic year. Like many others of the faculty and chiefs who withdrew when still vigorous, he too did not forget the college, and was summoned to take part in its councils. The words of Prof. Lincoln, recounting Caswell's labors at this time, may be here repeated:

After his resignation of the presidency of the university, Dr. Caswell was granted some remaining years of life, which, while relieved from the pressure of daily official cares, yet went on to the last in an uninterrupted discharge of various duties. He had reached old age, but it was a ripe and vigorous one; it was quite what Tacitus calls *cruda ac viridis senectus;* rather, I may say, it quite corresponded to Cicero's picture of old age, in that charming dialogue which our friend loved to read. It brought no infirmatives of body or mind; it withdrew from no active pursuits; it gave exalted pleasures and occupations; it imparted new dignity to the countenance and more weight to the character; and, while it was not far from the earthly end, it opened all the nearer visions of better life to come. At the meeting of the corporation, in which he retired from the presidency, he was chosen a member of the board of trustees, and, in 1875, a member of the board of fellows; so that it was his fortune to lend his active cooperation to a third college administration. And we have heard, in this place, the grateful acknowledgment of his successor, that he was his most cordial supporter, his trusted friend, and his confidential adviser.

Dr. Caswell died in the early part of 1877, and the university mourned for him as one of her loyal sons. No more fitting close to the sketch of his administration can be made than in the classic words of Prof. Lincoln, at the conclusion of his commemorative discourse:

It is good and ennobling to behold our departed friend in those heavenly scenes whither he has gone, there reunited forever to the associates and partners alike in church and college of his glorious earthly toils. If the Roman orator, unblessed by revelation, could break forth into exultant joy at the prospect of departing to the divine council of souls, surely, with the vision He places in our hearts, in whom *life and immortality have been brought to light,* we may see His redeemed ones united in high and holy converse in the heavenly world, beholding together His glory and enjoying the full felicities of His everlasting kingdom. To that blest kingdom and its sweet societies, into which entrance has been ministered to him, the heart of one of his pupils, who owes him more than any words of his own can express, would fain go after him now in filial salutation, while it cherishes the wish that his benediction might rest upon this service, which, all imperfect as it is, has yet been done in sincerest honor of his dear memory:

"Salve, care parens, alti nunc ætheris hæres,
Et fruere æternis, quæ tibi parta, bonis!
Discipulique tui vocem cognosce supremam,
Quæ voluit memores omnes esse tui."

PRESIDENT ROBINSON, 1872-1889.

In January, 1872, the special business of the corporation was the election of a president for the university. The committee recommended the name of Dr. E. G. Robinson, who was then president of the Rochester Theological Seminary. He was graduated from Brown in the class of 1838. Dr. Robinson had been engaged in pastoral and educational work and had been successful in each. In addition to the presidency, he held the chair of intellectual and moral philosophy. It was a cause for congratulation that Dr. Robinson had received his academic training under Dr. Wayland, and it was hoped that the methods so successfully begun by him would be continued by his successor.

Dr. Robinson fulfilled all the traditions for the qualifications of the presidency of Brown. He came from an institution with which he had been identified since its organization, so that he was a man of experience as well as of scholarship.

His purpose may be seen from the speech which he made to the alumni at the commencement of 1872:

GENTLEMEN AND BRETHREN OF THE ALUMNI: I hardly know why I am here; but I have come gladly and with all my heart. I have come for earnest work. Our dear old mother has said, "Come home," and I have come. I have come to prove myself a loyal son of dear old Brown. I have come with a reverence for the associations which gather about this institution. I propose to work in the same line in which my predecessors have worked; but I am not forgetful of the fact that great progress has been made and is rapidly making. A college of this day can not afford to stand where a college stood twenty-five years ago. The times not only have changed, but they are changing more rapidly than we are aware, till we stop and look back. I have come from teaching what is understood to be one of the dryest and most uninteresting of studies. I have been a teacher of theology. I do not propose to bring what belongs to a theological seminary to a college. College

BROWN UNIVERSITY—SLATER HALL.

methods are passing through a very rapid transition. There is no help for it. Physical science must be recognized in all its varied departments. It is impossible that Brown University should stand still and not open every conceivable avenue to its students in natural history and every department of natural science. There is at this time no successful work in teaching that does not recognize physical science at every step. We must do it here. And in so saying, we are not going, I trust, to lose sight of linguistic pursuits, and I for one, do not propose to lose sight of the studies of mental and moral philosophy. Physical science, to-day, is mixed up in all its various departments, with metaphysical and moral science, and it is impossible that we should separate them. They constitute parts of the grand curriculum. And, after all, I am satisfied that education which does not round out a man intellectually and morally is an education which, for this age is ineffectual.

SLATER HALL.

In 1879 an addition was made to the college buildings by the erection of Slater Hall, so named in honor of the giver, Mr. Horatio N. Slater. This hall is situated between Rhode Island and University halls, and is used for a dormitory. Being the newest of the three dormitories it was furnished with all the modern appliances. Nearly all the rooms are in suites of three. The growth of the college had necessitated such a building, so that its gift by Mr. Slater was very timely.

The gift was of additional interest because made by a citizen of the State, a fact indicating that the citizens of the State delight to honor and advance her university.

SAYLES MEMORIAL HALL.

The devotion and self-sacrifice of the founders of an institution are entitled to their full share of praise, and justly. Conscious that they will be unable, in all probability, to see the results of their labor, they must work for future generations to appreciate and build upon the foundations which they have laid.

When, therefore, the future years have demonstrated how well the foundation was laid and how wise was the early policy of the college, it is gratifying to record that the present generation recognizes its allegiance to the wisdom of the past and delights to assist in the growth of the institution.

Gifts of buildings and the endowments of professorships indicate a sense of gratitude to the *alma mater* and a recognition that the institution is worthy of honor.

Sayles Memorial Hall was the third building received by the university during this administration. The building was a memorial by the father, Mr. William F. Sayles, to the memory of his son, who would have graduated in 1878 had his life been spared. The letter containing the proposed gift was read on the commencement day of 1878:

I have selected this commencement, when my dear son, if living, would have graduated, for the expression of what I hope will be regarded with favor, in order that when his classmates are conferring credit on their *alma mater* his brief life may also not be without a beneficial influence on the institution he loved so well. -

The Memorial Hall was begun in 1879 and dedicated June 4, 1881. It is on the middle campus between Wilson Hall and the chemical laboratory. The architecture is Romanesque, and the building is cruciform. The exterior is ornate and the inscription in front, *Filio Pater Posuit MDCCCLXXX*, indicates the occasion of the structure. In the vestibule is a bronze tablet to the son, William Clark Sayles.

The building is of three stories; in the front part are the recitation rooms, eight in number. The rear contains the hall in which are held the academic exercises. The need for such a building had been impressive, and the gift was most timely.

At the dedication, June 4, 1881, the address in behalf of the building committee and Mr. Sayles was made by Prof. Lincoln. After a description of the inception of the building, Prof. Lincoln said:

This building, which, in its appointments and uses and its surroundings I have now briefly described, we gratefully recognize to-day as the generous gift of a new benefactor of the college; placed, too, at once by this gift in the roll of its most liberal benefactors. Like others, long known and venerated, who have gone before him in the good work of endowing this university, our new benefactor is a Rhode Island man by birth and residence and lifelong occupations, who, by the employment of his talents and skill and enterprise in those industrial pursuits in which Rhode Island has a kind of hereditary distinction, has acquired for himself an honored name and conferred additional honor upon his native State. Not himself a graduate of the college, but occupied from his early years in the exigent cares and labors of business life, he has generously come to its aid from his "appreciation," as he has told us in his letter to the corporation, "of the higher education which it affords," and has bestowed upon it this gift for the increase of its efficiency and usefulness in carrying forward this education. In no spirit of adulation, but of sincerest gratitude, may we all unite, as we are assembled here as members of the university and as citizens of Providence, in rendering our tribute of honor to William Francis Sayles for what he has done by the rearing of this building for the cause of science, and letters, and education in this college and in this community.

President Robinson accepted the gift of the building on the part of the corporation. In the concluding address Prof. Gammell noticed the growth of the college and of the interest it was holding in the community.

I speak to-day in the presence of the governor of the State, and that fact alone would remind me of the relations which have always existed between the university and the people of Rhode Island. It was a great enterprise when certain citizens of Rhode Island in 1763 and 1764, the year before the stamp act threatened the struggles of the colonies with the mother country, determined to ask a charter for a college or university of liberal education. There was no project of the time that could have had smaller promise of important results. The charter was granted, but it lay wholly unused for some two years. The college was at length begun in the town of Warren, and was established here in 1770 by the erection of University Hall, which was paid for by the contributions of the people of Rhode Island, very largely by the people of the county of Providence. That, may it please your excellency, is a fact in our history which I delight to mention in your presence. That University Hall and those narrow grounds remained scarcely changed for about fifty years, when Hope College in 1821 was built by that distinguished and most philanthropic citizen of Rhode Island, Mr. Nicholas Brown, at his own expense, and given to the college. In 1835 Manning Hall was also built by the same gentleman and presented to the corporation. In 1839 a subscription was begun for the building of Rhode Island Hall, for the building of a new mansion for the president, and for improving the college grounds. That subscription was commenced and nearly half made up by the contribution of the same gentleman, Nicholas Brown. It was completed by the contributions of the men and women of Rhode Island of that time. Some years afterwards the Chemical Hall was erected also by the contributions of people of Rhode Island— I may say almost entirely by people of Providence, and very largely by those who resided in the immediate neighborhood of the university. Then came yonder matchless Library Hall, the gift of Mr. John Carter Brown, as provided in his will and completed by Mrs. Brown, to whom the college owes a debt of gratitude for a benefaction which was prompted by a sentiment such as belongs to this which we to-day receive. It was the continuation of a work in memory of her husband. After this came the building of Slater Hall, the gift also of a Rhode Island man, Mr. Horatio N. Slater; for, though he lives just at present in Massachusetts, we shall never cease to call him a Rhode Island man any more than we shall allow his family name to be blotted from Rhode Island history.

And now we have this hall, our latest and crowning benefaction, by another citizen of Rhode Island, completing the list of eight halls that have been erected by people who belong to this State. Nor is this all. Our leading foundations for professorships, in like manner, all were given by citizens of Rhode Island. The first was given by Mr. Nicholas Brown, long ago, as the basis of a professorship of oratory and belles-lettres; another given by Mr. Rowland G. Hazard, as the foundation of the Hazard professorship of physics; another, given by Mr. William S. Rogers, a son of Rhode Island, as the foundation of the Newport-Rogers professorship of chemistry; another by the Rev. Dr. Elton, long a professor here, and a citizen of Rhode Island to the end of his life, as the foundation of a professorship as yet not completed, of natural theology; another of a lectureship on the fine arts, by Mr. Marshall Woods, and last of all the Olney professorship of natural history, which has just been received by the college. All these halls and these professorships, one and all, constituting the greatest benefactions which the university has ever received, have come from citizens of the State of Rhode Island. I do not by any means mean to forget, or to show the slightest indifference to the gifts which have come to us from beyond the limits of our little territory; but it is to the credit of the State and to the credit of her citizens that so much has been done by those who have lived just around the college. And I may add that the State itself, by its legislature, has appropriated the funds which were received from the United States for the use of the college, in the agricultural department. That, too, Mr. President, is to the credit— very highly to the credit of the State.

This Memorial Hall will now stand with the others, the glory of the college, and also the honor of the State—and I like to link the two together, for I can not think that they are separable. What adds to one, adds to the other; and what takes from one, takes from the other. If the State loses its high character it ceases to be so attractive a place for the education of the young. If the college is not able to fulfill its destiny the State is less worthy and less desirable as a place of residence or a home of learning. I am not indifferent in any way to the beautiful spots which our State presents, whether upon inland streams or by the shores of the sounding sea; I am not indifferent to the great works which genius and capital, combining with industry, have spread over all our territory, and made it such a hive of labor, and given it such a renown for the beautiful products which it sends over the world. Still less am I indifferent to our benevolent institutions—to our noble hospitals, to our homes for neglected infancy and for wearied and exhausted old age—but I know not where on the soil of this State the people have more cause for congratulation and pride than in these few acres of college grounds given by her own citizens, and covered with halls erected by their munificence, and dedicated to that science which is shaping the civilization of mankind; to that literature and those studies so fitted for the nurture of the young, so fitted to adorn human character and to dignify human life, and in every way so worthy of the civilization of which we boast. As it has been in the past, so let it be in the future. Let it still be true that the people of Rhode Island shall be the great and leading supporters of the college; let it ever be true, also, Mr. President, that the college shall be true and faithful, loyal and devoted to the interests and the fame of Rhode Island.

THE LIBRARY.

The new library building was the first of a series of three erected during the presidency of Dr. Robinson. The second was Slater Hall and the third Sayles Memorial Hall. The library building was the gift of John Carter Brown. The private library which bears his name is one of the most valuable for its collection of Americana, and the owner was always glad to open it to scholars.

There are certain names that are prominent in the life of a community or an institution. But still more worthy of note is the fact that a family from generation to generation identifies itself with the highest welfare of an institution. The changed name of the university to Brown University attests the grateful recognition of its indebtedness to the family in whose honor it has received its name.

John Carter Brown was the son of Nicholas Brown, who had done so much for the college. He had given books, money, buildings, and his personal interest. He had founded the permanent library fund. He had given Manning Hall. It was the great uncle of John Carter Brown, who was for twenty-two years the treasurer of the college, and who was the first to present to the library an important gift of books. His grandfather was one of the members of the corporation in 1764. It will thus be seen how closely allied to the interests of the university was this family. With such an example from his ancestors, to which was united a love of letters on his own part, John Carter Brown presented rare and costly books to the library of the university. Particularly valuable were the collections of Italian, French, and German books.

As has been stated in the description of the library proper, its home in Manning Hall was unsuitable, because the building was not fireproof, and the arrangements of the room were inadequate and inconvenient.

February 8, 1860, Mr. Brown subscribed conditionally $25,000 for the university. Of this $15,000 was to be used towards the erection of a fireproof building for the library. Previously he had bought the lot where the building was erected. In 1869 the conditions of his bequest of 1860 had been fulfilled, so that the library fund was now begun. Before the death of Mr. Brown, in 1874, he gave the lot and made provision in his will for the addition of $50,000 to the sum previously given by him.

The corporation at once took steps towards the erection of the building. Messrs. Alexis Caswell, Rowland Hazard, and J. C. Hartshorn were elected to serve as the library building committee. On the

BROWN UNIVERSITY—SAYLES MEMORIAL HALL.

death of Dr. Caswell, President Robinson was chosen to fill the vacancy. The personnel of this committee was a pledge that the work intrusted to it would be accomplished so as to insure the most satisfactory results. Work was begun on the building in 1875 and the edifice was completed in 1877. The architecture is Venetian-Gothic. The situation on a corner lot, opposite the campus, makes an imposing site and affords an admirable setting for this treasure house. The interior of the building has been described in connection with the working of the library. When dedicated the library contained nearly 50,000 volumes, now placed in a building in which the only wood construction is that of the shelves. Four inscriptions were placed on the walls, commemorating the benefactions of the donor of the building, the change of the name of the college, the erection of the building under the care of the corporation, and an extract from the Vulgate.

The inscriptions are placed in the north, west, east, and south panels, respectively:

>JOHANNES CARTER BROWN
>NATUS A. D. MDCCXCVII
>VIVUS HUJUS BIBLIOTHECÆ FAUTOR
>MORIENS ADHUC MEMOR
>HUNC LOCUM
>PECUNIAMQUE HUIC AEDIFICIO STRUENDO
>TESTAMENTO LEGAVIT.
>OBIIT A. D. MDCCCLXXIV.

>COLLEGIUM INSULÆ RHODIENSIS
>A. D. MDCCLXIV CONDITUM
>PROPTER LIBERALITATEM NICOLAI BROWN
>AB EJUS NOMINE APPELATUM EST
>UNIVERSITAS BRUNENSIS
>A. D. MDCCCIV.

>HOC AEDIFICIUM
>VIRI EX COLLEGIO ACADEMICO DELECTI
>FACIENDUM CURAVERUNT.
>A. D. MDCCCLXXV INCEPTUM
>A. D. MDCCCLXXVII FINITUM EST.

>MELIOR EST ENIM FRUCTUS MEUS AURO
>ET LAPIDE PRETIOSO
>ET GEMINA MEA ARGENTO ELECTO.
>BEATUS HOMO QUI AUDIT ME
>ET QUI VIGILAT AD FORES MEAS QUOTIDIE
>ET OBSERVAT AD POSTES OSTII MEI.
>Prov. VIII.—19, 34.

The total value of the building is $120,000. Alterations and unforeseen expenses had brought the cost of the building above the amount voted by the corporation. This additional expense was provided for by Mrs. Sophia Augusta Brown, who desired this amount to be added to the sum which her husband had given.

The present facilities secure accommodation for 100,000 volumes, and by a few changes room can be gained for an additional 50,000. The final act of the building committee was placing in the library a bust of the donor. This was also the gift of Mrs. Brown.

President Robinson said in accepting the keys:

This library stands here an enduring, a most worthy, monument to the munificence of its donor. It was fitting that he, who more than all others had enriched the library of Brown University, should close the long series of his generous deeds by providing the means for a structure that should be at once a safe repository and a perpetual memorial.

Great libraries, it is true, be they ever so large, ever so select, do not necessarily make either great or good universities. A university is made great, not by its library, not by the number of its students, not by the multiplicity of its departments of instruction, but by the character of its instructors and the quality of their work; and the highest style of work can never be produced except the instructors shall themselves be instructed by the productions of the best intellects that have lived. A great library is an indispensable adjunct to a great and good university. Such a library and a building suited to the best uses of it are now in the possession of Brown University. When centuries shall have passed, and we, now so full of animation, have passed away and been forgotten, youthful and aspiring minds will come beneath this roof eager in the pursuit of knowledge; they will gaze upon the features of that bust; they will read the inscription upon the uplifted walls of this dome; they will catch the inspiration of great thoughts and worthy deeds. The still air of delightful studies that will ever brood amid these alcoves will breed in their youthful minds lofty aspirations; and catching the inspirations that will come to them from these crowded shelves they will not be unmindful of their predecessors, and they will give thanks to God for the inestimable treasures that will here be stored for their use. Great will be their heritage, and great, we trust, will be in the future the results growing out of the erection of this building and the filling it with the best productions of the best minds of our race.

Honoring, then, the memory of him who has given this beautiful and majestic building, and thankful to the fast friends who have enriched or now are enriching the library which is here to be stored, let us still bear up and steer right onward.

PROFESSOR DIMAN.

In the early part of the year 1881 the college was called to mourn the death of one of the faculty, endeared to all who knew him—Prof. Diman. His death was a loss not only to the university, but to the State. At the close of the memorial exercises in the assembly, the house voted to adjourn, a token of respect seldom paid to a private citizen. But Prof. Diman was beloved by all who came within the sphere of his presence, and admired by all who knew him. He had held the chair of history and political economy since 1864.

Jeremiah Lewis Diman was born in Bristol, R. I., May 1, 1831. In recounting the life of a man, the biographer eagerly seeks information

BROWN UNIVERSITY — LIBRARY.

regarding the parents and the home life of the youth. Whence were derived those traits which made the man the scholar or the statesman? In what environment was his youth spent?

It was said that his grandfather was "peculiarly mild in disposition, gentle in manners, and domestic in his habits. He was a great reader, with a good memory, fond of investigation and argument, and was deacon of the Catholic Congregational Church for more than twenty years. His grandmother was a grandniece of Benjamin Franklin, as Frances Franklin, her grandmother, was sister of the philosopher. Diman's father was a man of strong character, with a fondness for antiquarian lore." His information in matters of local history was remarkable. He had been elected to serve as governor of the State and was held in high esteem by his fellow-citizens. His mother was characterized as "exceeding modest and retiring; it was her only ambition to be good and to do good."

In the words of his biographer, Miss Hazard—

Of such parents, with such an ancestry of pure, pious people, was he born. In him all the virtues of the various lines seemed to unite. His noble bearing spoke of the Puritan; his grace of manner of the livelier French blood; his philosophic mind was the true descendant of the first American philosopher; his tenderness of his sainted mother.

The anecdotes of his youth show that, although he was fond of study, he was a true boy in his delight for games and sports. Entering college at 16, he soon gave indications of his scholarly mind, so that he was honored by all. While in college he commenced a commonplace book, in which he was accustomed to write out an analysis of what he read, or jot down his reflections. Thus he made his own what he read, and stored away what in after years he used to such excellent advantage. These books show his fondness for history and philosophy. He also read extensively works of a religious character. His tastes were in the direction of literary rather than scientific studies. On graduating he delivered the classical oration on "The Living Principle of Literature."

It was his intention to devote himself to the study of divinity, after a year's study and intercourse in the home of Dr. Thayer, of Newport. The next two years he spent at Andover. Here was formed a little coterie of congenial spirits, and it was their testimony that Diman was the center of it. His training was further increased by a study of two years in the universities of Halle, Berlin, and Heidelberg. It was during these two years that he came in contact with the leading men of the universities, and that he received great inspiration from galleries and museum. These two years but widened and deepened his own catholic thoughts and convictions. In 1856 he was licensed to preach, and in December of the same year he was ordained as the pastor of the church at Fall River. He remained with this parish till 1860. That year he was married and established his home in Brookline as the pastor of the Congregational Church. Till 1864 he held this charge, when he withdrew to accept the chair of history and political economy at Brown University.

Prof. Diman was now 37. Trained in the best methods of his *alma mater*, to which were added his course of two years at Andover, and two years of European travel, he was a well-rounded scholar. In addition to that, he had been most acceptable as a pastor, a fact that was proven by the repeated calls he received from leading churches. All these facts conspired to make him a professor with all the noble traits of the Christian gentleman.

In addition to his college duties he preached from time to time. He lectured before the Normal School and the Friends' School. Perhaps his influence was as great in connection with the writing which he did for the Providence Journal from 1866 to the close of his life. A vigorous and scholarly writer, he could express himself as freely as he wished. His own idea of the function of a newspaper will best show the spirit of the man:

> The successful conduct of a daily paper, aiming to take high rank as a guide of public opinion, is attended with peculiar difficulties, difficulties which our readers can not fully appreciate. If we conceived that our only function was to wait on public sentiment and echo the prevailing sentiment around us, the labor would be greatly simplified. But believing that our readers look to us for an honest and straightforward expression of our own sentiments, we can not avoid the peril at times of offending some for whom we cherish the utmost respect, and of being misunderstood by others upon whose good opinion we place the highest value.

Too often the charge of exclusiveness can be brought against the scholar; that he does not let the community have the benefit of his attainments. But this could never be urged against Prof. Diman. For ten years he lectured at his home to classes of ladies of the city of Providence on historical subjects. He was one of the members to draft the rules and regulations of the Friday Evening Club, which consisted of but twelve members, nearly all of whom were men not in academic professions. He was the life of the club. Said one of the members:

> I may as well give up trying to translate that subtle charm of his talk, which is so easy and sweet to remember, and so hard to put into any fit description. The silver resonance of that voice still dwells in our ears, though it is silent forever. That fine sarcasm which I see now going down that speaking face, and into his nose and lips and tones; that incisive wit and wisdom which penetrated his very voice and manner; that swift passage of his mind and his talk from grave to gay, from lively to severe; that rich culture which made his words, his very manner of saying anything, music; that calm power which held listeners like a magnet—it is all like water spilled on the ground, which can not be gathered up again. Hardly a drop of it, in its fresh beauty, have I been able to recover; for how great and yet how indescribable the charm of our friend's conversation was.

He was a contributor to the leading reviews and quarterlies. He pronounced several orations, among them the Phi Beta Kappa oration at Amherst in 1869, and at Harvard in 1876. He gave a course of lectures at the Lowell Institute in Boston and at the Johns Hopkins University. Of his manner as a lecturer President Gilman says:

> He seemed to be talking to a company of friends on a subject of great importance, which he perfectly understood, with an unhesitating command, not only of names and dates, but of exact epithets and discriminating sentences. The ease with which he lectured, under circumstances of very considerable difficulty, was only equalled by the instruction and pleasure he gave the auditors.

Friday, January 28, 1881, Prof. Diman delivered his last lecture to the senior class in history. There was no suspicion that the pain in his face of which he complained would prove serious. But such was the case, and he died the following Thursday. The disease was malignant erysipelas. The news of his death came with startling surprise. The students looked at each other with wondering eyes querying if it were really so. Can Prof. Diman be dead? The exercises in the chapel on the following morning were particularly impressive, and the entire university showed by the solemnity and quiet their sense of sorrow at the great loss which it had sustained. Not only was his *alma mater* a mourner, but the city and the State felt that its favorite son had been taken. So closely had he identified himself with the city and the State that on any special occasion it was to him that the municipal and State authorities looked as the man to do honor to the event. This he ever was ready to do, because he believed that it was the duty of the scholar to keep in touch with the community. The representative men who gathered to pay the final respects to the dead showed how wide was the circle of mourners, not only in his own but in other States. So closely had he identified himself with academic circles that it was the general feeling that from the academy of letters had gone one whose loss would be keenly felt.

Resolutions of respect and condolence were passed by the assembly, the corporation of the university, the chapter of the Psi Upsilon of which he had been a member, and the senior class.

Among all the tributes to his memory, that by his friend, Prof. Murray, of Princeton, has been selected to conclude this sketch of Prof. Diman:

> He had been sought for pulpits in our principal cities by reason of his abilities as a preacher; for professorships in other institutions; repeatedly by Harvard College, where he was honored and beloved, as he was honored and beloved here; sought also for positions as the head of seats of learning. But our rejoicing is this, that his work was finished here in the university of which he had ever been a filial son, in the city which was proud of him, in the State which he loved, and with whose history he has forever linked himself.
>
> He was stricken down in the very flush and bloom of his power and plans. The summer vacation had been delightfully passed with his family and with dear lifelong friends among the mountains and lakes and by the sounding sea. Recruited apparently by it, he had gone partly through the winter's work. For the first time in his life did that work seem to drag him along with it, instead of being triumphantly lifted and borne by him. Disease came at length so treacherously that none feared it till it was too late, and then, on that winter evening, the shock—the pitiless, dreadful shock, the hush that settled in a hundred homes of the city, in

the very streets. Nothing could have been more touching and nothing could have been more significant.

Months have passed, and yet we ask ourselves, "Is he gone?" The vitality that was in him, so exuberant, so large, making itself felt in so many circles, giving a sense of his presence so strong and deep that we can not help recalling and repeating those lines of the "In Memoriam" so closely applicable to our beloved dead:

> "If one should bring me this report
> That thou hadst touched the land to-day,
> And I went down unto the quay
> And found thee lying in the port;
>
> "And standing muffled round in woe,
> Should see thy passengers in rank
> Come stepping lightly down the plank
> And beckoning unto those they know;
>
> "And, if along with those should come
> The man I held as half divine,
> Should strike a sudden hand in mine
> And ask a thousand things of home,
>
> "And I should tell him all my pain,
> And how my life had drooped of late,
> And he should sorrow o'er my state,
> And marvel what possessed my brain,
>
> "And I perceived no touch of change,
> No hint of death in all his frame;
> But found him all in all the same,
> I should not feel it to be strange."

We buried him in the snows of winter. The sky over our heads as we bore him to the cemetery was full of blessed sunlight. There was "calm and deep peace in the wide air." There was calm and deep peace, too, in our hearts as we remembered the noble life and recalled the words, "Blessed are the dead that die in the Lord." We thought of the coming spring, in which he always so delighted, and the spring has come to us. He is, in the language of a favorite hymn, where

> Everlasting spring abides,
> And never withering flowers.

Yet he himself has uttered words in one of his sermons which are so deeply true and so touchingly pertinent that they prove the fittest conclusion to this commemorative service.

"Even when in middle life the strong man is suddenly stricken down, dying in the midst of the battle, with harness on, there are many aspects in which the sorrow is full of comfort. It is the death which the good soldier never shuns. The memory left is not of decay, but of the fullness of manly strength. The image which affection cherished is a grateful one. And especially is this the case when into the zealous and faithful labor of a few years have been compressed the work of a long life. We need not length of days to do well our life work. The most consecrated souls are often called soonest away."

PROFESSOR CHACE.

A famous man once said, "I have learned more from men than from books." In the history of an institution there are certain men who stand forth prominent for their moral worth and for the impression they make on their students. One of the benefits derived from contact with a great teacher is the personality which he impresses by example and precept. Too often the student in college may not appreciate how great has been this influence, but sooner or later his recognition of it will come, and the loving tribute of appreciation will be paid.

If any excuse need be offered for the biography of men prominent in the college, it can be urged that only as their lives are known can be seen the motives and purposes which have given them the influence they wielded.

. Said Prof. Diman on one occasion:

> Admirable culture of whatever kind must have its roots in the moral sentiment. Scientific training, unless regulated and qualified by broader culture, can only end in debilitating instead of enlarging the spiritual nature * * * for education must receive its shape from above, not from beneath.

Particularly appropriate were these words to the character exemplified by Prof. George Ide Chace, who for forty years was identified with the college in all the grades of academic work from tutor to president.

The subject of the following sketch, George Ide Chace, was born in 1808 in Massachusetts. Entering the sophomore class in 1827, while Dr. Wayland was president, he proved himself an enthusiastic student, graduating with the highest honor. He determined upon teaching as his vocation in life, and his after career showed how wise was this choice. He accepted the principalship of an academy in Waterville, Me., but remained there for a brief period, having accepted a position as tutor in mathematics at Brown. This was in 1831. In 1833 he was advanced from tutor to adjunct professor in mathematics and natural philosophy. From this time his instruction in the natural sciences began. The next year he held the chair of chemistry, and in 1836 the department was enlarged so as to include geology and physiology as well as chemistry. This position he held till 1867.

The natural sciences at that time were not given such an important place in the college curriculum, but even then for one man to combine so many in his instruction showed that he had rare ability. Prof. Chace was a man of ability in several subjects, but it was admitted that if he had devoted himself entirely to pure mathematics he would have held a foremost position among the ranks of mathematicians.

After the resignation of President Sears, Prof. Chace held the presidency of the college for 1866–'67.

There was a feeling that as all the other presidents had been clergymen such a precedent should be followed. This was the reason of the appointment of Dr. Caswell to the position of head of the college. This change involved another in the instruction, namely, that Prof. Chace should take the chair of moral and intellectual philosophy. His presidency of the college during the one year he held it showed his wisdom and devotion. The change from the department of the sciences to that which he now held was made in the confidence that his work would be well done. Nor was this trust misplaced. The hold which he had upon his classes in this department may be seen from a quotation from the petition of the class of 1872, when there was a prospect that he would not be able to complete the course of that collegiate year:

* * * Your instruction can not, we feel, be replaced to us; still less can be filled the place which you occupy in our hearts. We desire, therefore, as a class, to return to you our heartfelt thanks for the past; and while expressing our preference for your instruction over that of anyone who might succeed you, we sincerely hope that it may be within your power to complete our course of instruction in moral philosophy, when we shall consider it our honor to leave the university with you. (Signed by the class.)

The class had the privilege of his instruction through the year, but in the same year, 1872, he decided to sever his connection with the college. For forty-one years he had served on the faculty. His retirement was the result of mature deliberation. In 1867 he had written to his sister:

I prefer to close my professional career while I am in full strength and vigor, and while I have still freshness of interests enough to find other occupations attractive.

Prof. Chace was one who brought his academic culture into the community. He lectured before the Peabody Institute and the Smithsonian. Under Dr. Wayland the methods of university education were reorganized, and scientific instruction in the processes of the arts was to be given to the community. Accordingly, Prof. Chace delivered a course of lectures for the benefit of those engaged in the working of metals. The course was eminently successful, and those who attended expressed their appreciation by presenting the professor with a silver pitcher. He was one of the original members of the Friday Evening Club, of which Prof. Diman was such a valued member. Here, in the discussions and in the papers which he presented, was seen the wide range of his scholarly mind. He was also a contributor to leading reviews. Perhaps the most successful of his addresses was that commemorative of Dr. Wayland. This was delivered in 1866, and extracts have been given in connection with the sketch of Dr. Wayland.

After leaving the university he spent two years in foreign travel. On his return he was chosen to the chairmanship of the State board of charities, and the remainder of his life was spent in philanthropic work. The respect and the esteem in which he was held by his fellow-citizens were shown by the tributes to him from all sides. Mindful to the last of his devotion to his *alma mater*, he left $9,000 to be devoted to two scholarships. His death occurred April 29, 1885.

The following extract from a resolution offered by Prof. Lincoln, on the part of the alumni, will indicate the opinion of his colleagues:

His rare ability in the sciences, both in the investigation and in the communication of truth; his clearness and fullness of comprehension in the statement of principles, and his skill and aptness in their illustration; the stimulating influence of his instruction toward the pursuit and acquisition of sound knowledge, and their molding moral force in producing right habits of thinking and noble forms of character—all these will ever be cherished by his pupils among the choicest memories of their college education, and be treasured in the history of our university among the best elements of its fame and usefulness. And while we thus recall, as alumni of this university, the useful services of Prof. Chace's long professional career, we would not forget the new course of service, no less useful, on which he entered at the completion of that career. He might reasonably then have sought a studious retirement, where he might spend his declining years in meditation upon the elevated themes of philosophy and religion so familiar to him by nature and by habit. But so strong were his tendencies to useful action, he saw so keenly the need of such action in the world, the good that imperatively needed to be done and the evil to be undone, that he then gave himself with fresh zeal and devotion to the promotion of the great interests of philanthropy, morality, and religion, in connection with charitable and public institutions in Rhode Island. This feature of Prof. Chace's life and character reminds one of the words of a Latin poet, said of a great Roman, who was a man alike of action and of thought: "*Nil actum credens, dumquid superesset agendum.*" So it was with Prof. Chace, that he thought "nothing done so long as anything remained to be done." So was it also with him as a Christian man, that with the aim and spirit of a life to be lived not for self, but for others, he gave his best thoughts and efforts to wise and beneficent measures for the cure of the sick, for the care of the insane, for the instruction of the ignorant, and the reformation of the vicious. Such was the end that crowned the work of his life.

PROFESSOR GREENE.

In January, 1883, occurred the death of Prof. Samuel S. Greene. From his identification with the higher educational interests in the State, not only at the college but in the city, mention should be made of what he did.

He, too, was a graduate of Brown, of the class of 1837. He taught till 1849, when he was appointed agent of the Massachusetts board of education. After the adoption of the new system, he was appointed professor of "didactics" at Brown. In addition to his duties there he commenced a course of lectures to teachers, which was the germ of the normal school. In 1855 he was appointed professor of mathematics and civil engineering at Brown, having resigned the position of superintendent of the city schools.

Perhaps he is as widely known through his text-books: Analysis of the English Language, First Lessons in Grammar, Elements of English Grammar, English Grammar, and Introduction to English Grammar.

The minute which was entered on the records of the faculty will show the esteem in which he was held by those who were associated with him.

His extensive and accurate acquaintance with literary as well as with scientific subjects, and his enthusiastic devotion to the cause of education, both in the public schools and in the university, are widely known and are appreciated, and have contributed largely to the reputation and dignity of this institution. We recall, too, his almost unequaled skill as a teacher of abstruse and difficult sciences, his unwearied efforts in imparting knowledge, the noble serenity and dignity of his Christian character, which left so deep an impress on all his pupils, and we feel that, as a corps of instructors, we have met with a loss well-nigh irreparable.

THE COLLEGE IN 1889.

The last report of Dr. Robinson to the corporation in 1889 gathered up some of the experiences of the college since he had assumed the presidency. Attention was called in it to the fact that for the first time in its history the degree of doctor of philosophy had been conferred on two students who pursued special courses of resident graduate study.

On this side of the university work he continued:

It is earnestly to be hoped that courses of graduate study, to be rewarded by higher degrees, which have thus been begun, will hereafter become permanent parts of the educational opportunities afforded at Brown University, and that these courses of study will be so far multiplied and extended as to embrace the chief branches of literature and science. Surely a college that has existed for a century and a quarter, has existed in the midst of a rich and populous city from which it derives a large percentage of its students, and a college that for three-quarters of a century has borne the title of university, ought by this time to do something more than to repeat an endless routine of elementary studies.

In thus advocating an enlargement of the sphere of work, and pleading that provision be made for advanced instruction, nothing is further from my thought than that the distinctive work of the college should in any way be interfered with, or its courses of study or standards of excellence be in any way changed. The thorough work of the college is indispensable as a preparation for advanced work in any department whatever. Nothing in the matter of education seems to me more irrational than a proposal to supplant the college with the university, or to attempt instruction in the higher ranges of knowledge without a thorough grounding in its elements.

With reference to the deportment of the students the president says:

College pranks and disturbances by night, so common years ago, have for the present ceased. I hardly know how the same number of young men could be expected to conduct themselves with more uniform decorum and propriety than our students have done during the last year. For ten years or more there has been a steady and uniform improvement of manners and deportment. The contrast between the deportment of students the past year and seventeen years ago has been too marked to escape the notice of the most casual observer. I wish I could speak with equal confidence of a corresponding improvement in studiousness and attainments. In saying this, however, I would by no means be understood to imply that there is less devotion to study than formerly, or even that there is not more. But increase in the amount of thorough scholarship, and in the number of students whose aims are high and generous, has not in any college in the country, so far as I can learn, distinctively characterized the so-called progress of recent years; has not kept pace either with the multiplication of departments of knowledge, or with the increase of means for exploring them. That the social and festive element of college life has largely and very generally increased is manifest to all men. The increase of this element doubtless to some extent accounts for the diminution of the spirit of disorder once so common in all the colleges. So far as this college is concerned I think there has also been an increase of manliness and self-respect. Student life with us has been brought into closer relations than once existed with the social life of the city. The influence of this has been restraining and refining, though it may not always have been intellectually quickening.

In conclusion reference was made to his withdrawal from the presidency:

In resigning the presidency of the university, I retire with the consciousness of having labored honestly for its best interests; and with the conviction that, while its progress, from causes which ought never to have existed, has not been all that I had labored and hoped for, there has nevertheless been an advance in the kind and extent of its work; it has never been in more favor with those who are disposed to supply it with needed funds than it now is; and it never had a better prospect of usefulness and of patronage from all parts of our country than has recently been opening before it.

At the meeting of the corporation, when the resignation of Dr. Robinson was presented, and a committee chosen to select his successor, Prof. Gammell made the following remarks:

The funds of the university, which in 1872 were, $552,430, were, in 1888, $960,411, not including the gift of Mr. Duncan, $20,000, and a more recent gift of $20,000, and other gifts, which would make the total about $1,018,000. The endowment has been very nearly doubled (not counting the Lyman bequest, from which $60,000 or $70,000 will be realized). These gifts have come very largely from the community in which the college is located.

For this prosperity we are greatly indebted to the judgment, the fidelity, the ability, and the diligence of President Robinson. During those seventeen years he has never been absent from a college duty, from a recitation, or from a chapel exercise, except when called away by public duties. How few professional men have a similar record.

Of his instruction I may speak with confidence, having had two sons under his instructions, and it having been my duty in various ways to know the internal history of the college. The instruction has been of a very high order. He has done much to raise its standard; he has restored largely the spirit of the instruction of my old teacher, President Wayland. I consider this a fair statement of the results of Dr. Robinson's instruction.

President Andrews, 1889.

Upon the resignation of Dr. Robinson, a committee of 9 was chosen to elect a new president. The task was difficult on account of the numerous candidates that were before the committee. After due consideration, the unanimous choice of the committee was in favor of Elisha B. Andrews, who was then holding the chair of political economy at Cornell.

Dr. Andrews was graduated from Brown in 1870, and from Newton Theological Seminary in 1874. He held a pastorate in Beverly, Mass., for one year, and was the president of Denison University till 1879.

For the next three years he was at Newton Theological Seminary. He was then called to the chair of history and political economy at Brown. This position he held for five years, going to Cornell in 1888.

Of the many comments which appeared with reference to the new president of the university, the following will give a very good idea of the man:

While under 45, he is the senior by fourteen years of Dr. Wayland, when that celebrated educator was first elected to his position. Brown has had very young as well as very aged presidents, and it is now returning to one of the best traditions of its honorable history in summoning to its chief seat Dr. Andrews, in the prime of his manhood.

Dr. Andrews is not a narrow-minded or bigoted denominationalist, but a man of broad catholic sympathies, comprehensive learning, and commanding force. He is singularly well adapted for the work of completely emancipating that college from sectarian influences and establishing it on the broad foundation of higher scholarship and good letters. Under his predecessor, Brown has made remarkable progress during the last seventeen years, and he will enter upon his work under the most favorable auspices, a new gymnasium having been already practically secured. Dr. Andrews, however, is not an educator who is dependent upon rich endowments or the size and number of college buildings. He belongs to the same class of teachers as Dr. Arnold, who could have established a great school if he had started it in a barn. He is a man endowed with a genius for teaching and for commanding the sympathies of young men.

The personality of the head of an institution will be impressed on its working force. A man of broad ideas, progressive and energetic, can do much to bring an institution of learning into the front ranks. It is not enough to have collected a faculty who shall all be eminent in their departments—a fine equipment of laboratories and libraries will not bring a college to the front—but there must be a man at the head who can see into the future. He must plan now for what is to come; he must secure the cooperation of the academic staff, and have the enthusiastic admiration of the students. In addition to these essentials within the college walls, he must bring the college into touch with the life of the city. The college is an institution of the city, and to the extent the citizens feel a pride in it, will its sphere of usefulness be increased. In the opinion of the friends of the institution, such qualifications are happily united in its present leader. Coming to the university as the unanimous choice of the committee who were chosen to elect a president, it is confidently believed that under his administration an era of prosperity is opening up before the university.

A college must depend for its main support on the body of its alumni. Those of Brown are to-day holding positions of trust and honor in all the States of the Union. Although the college is denominational, it is not sectarian. There is every reason to suppose that very few measures in its administration have been advanced or withdrawn on strict sectarian grounds. The interest which the alumni evince is shown by the readiness with which the Lincoln fund was secured.

Wilson Hall was ready for occupancy in 1890. The Ladd Observatory was built, and plans for the new gymnasium had been accepted. The history of the beginning of these additions belongs to the previous administration, but the results will be an integral part in the increased facilities of the university in the immediate future.

COURSE OF STUDY.

In 1889 two students received the degree of doctor of philosophy after special courses of study in residence at the university. The degree of master of arts is bestowed upon a candidate, already a bachelor of arts, who has completed a thorough course of liberal graduate study, sufficient in amount to constitute a fifth year of college work and has passed

satisfactory examinations thereupon. The degrees of bachelor of arts and bachelor of philosophy are conferred at graduation. Students may pursue a select course without becoming a candidate for a degree. The attendance in the class room must be at least sixteen hours per week. The course is one of four years.

The courses of instruction form a system of required and elective study. The studies of the freshman year are all required, with the exception that a choice of courses is offered candidates for the degree of bachelor of philosophy according as they do or do not pursue the study of an ancient language. In the sophomore and junior years the required studies occupy seven of the sixteen hours of instruction each week, and in the senior year five of the fourteen hours. The required studies of the freshman year are selected for their disciplinary value, in order that the students may the more profitably pursue those of subsequent years, whatever they may select. The required studies of the sophomore, junior, and senior years are restricted to English, German, history, and philosophy, the pursuit of which is deemed necessary for all students who are to be recommended for a collegiate degree.

The elective studies offer the student a large number of subjects, and are so placed in the curriculum that freedom of choice is allowed within the necessary limitations of the schedule of lectures. In this schedule a number of parallel courses, extending through the three years, are made available, and to these each student is advised to conform in selecting his studies.

In addition to the regular courses of instruction, special honor courses are offered, which are open to students who desire to do extra work in any particular department. These honor courses consist mainly of additional reading supplemented by essays, and examinations are held at the option of the several professors.

THE DEPARTMENTS OF INSTRUCTION.

PHILOSOPHY.

The primary aim in the required philosophical studies is to strengthen and discipline the pupil's mind, and as far as possible to render him a safe, strong, independent thinker and investigator. Along with this goes a practical purpose, especially pronounced in ethics, to aid pupils in mastering those important problems in this department which are basal to all high intellectual life and to conduct. Great attention is given to the topics of practical ethics and casuistry, now of such peculiar interest to the world. In the history of philosophy, which is elective, effort is made, by one year more in ancient philosophy, from Plato as center, the next in modern, with Kant as the fixed point, to reveal the concatenation of philosophical systems, the march of systematic thought from master to master. The teaching is not merely analytic or historical, but positive and constructive, the reverse of skeptical. The evolution of religion and the course and meaning of divine revelation are pointed out and emphasized.

GREEK LANGUAGE AND LITERATURE.

The studies in this department are prescribed for the freshman year and elective for the sophomore, junior, and senior years.

The courses of instruction and study aim to give the student a critical knowledge of the language, to secure for him facility in reading and appreciating Greek authors, and to interest him in the study of the literature, civilization, and life of the ancient Greeks.

The courses of reading may be greatly extended for those who are either candidates for the higher degrees or are studying for honors.

The president's premiums for excellence in preparatory Greek are awarded after a special examination at the beginning of the freshman year.

The Foster premium for the highest excellence in the Greek language is awarded after a critical examination at the close of the senior year.

LATIN LANGUAGE AND LITERATURE.

The studies in this department, as in Greek, are prescribed for the freshman year, and elective for the sophomore, junior, and senior years. The courses of study have been specified, but other authors than those named may be read in different years.

It is intended that lectures be given to the freshman and sophomore classes, on the ends and scope of the studies of the department, and on the literature pertaining to them; also on the authors read and their contemporaries in Roman literature. In connection with the study of Horace, lectures on Rome and the Romans of the time of Augustus will be given. The elective courses in the senior year are accompanied by lectures.

The chief objects aimed at in the instruction may be briefly stated as follows: To secure for the student by grammatical and exegetical study, and by sight reading, the ability to read Latin with facility; to cultivate by faithful translation his power of expression in English; and by uniting continuous historical and literary illustration with the reading of classic Roman writers, to make the study of Latin a means of increasing his mental discipline and literary culture.

The president's premiums for excellency in preparatory Latin are awarded after a special examination at the beginning of the freshman year.

CLASSICAL ARCHÆOLOGY.

In connection with the work in Greek and Latin an elementary course of instruction in classical archæology is offered to the senior class as an elective study for the first half-year. It consists chiefly of a study of the history of Greek sculpture. The text-book, Collignon's Manual of Greek Archæology translated by Wright, is supplemented by lectures and by extensive collateral reading. The plaster casts in the museum of classical archæology, photographs, engravings, etc., are used by the instructor to illustrate the subject.

RHETORIC AND ENGLISH LITERATURE.

The aim of the course in rhetoric is to give a thorough and systematic training in the principles and practice of English composition. The different kinds of composition are set forth in their logical relation to each other; and essays, whose plans are based on specific rhetorical methods, are required from the student.

The subject of style is discussed both theoretically and practically, and the elements of rhetorical criticism are applied in the analysis of the work of a standard author.

There are two parallel courses in English literature, one general, discussing the uniform and progressive development of the literature from the fifth to the nineteenth century; and the other special, embracing the reading and literary criticism of leading authors from the fourteenth to the nineteenth century. The aim of the courses is to inculcate the unity of the literature, and also to cultivate the literary taste of the student that he may appreciate the classics of our English tongue. In connection with the elective course in the senior year lectures are given on early American literature.

For rhetorical work in the junior year the student is required to prepare essays in connection with both the courses in literature, and also to deliver orations, which have been privately rehearsed before the instructor in elocution.

In the junior year a voluntary class is formed for the study of Anglo-Saxon.

The course in elocution includes the acquirement of the principles of the art, and such a drill in vocal development and delivery as to assist the student to become an effective speaker.

HISTORY AND POLITICAL SCIENCE.

The course of instruction in history and political science continues through the junior and senior years. Throughout the former, history is a required study; throughout the latter, there are electives in political science, in which, however, much attention is given to historical matters.

During the first term of the junior year, the mediæval and modern history of Europe are studied. Lectures are first given upon the history of the Roman Empire from the death of Marcus Aurelius to the latter part of the fifth century. A text-book is then used, by means of which, in connection with informal lectures, class-room reports, and supplementary reading, the history of Europe is pursued down to the beginning of the eighteenth century. During the second term the same subject is continued until the history of the present year is reached; the term is thenceforward devoted, after similar methods, to the study of the political and constitutional history of the United States, especially since the year 1783. This study, also, is brought down to the present time.

The elective course of the first term of the senior year is occupied with the subject of constitutions, European and American. The forms of government of the chief European states are considered. The study of the American Constitution, next succeeding, is not confined to comment on the document called by that name, but aims to insure a comprehensive knowledge of all the most important institutions of government actually existing in America. The study is accompanied by efforts to give a clear historical knowledge of the internal politics of European and American states in recent years. The subjects of the elective in the second term of the senior year are the history of law, and international law and the recent history of diplomacy. Lectures treat of ancient law, and of the history and development of Roman law and of English law. A small text-book of international law is then employed, the study of which is accompanied by lectures and reports on important topics of recent diplomatic history. Thus, the first elective being accompanied by a study of the recent internal history of European and American states, the second is accompanied by the study of the recent history of their external relations. The adjustment of a revised curriculum to the conditions presented by existing classes has caused some deviation from this programme during the present year.

POLITICAL ECONOMY.

The course in political economy comprises two parts: (1) An elementary course, occupying three hours a week during the first half of the senior year. (2) An advanced course, occupying three hours a week during the second half of the senior year. The elementary course is based upon a text-book, supplemented by lectures on the part of the instructor, and by reading in standard authors and investigations on the part of the class. Some of the more important economic problems of the day are discussed, and their relation to underlying economic principles shown.

The advanced course is intended to vary somewhat from year to year, one of two objects being kept in view, either to introduce the student to the careful and detailed study of some special field of economics, or to show the science in its broad historical relations. Two hours a week are devoted to the history of the science, with Ingram's History of Political Economy as a text-book, and lectures by the instructor on the history of economic life, and the relation between that life and the development of economic science. The students are required to read extensively in the more important authors dealt with. One hour a week is devoted to a discussion of economic problems, involving important principles, with the purpose of reviewing and fixing firmly in mind the work of the elementary course. The endeavor is made to give these problems as practical a character as possible, in order to train the student in the application of economic principles to the questions of modern economic life.

In addition to the regular course, a class of 10 or 12 students, especially interested in economics, meets the instructor two hours each month for seminary work along some special line of study, varying from year to year. The work is based upon Walker's Money, Trade and Industry, and Jevons's Money and the Mechanism of Exchange. Investigations are made and essays presented upon topics which are suggested by these works.

MODERN LANGUAGES.

The department of modern languages includes German, French, Italian, and Spanish. The main aim is twofold: to lay a broad and firm foundation in the forms and syntactical structure of the language studied, and to furnish an introduction to an appreciative acquaintance with the literature. A subordinate and auxiliary aim is to afford practice in writing and speaking the language. These aims are modified somewhat by the subject studied, the length of the course, and the number in the class.

GERMAN.

This study may be pursued three years, in recitations three times a week, from the beginning of the sophomore year to the end of the senior year. It is a required study only during the sophomore year. The following courses are offered:

(1) *Introductory course of one year.*—Careful attention is here given to the language, to forms and to syntax, enforced by daily drill in inflection and in parsing, by written exercises, and by practice in speaking. A variety of selections is read from the best authors, each passage being pronounced aloud in German, translated, analyzed, and construed. Proper attention is bestowed upon literary quality, but more upon the linguistic side of the study. One hour each week through the whole year is devoted to conversation and composition.

(2) *Course in Schiller, of one-half year.*—Less attention is now given to the grammar and more to the literary elements, to the thoughts presented, to the beauties of style, to the versification, and to a comparison of Schiller with other writers. The aim is to introduce the class to an acquaintance with Schiller. One hour each week through the half year is devoted to conversation and composition.

(3) *Course in Lessing, of one-half year.*—The literary aim is here the dominant one. The study of the grammatical side of the German is, however, not lost sight of, though very little time is given to class-room drill.

(4) *Course in Goethe, of one year.*—In this the literary side of the study absorbs the whole attention. There is no study of grammar merely as grammar, though the student is held responsible for the most accurate translation and interpretation of all the work set before him. As in the preceding courses, all the work must be read at least twice in the original.

(5) *Course in literature.*—During the middle year occasional lectures are given upon the pieces of literature studied. During the last year there is a course of thirty lectures upon the rise and development of German literature, with special attention to the period beginning with Klopstock and ending with Goethe. The class is required to take notes, to pursue a course of reading upon the subjects studied, and to submit written essays upon assigned topics.

(6) *Honor course.*—This course extends over the entire three years, and is open only to those who maintain in German a rank of 95 per cent. The course consists of a careful preparation upon selected pieces from the authors read in the class room, equal in amount to the work performed by the class. Upon this work the student is from time to time examined.

(7) *Graduate course.*—An advance course is already opened for those who desire to pursue German in connection with other studies, for the master's or the doctor's degree.

In the year 1890 there will be offered to graduate students a course in the middle high German, including:

1. A course in middle high German and its relations to old and new high German.

2. A course of readings in the Minnesänger, Walther von der Vogelweide, and Wolfram von Eschenbach.

3. A reading and critical study of the national epic, Das Nibelungenlied.

FRENCH.

Candidates for degrees are examined at their entrance to college upon French grammar and upon easy French prose. They are then separated into divisions based upon scholarship. The course extends over the first two years, three hours a week. The general aim is the same as that already set forth in German.

(1) Elementary course, of one-half year. The second and third divisions of the freshman class are given a course in grammar work and in the reading of easy prose, in which grammatical drill is the prominent feature.

(2) Course in Racine, of one-half year, open to the first division of the freshman class during the first half year, and to the second and third divisions during the second half year. In this course attention to the literary work and to grammatical analysis are given equal prominence. Especial attention is given to reading in the original, to translation, to versification, to grammatical and critical anaylsis

(3) Course in Corneille, of one-half year, open to the first division of the freshman class during the second half year. The main work is a careful study of the author's masterpieces, on the literary side, though considerable time is given to the study of the language.

(4) Course in Molière, of one-half year, open only to those who have completed course 3. Several of the masterpieces of Molière are read, with a careful examination of the style and the peculiarities in language.

(5) Course in Voltaire and later writers, of one-half year, open to those who have completed course 4.

(6) Honor course, of two years, open on the same conditions as the similar course in German, to which the work corresponds in quantity and character.

(7) Graduate course, corresponding to the parallel course in German.

SPANISH.

This study is offered as an elective during the first half of the senior year. The aim is to impart a facility in reading and translating readily and accurately easy prose and verse.

ITALIAN.

This study is at present offered during the last half of the senior year as an elective. The aim is similar to that in Spanish.

MATHEMATICS, PURE AND APPLIED.

The full course of mathematics occupies four years.

Pure mathematics.

First year.—(1) Geometry, solid and spherical, with original propositions, taught by means of oral recitations and frequent written exercises. (2) Trigonometry, analytical, plane and spherical, the use of logarithmic tables and trigonometrical formulas, and solutions of practical problems. (3) Algebra, embracing the theory of quadratic equations, permutations and combinations, undetermined coefficients, the binomial theorem for negative and fractional exponents, summation of series, and logarithms.

Second year.—Analytic geometry, comprising the straight line, the circle, the parabola, the ellipse, the hyperbola, the general equation of the second degree, higher plane curves in analytic geometry of two dimensions, and the point, the straight line, the plane, and surfaces of space, revolution in analytic geometry of three dimensions.

Third year.—(1) Differential calculus, comprising the differentiations of algebraic and transcendental functions, successive differentiations, the evaluation of indeterminate forms, maxima and minima of functions of a single variable, and the development of functions in series. (2) Integral calculus, comprising the elementary methods of integration and their application to the determination of areas and volumes, and the rectification of curves.

Fourth year.—(1) A continuation of the course in integral calculus and the general theory of equations.

Applied mathematics, including engineering.

The full course in this department occupies four years, but a longer or a shorter course may be pursued if the student so elects. Those not wishing to pursue the full course will find the studies so arranged that the knowledge and practice acquired in a partial course will be practical and available. Ample provision will be made for the instruction of any who desire a more extended course than is here indicated in engineering and in higher mathematics. Any part of the engineering course is open to all students as an elective, if they are prepared by previous work to pursue it to advantage.

The following is the order of study for the regular course:

First year.—(1) Geometry, trigonometry, and algebra, as indicated in the first year of pure mathematics. (2) Plane geometrical problems, consisting of both recitation work and mechanical construction. A thorough discussion of the various methods of constructing complicated problems, involving original work, is required. Mechanical drawing, consisting of instruction in the use of instruments, line drawing and pen shading, construction of plane geometrical problems, and the more complicated plane curves, the principles of projection and their application in model drawing. (3) Free-hand drawing, consisting of crayon drawing of lines, simple outlines of figures, shading, drawing of models of machinery, and architectural drawing. (4) Surveying, comprised in three parts, viz, recitation work, field work, and plotting. In these are embraced a study of the construction, use, and adjustment of engineering instruments, compass and transit surveying, computation of areas, supplying omissions, laying out and dividing land, section leveling, cross-section work, computation of earthwork, topography, and the laying out of railroad curves.

Second year.—(1) Analytic geometry is indicated in the second year of pure mathematics. (2) Descriptive geometry, comprising recitation work and mechanical drawing, discussion and proof of the methods of representing (1) geometrical magnitudes, and (2) the solution of problems relating to these magnitudes in space, and the application of descriptive geometry in machine drawing from models. (3) Shades and shadows, linear perspective, and isometrical projections.

Third year.—(1) Differential and integral calculus, as indicated in the third year of pure mathematics. (2) Advanced surveying, comprising recitation work, field work, and plotting, construction, use, and adjustment of instruments not considered in the first year, land surveying, topographical surveying by the transit and stadia, hydrographic mining and city surveying, the measurement of volume, geodesic surveying, and projection of maps. (3) Theory of structure, embracing the construction of foundations in all classes of soils, pile foundations and substructures, stability of blocks of stone or brick entering into the structure of walls of buildings, arches, retaining walls, and piers, and trigonometrical calculations of strains on different varieties of framed structures, including trussed and suspension bridges, with both steady and rolling beds. (4) Graphical analysis of strains on roof and bridge trusses and other framed structures, and strains on cables and other portions of suspension bridges.

Fourth year.—(1) General theory of equations as indicated in the fourth year of pure mathematics. (2) Weisbach's Mechanics. The following are among the subjects considered: The laws governing motion and force, statics of rigid bodies, theory of the center of gravity in surfaces and solids, equilibrium and dynamical stability of bodies rigidly fastened, resistance of friction, elasticity and strength of flexure, hydraulics, embracing the structure and use of hydraulic machines, the investigation of the laws which govern the flow of water from reservoirs, and the flow of water in rivers, canals, and conduit pipes, and water as a motor. (3) Lectures on the history of architecture and architectural construction. (4) Special classes, open to all students in mechanical drawing, are arranged according to the wants of the applicants.

Students desiring admission to this course are subjected to an examination on the same amount of mathematics as is required of candidates entering for a degree.

The objects sought to be attained are, in the freshman mathematics: (1) A thorough knowledge of the elementary principles of mathematical science, which will prepare the student for any advanced mathematical work. (2) A discipline of the mind to careful analysis and strict logical methods of thought and the development of the reasoning powers.

In the higher elective classes in pure mathematics: (1) Mental discipline for those students who do not intend to pursue the subject further. (2) A thorough mathematical foundation for all students who desire to make mathematical studies a specialty.

In applied mathematics: (1) The application of the principles of pure mathematics to the practical problems of mechanical work and investigation. (2) To make such use of those mathematical and mechanical works within the time allotted to the course as will enable the student in the future to pursue by himself more extended works. (3) To prepare students in engineering to enter at once upon field and office work.

CHEMISTRY.

The chemical laboratory is open to students from 8:30 a. m. to 2:30 p. m. on every week day except Saturday. It is the design of this department to afford instruction in the general principles of chemistry, in analytical chemistry, and in the practical applications of the subject. Attention is given to metallurgy, medical chemistry, agricultural chemistry, and the application of chemistry to manufacturing processes.

The courses are not confined to undergraduates—other persons, if prepared to pursue the study to advantage, being admitted; but a knowledge of the general principles of chemistry is absolutely necessary to profitable study in any of the more advanced courses.

All students in the working laboratory are required, in addition to their experimental study, to attend weekly exercises covering a review and discussion of topics in general chemistry. The subject is treated in two grand divisions—inorganic and organic. One term of the year it includes the study of the metals and nonmetals; the other term, organic chemistry. These exercises are supplemented by lectures, explaining recent progress in chemical theory, and new applications of chemical substances and new inventions.

PHYSICS.

The course in physics begins in the first term of sophomore year, with the study of the principles of mechanics. The text-book used is Dana's Elementary Mechanics, which is supplemented by experimental illustrations in the class room. Three hours per week during the term are devoted to this subject.

Sound, light, heat, and electricity are discussed in the second term of sophomore year, three hours each week, in lectures abundantly illustrated by experiments. Frequent examinations, both oral and in writing, are held to test the progress of the class.

PHYSICAL LABORATORY.

Wilson Hall, named in memory of its donor, the late Mr. George F. Wilson, of Providence, is now completed and serves as the physical laboratory of the university. The structure presents a front on the middle campus of 84 feet, and extends eastward 106 feet, with a height of 70 feet. It is built of granite and sandstone, with special regard to the solidity required for the purpose in view in its erection. It contains rooms for laboratory and class work, a large lecture room, a workshop for wood and metals, and also private rooms for special researches; and it is liberally supplied with the appliances and apparatus required in experimental mechanics and physics.

After the completion of this building ample opportunity was provided for laboratory work in physics. The following laboratory courses are now offered: (*a*) A course in mechanical experiment and construction, intended to meet the needs of those expecting to follow mechanical pursuits. (*b*) A general experimental course in sound, light, heat, and electricity, intended for such as propose to teach these subjects. (*c*) A special course in electricity.

Opportunities for special investigations are afforded for advanced students.

BROWN UNIVERSITY—CHEMICAL LABORATORY.

ASTRONOMY.

The courses of study at present offered in astronomy are two: (1) A lecture course in descriptive astronomy. (2) A laboratory course in practical astronomy. The former is designed to acquaint the student with the fundamental conceptions of the science, the methods of its professional study, and the present state of our knowledge of the heavenly bodies. A general treatise of astronomy is made the basis of the course, and is supplemented by lectures and by abstracts prepared by members of the class upon assigned topics. The latter is a technical study of the theory of astronomical instruments and practice in their use. The sextant, transit, zenith telescope, and equatorial are taken up in turn, and problems, such as the determination of time and latitude, are solved by actual observation and calculation.

THE LADD ASTRONOMICAL OBSERVATORY.

The facilities for instruction in astronomy were greatly increased by the erection in 1891 of an astronomical observatory, through the liberality of his excellency, Governor H. W. Ladd. The observatory is equipped with an equatorial telescope of 12 inches aperture, supplied with a micrometer, spectroscope, and other attachments; two transit instruments, one of which can be used as a zenith telescope; astronomical clocks and minor instruments. On the completion of this observatory additional courses of undergraduate study were offered, and opportunity was given for advanced study leading to graduate degrees. It is also expected that certain astronomical investigations will be regularly carried on.

ZOOLOGY AND GEOLOGY.

Zoology is taught in the second college half year by lectures, frequent examinations, and laboratory work. It is the aim to adapt the lectures to the needs of the general student. It is taken for granted that no liberally educated person should be without a general knowledge of the principles of biology, the laws of animal morphology, the relations of animals to the world about them and to man, and the probable mode of their origin.

The laboratory work is a course on comparative anatomy. The student is required to draw and to dissect the most important types of the animal kingdom, viz., a starfish, clam, lobster, grasshopper, beetle, butterfly, a fish, frog, bird, and mammal. He is required to examine and draw portions of the skeleton of each type of vertebrates, including a comparative study of limbs. The structure of cells and of the protozoa, as well as of the sponges, is demonstrated. The course is designed to be of value to one intending to study medicine, as one-half of the term's work is devoted to a study of the vertebrate animals. The course has been enlarged, and more time is given at the end of the course to anthropology, or the natural history of man.

Special facilities are offered to anyone desiring to do more advanced work in zoology.

Specimens of the following rarer types have lately been added for use in this department: African lung-fish (*Protopterus*) *Polypterus*, *Siren*, *Amphiuma*, *Cæcilia*, and a skin and skeleton of the Australian spiny ant-eater (*Echidna*); also skeletons and other osteological preparations of fishes, batrachians, lizards, birds, and mammals. Collections illustrating the invertebrate, crustacean, fish, amphibian, reptilian, and bird fauna of Rhode Island have been set apart in the museum; and valuable histological and embryological preparations have been added.

Instruction in geology is given during the first college half year by means of lectures, laboratory work, and field excursions, with especial reference to the geology, structural and economic, of Rhode Island. The lectures are illustrated by diagrams, models in wood and plaster, and fossils. During 1885 the paleontological collection was rearranged and labeled for the use of students. The fossil flora of Rhode Island is fully represented, and important animal remains of the Rhode Island carboniferous rocks were added in 1888 and 1889.

The laboratory work comprises an elementary course in mineralogy and lithology. Many duplicate crystals have been purchased, and the students are allowed to use them freely in their work. A special collection of Rhode Island minerals and rocks has been formed and additional European educational specimens secured.

Two large models, including one of the Atlantic Ocean bottom, and a model of the Caribbean Sea bottom, from the office of the U. S. Hydrographic Bureau, Washington, were deposited in 1889 in the lecture room, through the kindness of Commander Bartlett, U. S. Navy.

The lectures on prehistoric anthropology, at the close of the geological course, were in 1889–'90, illustrated by prehistoric implements of stone, bone, and bronze, with casts, models, and photographs, either collected or purchased by the professor in charge of this department in 1889 in France, Italy, and England, and especially from the lake dwellings in Switzerland. The funds for these purchases were furnished by an alumnus of the university.

PHYSIOLOGY.

During the first half year a number of lectures are given the freshman class upon matters relating to personal hygiene. Attention is called to the important laws of health, and practical advice given in regard to exercise, hours for study and sleep, the care of the digestive functions and the eyesight, and other matters in which the habits of students are so often faulty.

In the junior year elementary instruction is given in anatomy and physiology, the subjects being considered from a scientific rather than from a practical standpoint. The object of these lectures is to lay the foundation for a study of the morphology of the lower animals, those organs and functions which are of particular interest in this connection receiving the most attention.

BOTANY.

Instruction in botany is given by means of lectures and laboratory practice. The course occupies two years.

The first year is devoted to general morphology, practice in analyzing and describing plants, and the preparation of a small herbarium. A few difficult families, such as *Compositæ, Cruciferæ,* and *Umbelliferæ* are specially treated. Field excursions to neighboring points of interest and visits to conservatories are made. Collateral reading is required. For this purpose every student must read and prepare a digest of at least 2 books from a given list per term.

In the second year the study of the more difficult families is continued for a few weeks. Histological work is then taken up, and the preparation of microscopic objects. At the same time there are lectures on vegetable physiology, geographical botany, etc. Collateral reading is again required, with an occasional paper on some given subject.

Each student is expected to pay a small fee per term for the purchase of specimens used in class work. Original work and observation is encouraged. Students are required and encouraged to make illustrative drawings from the objects studied. It is designed in all cases to foster independent reasoning and thoughtful comparison.

THE HERBARIA.

The large and extremely valuable collection bequeathed to the university by the late Stephen Thayer Olney is housed in Manning Hall. The botanical lecture room is adjoining, with its appliances for study. To the original herbarium there have been added those of Mr. James L. Bennett, of Providence, Dr. C. M. Brownell, of Hartford, and the cosmopolitan collection of ferns presented by Miss Stout, of New York, in memory of her brother. There is also a yearly increment from exchange, and from the additions made by the curator to his personal gift. Under proper restrictions the herbaria are made accessible to the public and to students. An increasing number of professional botanists consult it, and every courtesy is extended to them and to visitors generally.

AGRICULTURE.

The course of instruction in agriculture includes the courses in the preparatory branches, chemistry, physics, botany, physiology, zoology, and comparative anatomy. It also embraces special lectures on agriculture. These relate to the study of soils and to applied economic zoology, according to the following schedule of topics:

Introduction: History of agriculture, tracing its development through the Jewish, Grecian, Roman, Spanish, and English nations to the formation of agricultural and horticultural societies in the United States, with a brief account of the earlier ones formed within the years from 1785 to 1829, inclusive. The subject is then continued by the discussion of the following topics: (1) Primary condition of matter; (2) formation of soil from inorganic elements; (3) source of organic matter; (4) constituents of plants required by soil; (5) constituents of soil in the mass; (6) results of experiments with unfertilized and fertilized soils; (7) composition of fertile soil; (8) cardinal law in agriculture; (9) rotation of crops; (10) discriminating application of fertilizers.

Under the general head of economic zoology are discussed the distinctive characteristics of the most approved breeds of both neat cattle and horses. Practical instruction is given by the visiting of farms and in obtaining and preserving specimens in natural history. Taxidermy is also taught when desired by the class.

WILSON HALL.

By the will of the late George F. Wilson, of Providence, the sum of $100,000 was bequeathed to the corporation of Brown University, "for a building devoted to scientific purposes." It was decided that this sum should be applied to the construction of a physical laboratory, to be called Wilson Hall. In June, 1887, a committee was appointed by the corporation to obtain plans and superintend the erection of the building. The plans submitted by Messrs. Gould and Angell, of Providence, were accepted by the committee in November, 1888, and work was begun June 6, 1889. The building is designed in a style of Romanesque architecture, modified to suit the special purpose for which it was erected. Its exterior is of granite and sandstone, and has a front of 84 feet and a depth of 106 feet. The total floor area is about 14,600 square feet. It is constructed in the most thorough manner with a view to the greatest solidity and freedom from vibration. In front and rear the building contains three stories, while in the central part there are four. By this arrangement a number of smaller rooms are provided for storing apparatus—for special research—private rooms for the professors and assistants, while the class rooms are ample and lofty.

The building is heated by direct radiation from steam pipes, steam being supplied from an outside station, so that there is no dust from coal or ashes to be feared. In that portion of the laboratory devoted to magnetism both steam and gas pipes are of brass.

In the lower laboratory stand two piers, one 14 feet long by 3 feet wide, built up of solid masonry from the ground to the height of an ordinary working table, the other 10 feet long by 4½ feet wide and of the same height as the preceding. This not only serves as a good working pier, but also supports an arch of solid masonry, surmounted by a beveled slab of stone 11 feet long by 3 feet wide, which comes flush with the laboratory room above. Upon this slab the working table may be placed, or be removed at will, leaving the entire floor space free. In the lecture room the lecture desk is supported on a similar slab, 12 by 3½ feet, resting on a pier of masonry and flush with the platform. All the piers are kept entirely free from the flooring. Besides the piers, stone slabs supported on brackets built into the outer walls have been provided as working tables, since experience seems to show that their stability compares very favorably with that of the piers themselves. Similar slabs are provided outside of such windows as seemed likely to be available for the heliostat.

One 10-horse power Otto gas engine furnishes power for the mechanical and electrical work to be done, and it is proposed to give special attention to these branches of physics. For the present a larger share of purely constructive work is planned for than perhaps properly belongs to a physical laboratory in the higher sense, but a movement is on foot which promises ultimately to enable us to create a special department of applied mechanics, in which case such work will be transferred to another building.

PRESENT POLICY.

In an interview with President Andrews with reference to what, so far as he could say, would be the policy of the university, he said that it would be his aim to make Brown the peer of any college in the land. A movement is now on foot to raise funds, half a million or more, as may be necessary, which are to be devoted to the organization and maintenance of a school of applied science. A large class in the community is obliged to go out of the State for a technical training. There is a demand for such a school and it would receive the support of all those interested in industrial pursuits. Such a school should have a department of design to which a student could come for that one branch. He would favor that those following its regular courses should take courses in political economy, English literature, and the modern languages, in order that the student might come out not merely with an education that will enable him to earn a livelihood, but with a liberal education.

The university is the only one in the State, and it should be made a factor for good to all. A liberal education is of necessity acquired but by few in a community, and is not fully appreciated by the many. President Andrews favors such a movement as one that would deepen the hold of the college on the people. We would like to inaugurate this very winter, if possible, and, if not, as soon as it may be possible, a system of university extension. We would have instructors from all of the departments of the university go to Pawtucket, Newport, Fall River, or any part of the State where classes might be formed. In this way the university could be brought to the people and they would be made to feel its influence.

At the opening of the academic year of 1890, arrangements will be made for obtaining instruction in electrical engineering, under the charge of a competent instructor. Wilson Hall contains the latest and most improved facilities in the department of physics.

Then, too, there are exceptional advantages in the city of Providence for what the university would offer were there a faculty of law.

To begin here a good course in law would not, however, be costly, and there is much not only to render effort in that direction desirable, but also to assure its success. The university once had a law department, or at least a professor in that branch. The common law preferences and procedure characteristic of the Rhode Island judicial system render a law school almost a necessity in this State. A noble law library is at our doors. Courts in all varieties, Federal, State, and municipal, before which are to be heard some of the greatest lawyers of the land, are in operation within ten minutes' walk of our chapel. At the start, three new professors would suffice; and we should have a law class of 40 or 50 the first term.

But while there are magnificent opportunities from a school of applied science, from university extension, and from a faculty of law, it has been and still is his cherished purpose to broaden and deepen the present foundations. The courses in Latin, Greek, the sciences, mathematics, and modern languages would be made so broad and thorough that Brown would rank among the leading colleges of the land. The education should be such that the student while specializing would not be a mere specialist. He should be taught to use his mind. Laboratories, while showing him how to do so, should be so utilized that the mind would be made still more effective. The whole trend of the education should be towards the development of the mind by the roundness of an education truly liberal. Brown is cosmopolitan in the personnel of the students. Although the college is denominational, students representing nearly all the various denominations come here. The contact of the men from the various sections of the country is an important element in the education which is here received. A student thus learns that there are 44 States besides his own comprising the Union.

The following extracts are made from President Andrews's report to the corporation for 1889-'90:

We do well, in view of this and such positions which we shall have to equip as the years pass, to direct, so far as possible, whether at home or abroad, the advanced studies of our most brilliant graduates. A system of home and traveling fellowships would immensely aid us in this. Four hundred dollars a year would support a graduate student at home; $500 abroad. Gifts of these sums for these purposes, or, better, of foundations assuring them, would be among the most acceptable means for promoting high scholarship among us. While I hope that we shall never fill our faculty with mere specialists, it is no longer safe to depend for men to become professors upon specially apt general scholars, promoted without particular training, from the ranks of the various learned professions. Nor is there any excuse for doing this, since there is talent enough available for all required teaching, if it is only sought out and guided. Our range of choice being so wide, contracts with instructors should be strictly construed as holding only from year to year, so that none need be retained who do not give promise of uncommon success. New professors, too, unless men of settled reputation, should be engaged at first for but three or five years, leav-

BROWN UNIVERSITY—PRESIDENT'S HOUSE.

ing the university in condition to relieve itself of any who may prove inert, inapt, or without ambition. The literary institutions of the country suffer distressingly to-day from professors and other officers who, sure of their tenure, have remitted zeal and come to treat their positions as a mere convenience.

Let none of the above suggestions touching our needs be taken as a complaint. The prospects for our university seem to me to be, on the whole, very encouraging. We may look for a considerable accession, in the course of years, to the number of our students; and if we display progress, proper enterprise, and sound financial wisdom, we shall, I believe, secure abundant funds.

Supposing that we may hope for advance, what ought to be our policy? My sentence is that we should toil primarily, sedulously, unremittingly, and always to enlarge and strengthen the old plant, to make even better, richer, wider, that genuinely liberal education which it has for a century and a quarter been the pride of Brown University to give. However the curriculum may expand, the aim in this part of our work should never change.

But to perfect the plant as is desirable, not to speak of remote requirements, several new professorships are needed—a professorship of European history, a professorship of political and social science, a professorship of philosophy, a professorship of English and American literature apart from rhetoric, and a professorship of the history and criticism of the fine arts. We must speedily have, besides, an assistant professor in chemistry and another in physics.

With such an increase of force—indispensable, whether we wish to furnish the ideal liberal education or only to compete with other good institutions—we shall be enabled to attain a second most valuable end—the establishment of a graduate course.

HISTORICAL AND ECONOMIC ASSOCIATION.

The University during the year 1888–'89, under the auspices of the Brown University Historical and Economic Association, maintained two courses of lectures. These were held in Manning Hall, and were open to the public. Large audiences showed the interest which was manifested.

In 1889–'90 there were two courses, one of 6 lectures on The State and Social Reform, and the other of 4 lectures on Railroad Problems. The lecturers in the first course were: Prof. Woodrow Wilson, LL. D., of Wesleyan University; Rev. John G. Brooks, of Brockton, Mass.; Hon. Francis Wayland, LL. D., of Yale University; Prof. F. W. Taussig, of Harvard University; Gen. Francis A. Walker, LL. D., of the Massachusetts Institute of Technology; Rev. Edward Everett Hale, D. D.; and in the second course Prof. Davis R. Dewey, of the Massachusetts Institute of Technology; Edward Atkinson, esq., of Boston; Prof. Henry B. Gardner, of Brown University; Dr. Edwin R. A. Seligman, of Columbia College, and Alfred Stone, esq., of Providence.

During the winter of 1890 '91 there were two courses, the first on the History of Political Parties in the United States; the second on Money. The lecturers in the first course and their subjects were as follows: Hon. Andrew D. White, LL. D., ex-president of Cornell University, The Influence of America on the French Revolution; Prof. Anson D. Morse, of Amherst College, Political Parties; their Nature, Uses, and Claims; Prof. J. F. Jameson, of Brown University, The Origin of Parties in the United States; Prof. Anson D. Morse, The Parties of the

Federalist Period; Prof. Charles H. Levermore, of the Massachusetts Institute of Technology, The Rise of the Whig Party and of Jacksonian Democracy.

The lecturers in the second course and their subjects were as follows: Dr. E. B. Andrews, president of the University, The History of Our Silver Dollar; Prof. F. W. Taussig, of Harvard University, The Silver Situation in the United States; Hon. Nelson W. Aldrich, of the United States Senate, The Future of Silver; Mr. Willard C. Fisher, instructor in Brown University, Do We Need More Money?; Prof. J. Laurence Laughlin, of Cornell University, The Subtreasury System.

UNIVERSITY EXTENSION.

As early as 1785 a course of public lectures was given in the State House, under the auspices of the university. Under the presidency of Dr. Wayland, the professor in chemistry offered to the mechanics and artisans of Providence a course of 8 lectures in The Chemistry of the Precious Metals. Within recent years courses of a general nature have been given in Manning Hall, and the public has been invited. The Historical and Economic Association of Brown University, for the last five years has offered 2 courses each year in the field of history and politics. But in the winter of 1890–'91 a course in university extension was started in Pawtucket, a manufacturing and industrial center. This course was experimental, but so successful as to encourage the introduction of similar courses in other cities in the State.

The following announcement of the scheme was given a wide distribution in the city:

RHODE ISLAND UNIVERSITY EXTENSION.

After the example of the great English universities, it is proposed to open in the high school building in Pawtucket, soon after January 1, 1891, provided that by this date fifteen applications for each course have been received, two courses of thorough scientific lectures by members of the faculty of Brown University, one on astronomy, the other on botany, each course consisting of 12 lectures. If they prove to meet a public want, these courses will be followed in subsequent years by the same and by similar ones on other subjects, covering in a few seasons the entire round of science, philosophy, and literature, so far as such subjects can be presented in the English language. The lectures, while as free as possible from mere technicalities, and open to persons of both sexes and all ages, will be intended not for the curious, but only for thoughtful and studious people, clergymen, teachers, clerks, mechanics, and others who are willing to pursue attentively at least one entire course. At the end of each course pupils who desire will be examined, and, if they pass, receive a certificate of that fact. Those who pass in ten courses, making up a "cycle," will receive an engraved diploma, constituting them members of the Rhode Island University Extension.

The fees will be $3 for each person for each course, with 50 cents additional per person for each examination. Persons desiring to take one or both of the above courses are requested to register their names at once with the superintendent of schools, Pawtucket. For further information apply to

E. BENJ. ANDREWS.

BROWN UNIVERSITY, *November 1, 1890.*

The superintendent of public schools sent circulars like the following to the manufacturers, who put them in the hands of their operatives:

PAWTUCKET, R. I., *December 18, 1890.*

In cooperation with President Andrews, of Brown University, I am trying to spread the knowledge of the university extension as widely as possible. It is desired especially to reach the more intelligent laboring classes.

May I trespass upon your good nature to the extent of asking you to post one of the inclosed circulars where it will be seen by your employés, and to have the others handed to persons likely to be interested. I shall be glad to send more circulars if desired.

Trusting that you will be interested in advancing the movement, and thanking you for your trouble in the matter, I am,

Yours, sincerely,

HENRY M. MAXSON,
Superintendent of Public Schools.

The programme of the courses given stated:

In carrying out the proposed plan of putting the advantages of the university within the reach of every person, without regard to his residence or circumstances, the president and professors of Brown University have arranged for this year the following courses of lectures to be given at the Pawtucket high school. There are 12 lectures in each course, one occurring each successive week at 8 p. m., astronomy beginning January 12; botany, January 14; German literature, January 17.

Astronomy, by Prof. Winslow Upton.

The course will treat upon the motions of the heavenly bodies, the diurnal motion of the heavens, the annual motion of the sun, the motion of the moon, planetary motions, and stellar motions, describing each in its turn and referring it to its true cause. The results of their combinations will be discussed and certain practical applications shown as they are used in measuring time and arranging the calendar.

Botany, by Prof. W. W. Bailey.

This course will be essentially practical, the aim being to give each member of the class the ability to take up and continue the study and classification of plants by himself after the course has been finished. The class will be set to work, flower and microscope in hand, after the class-room method used in the university.

German literature, by Prof. Alonzo Williams.

Considering the place of literature in education, the land, the people, language, and literature of ancient Germany, the great epics of the language, with a treatment of the various eras and possibly some verse translations and discussion of the Niebelungenlied and Parzival. This course will be given in English and will be interesting and instructive to those who know nothing of the German language, as well as to those who do, and should appeal to every student and lover of literature. It has been decided to hold this class also in the evening instead of the afternoon, as at first talked.

Each student can take one course or more, as he wishes; he can devote extra time to study or not, as his circumstances permit; there will be no examination except for those who desire it.

It is not a money-making scheme, nor, on the other hand, an ordinary lecture course. It is simply and solely a plan to give everyone, regardless of occupation or circumstances, an opportunity to get some of the benefits of a college education.

The fee is $3 for each course of lectures. It is desirable that names should be previously sent to me at Music Hall, but persons may join the opening night if this is not convenient.

The specimen card gives the details of the course affecting the student:

[Preserve this.]

RHODE ISLAND UNIVERSITY EXTENSION.

CARD OF MATRICULATION.[1]

The holder[2] of this card, M ———— ————, of ———— ————, has been enrolled and examined[3] in
[Name in full.]
Rhode Island University extension courses, as indicated below:

Name of course.	Date of beginning.	Fee, $3.[4]	Signature of instructor.	Date of examination[5] and result.	Signature of examiner.	Fee, 50 cents.[6]
....	....	....	....	....	....	....
....	....	....	....	....	....	....
....	....	....	....	....	....	....

[1] No person is a member of the class who has not a matriculation card. Each card has spaces for 10 courses, or a cycle.

[2] Let the pupil write his or her name in full, and residence. The instructor will then write in the proper places the name of the course, the date of beginning it, and the word "paid" when the fee is collected.

[3] No examination is required, but any pupil who desires can be examined in any course. Examinations passed in 10 courses, or a cycle, entitle to a diploma.

[4] Fees are due in advance. The word "paid" in this space, in the handwriting of the instructor, is a sufficient receipt for the fee.

[5] Write "passed" or "failed." Fee must be paid in either case.

[6] The word "paid" in this space, in the handwriting of the examiner (usually the same as the instructor), is a sufficient receipt.

While these courses are experimental, the indications show a spirit of appreciation on the part of those following them. By February 1, 1891, the average attendance was 30, a few students taking the 3 courses, but the majority following 1. The students are chiefly from the professional classes, and the cooperation of those engaged in industrial pursuits has not been so largely secured as could be wished.

President Andrews expressed himself as pleased with the initiative courses, and has organized others in different parts of the State.

PROFESSOR GAMMELL.

In the history of an institution of learning there are certain professors who stand out in bold relief. They have not been content simply to do well what have been their allotted tasks, but they have recognized the high possibilities of their calling. Men of strong personality, they have left impressions of character on their students, who will remember these lessons long after those of the class room have faded from memory.

Such men knew that they had the possibilities of molding the lives and shaping the character of their pupils. How well they succeeded may be seen in the tributes of respect and gratitude which are paid by their students when they learn that they, in common with their college, are called to mourn the departure of an honored teacher. Many such tributes bear testimony to the fact that aspirations were aroused and noble purposes were deepened by the contact and by the influence of a manly professor.

It has been the rare good fortune of Brown that she has always had men like these, either in the active labors of the academic staff or in the prudent counselings of governing boards. Many of these men came under the influence of Wayland during his presidency, and they in turn testify their indebtedness to him. It is admitted that the influence of Wayland in the history of the college has been most productive of good, and his successors, as they have approached his characteristics, have received an additional word of praise.

Prof. William Gammell, whose death occurred in 1889, was one of the names that the university will cherish. Although he left the academic chair in 1867, he had not ceased to identify himself with the university. After thirty-two years of service, as tutor and professor, he withdrew in the prime of his powers. His influence may be said to have continued, in that his successor to the professorship of history was Diman, his pupil. Prof. Gammell's connection with the university was contemporaneous with some of the most honored and brilliant men who were called to preside over or guide the instruction. He was associated with Wayland, Sears, Chace, Dunn, Caswell, Lincoln, Diman, and many others who had the best welfare of the college at heart.

Graduating in 1831 with the highest honors of his class, he was called the following year to a tutorship at the college. He was called tutor and lecturer in the Latin language and literature. His promotion to the assistant professorship of belles-lettres followed in 1835. He was associated in this chair with Prof. William G. Goddard. In 1837 he was appointed professor of rhetoric, and the chief labor of the department devolved upon him, owing to the poor health of Prof. Goddard.

The "new system," as planned by Wayland in the reorganization of the instruction of the college, constituted a separate department of history. To this chair Prof. Gammell was transferred and held the professorship of history and political economy till his withdrawal in 1867. But his withdrawal from the duties of a professor by no means withdrew him from the heartiest cooperation in the interests of the college. He was elected a member of the corporation in 1870, and was actively identified with the management of the college. After his resignation from his professorship he devoted himself to labors in behalf of public charity and philanthropy. This President Wayland and Prof. Chace had also done.

In the biography of Prof. Gammell appears the following letter, of which a part is quoted. It was written by Dr. Thayer, of Newport:

NEWPORT, *March 15, 1890.*

I have been asked to join in a testimonial to Prof. Gammell. My increasing intercourse with him of late years has made me feel his loss too much not to comply with the request. One shrinks from a formal tribute to a friend. Yet it is a real tribute which I pay Prof. Gammell in saying that through all the changes about him he preserved his identity. For all agree that a wonderful process of assimilation is going on, and everybody is becoming like everybody else. Perpetual contacts with all sorts of people are unconscious attritions that rub down personal peculiarities to an uninteresting sameness. Fashionable life renders its votaries indistinguishable by the enamel it puts on them. Politics bring men into disgusting resemblance, while our literature of all kinds is strangely alike and forms its readers to its own average. What wonder, then, that men lose or greatly qualify their identities, that colleges are conforming to the pattern of the age, and that presidents and professors are becoming like the rest of mankind—the presidents largely employed in collecting funds, and the professors no longer living and working in the college only, but playing the scholar in politics and acting in peripatetic universities. But Prof. Gammell was wholly formed in Brown University when—defects and all—it was the old American college, and his life was concentrated there with singular devotion. That cast of character he never lost, not obtrusively, but decidedly it impressed you, and it was easy to conceive him in the classroom. His opinions were positive and given emphatically, but not offensively *ex cathedra*. He loved racy good English, taught it and used it, though I doubt not he exercised literary charity for his pupils and friends who have come to prefer poets and thinkers whose meaning is not plain to their readers nor probably was to themselves. The professor was a "gentleman of the old school," and to those who did not know the man he might have seemed reserved, but from the testimony of his pupils he had a warm fund of sympathy and a genial interest for them. He was a member of the "Friday Club," and his interest and devotion to it contributed to the success of the gathering. Some of the papers there presented have been printed.

THE LIBRARY.

The historian of an institution is able to appreciate the benefit to it of founders who were men of wisdom. President Manning appreciated the need of books for the college. The culture and learning of the day were in books, and these were expensive. The professors were not able to provide themselves with such books as were necessary for their own libraries in the various departments. It was necessary that the centers of learning should have libraries, not only for the use of the students but for consultation by the instructors.

If Rhode Island College was to be an influence in the community and if it was to be a center of learning, it must have a working library. President Manning clearly saw the necessity for this and very early used his influence towards its accomplishment. The success which attended his efforts has been evinced by the steady growth in the college and the formation of the nucleus of an excellent library.

Two years after the removal of the college to Providence the number of books was 250, "not well chosen, being such as our friends could best spare."

BROWN UNIVERSITY—INTERIOR OF LIBRARY.

In 1782, at the reorganization of the college after the interval of the Revolution, there were 500 books, "most of which are both very ancient and very useless, as well as very ragged and unsightly." By subscriptions and by the gifts of friends additions were made so that the number was increased to about 4,000. It is of interest to note that several donations of books were made by Englishmen, showing their interest in the college, although the incidents of the Revolution were still fresh in mind.

The library was placed in the east room on the second floor of University Hall, till it was removed to Manning Hall. The books composing the library were theological and biographical chiefly, although some were scientific and historical. Very many of the early accessions were obtained by purchase, the money having been subscribed by friends, so that the deficiencies of any department could be supplied.

From the by-laws adopted in 1785 are taken the following extracts:

The librarian shall keep the library room neat and clean, and in delivering out books he shall suffer none of the students to derange or handle them on the shelves.

He shall demand and receive a fine of sixpence for every time that any student hath suffered a library book to be uncovered in his possession.

He shall open the library room on such day of the week as the president shall from time to time direct, and shall keep it open from 1 to 3 o'clock in the afternoon.

The sum of $25 was paid the librarian in 1792, and in 1796 the freshman class was admitted to the use of the library on the same terms as the other students.

The friends of the college remembered the library, and legacies of valuable books were left to it. That of the Rev. William Richards, of Lynn, England, was rich in books illustrative of Welsh and English antiquities. Other smaller but valuable bequests were made.

In 1831 an effort was made to raise $25,000 for the purchase of books and apparatus for the philosophical and chemical departments. Nearly $20,000 was secured and invested till it should reach the desired sum of $25,000. The room in University Hall was by this time "crowded to excess, unsightly, and wholly unsuited for the purpose to which from necessity it was devoted."

In 1835 Manning Hall was dedicated. This building had been erected by the generosity of Nicholas Brown, and was to serve as a chapel and library. This building afforded more room, but was not conveniently adapted for a library, nor was it fireproof. However, the library remained in this building till 1878, when it was removed to the present building. In 1843 the number of volumes was about 10,500.

In the next decade valuable additions of French, German, and Italian books were added, having been carefully selected by Prof. Jewett, who was at the time in Europe. He was also successful in securing a valuable collection of English books, including one of Shakespeariana. A collection of patristic works was commenced in 1847. This was enlarged by the efforts of some of the city clergymen, and a very complete set was secured.

Such was, in outline, the growth of the library till its removal in 1878 to the present building. The words of President Robinson at the dedication of the building fittingly characterize the library. "Admirable, spacious, complete, massive, imposing, enduring as is this structure, the library which is to occupy it is not unworthy of its place. No college library perhaps in the country is better fitted to the uses for which such libraries are supposed to be gathered. It has never been the receptacle of cast-off books; it has never been encumbered by gifts of unsalable private libraries. Its 50,000 volumes have been selected under scrutinizing eyes with unremitted care that the best authorities in every department of learning should find a place on its shelves. Even its largest purchases have been made with extremest care and by well-read men." These facts bridged a mighty chasm between the present and that early day, when the library had but 250 volumes, "not well chosen, being such as our friends could best spare."

The present building is fireproof, and the plan is that of a cross with octagonal radiating wings. The reading room is in the center. Light is obtained from the large windows of the cupola and also by small windows in each alcove. Particular attention was paid to lighting and ventilation, two excellencies which here have been secured. Each of the three wings, octagonal in shape, contains 24 alcoves. The west wing is devoted to history. Over the window in each alcove is the general classification: Biblical literature, theology, religious history, biography, voyages and travels, American history, English history, general history. The north wing is devoted to science, with the following classification: Jurisprudence, political economy, philosophy, natural history, medical science, useful and fine arts, mathematics, chemistry, physics. The east wing is devoted to literature. The classifications are: Bibliography and literary history, philology, Greek and Latin classics, collected works, English and American literature, foreign literature, periodicals.

Each alcove is supplied with a table and chairs so that the book can be consulted there. The students have free access to all the alcoves on the ground floor, and may obtain permission to consult books on the two upper ones. Regarding the free access of students to the books the librarian says:

It was early my conviction, and an experience of forty years as a librarian has only served to confirm it, that the books of a college library should be so arranged as to allow the students to consult and handle them freely. Catalogues, however necessary and accessible and however carefully and skillfully prepared, can never take the place of the books themselves in a collegiate institution. It requires, moreover, no small degree of knowledge and patience to consult a modern catalogue of a large collection of books. Hence, the president of Harvard College, at a recent meeting of the American Library Association, facetiously remarked that although he might claim to be as intelligent as the ordinary frequenters of a library, he did not know enough to use a card catalogue.

The library has open shelves where the books can be readily handled by all, and quiet, well-lighted alcoves, with convenient tables and seats, inviting to study and research.

This arrangement is of great advantage to the student, for he can see very quickly whether a book is one that he may want. In addition he gains some knowledge from the titles, for he knows where to go for a book although he may not need it at once. Alumni from neighboring cities have come to consult this library simply because they had free access to the shelves, and they have been rewarded by finding books of which they had no knowledge. One member of the class of 1858 felt indebted to the library to such an extent that he presented a valuable collection of works on pedagogics.

The catalogue is of the card system, arranged so as to show titles, authors, and subjects. The books are recorded by numbers which show the alcove, press number, shelf number, and the number of the book on the shelf. Thus 6-1-9-26 means alcove six, press one, shelf nine, book twenty-six. On the ground floor there are 9 shelves in each alcove, and 7 on each of the alcoves on the two upper floors. Each shelf is 30 inches long. Each book is charged to the student, who signs the register in which it is recorded.

The library funds amount to $46,000. Of this amount $10,000 is a bequest from the late Prof. Gammell, for the purchase of books relating to the history of the United States. Ten thousand dollars constitutes the "Olney fund" for the purchase of botanical books and plants. The balance, including a bequest of $500 from the late President Wayland, was raised by subscription in 1831, and is called the "library fund." To this the Hon. Nicholas Brown contributed $10,000.

The library is open in term time each week day, except Saturday, from 10 to 4; on Saturdays from 10 to 1; during vacations on Saturdays only. The central part of the library is open also from 7 to 10 each week-day evening, except Saturday, not, however, for the drawing and return of books, but for reading, consultation, and research.

Members of the corporation and of the faculty, also every donor residing in Providence, of $500 or more to the funds of the university, may use the library without charge. The library committee can grant this privilege to others, but by vote of the corporation, persons not exempted in any of these ways, including students and graduates, pay for library privileges the sum of $5 each, per annum.

During the year 1890 the library was increased by the addition of 575 volumes by purchase and 540 volumes and 1,884 pamphlets by gift. It now numbers about 80,000 bound volumes and 20,000 pamphlets.

There has been placed in the rotunda of the library building an additional long table, upon which are placed a large number of books for ready examination by students. This collection, varying from time to time, includes recent accessions to the library, books recommended by professors for consultation by students in connection with topics discussed in the lecture room, also works illustrative of archæology.

Any mention of the library would be incomplete without reference to the librarian, Dr. R. A. Guild.[1] He is one of the best friends of the students, nor does he forget them after they graduate. Each alumnus as he returns to the university invariably finds himself at the library, where he is sure of a cordial welcome and a genuine interest in what he has been doing, on the part of the librarian. It would seem as if Dr. Guild spent nearly as much of his time on the steps and vestibule of the library as in his room, so reluctant is he to allow his friends to depart, and such hard work is it for them to get away. He is sure to make some inquiry regarding a classmate, or relate some anecdote concerning an alumnus or a friend of the college. He is always willing to do all he can for the students, in aiding them in their use of the library, and more than one, on his return in after years, has made recognition to the doctor of the obligation which he felt towards him. He is a loyal son of his *alma mater*, and no one is more conversant with her past.

BROWN IN 1861.

Reference should be made to the part which the university took in the scenes of 1861–1865. The echoes of conflict are now growing fainter and fainter, so that mention can be made of events which reflect credit on the college, without exciting aversion from those who took opposite sides.

The enthusiasm was intense among the students, and they all acted in accord with what each considered the duties of the hour. The spirit which had animated the early years of the college, when the buildings were given up for barracks and hospitals in the Revolution, still seemed to be present.

When, after the close of the strife, it was desired to recall and commemorate the sons of Brown who had shared in the conflict, and who had given up life itself, the choice of the students was the erection of a mural tablet in the chapel. At the commemorative exercises in the chapel, the address was given by Prof. Lincoln. It is presented entire, because it is a refutation of the charge that the scholar takes no part in politics; that liberal studies withdraw the student from interest or activity in passing events that concern his fellow-men or his country:

If I speak at this time in behalf of the faculty it is for the purpose of making it distinctly understood that their part in the work now consummated has been merely formal. To the undergraduates all the praise belongs. From them the suggestion came, and save that to my colleague, the professor of Latin, they owe the terse and admirable inscription, they have had the matter wholly in their own hands. I need hardly say that this gives a peculiar interest to our present services. So far as I am aware, no such tribute has been paid in any of our sister colleges. Some, with imposing ceremonies, have commemorated their unreturning dead. One has with great propriety decided to devote a chapel to the precious memory of sacrifices which, in an earlier age, would have swelled the lists of saints and martyrs, while our most ancient university seeks expression for her proud sorrow in a memorial

---

[1] Dr. Guild and the late Prof. Diman had much to do with building up the library collections of Brown University.—ED.

hall, whose stately front will bear the names of her heroes, while its inner walls will be eloquent with their pictured lips. But such costly offerings can come only from the whole body of alumni, while the simple tablet which we set up to-day derives its distinctive value from the fact that it is a student's tribute. And if, as the Roman historian holds, next to the doing of great deeds must be reckoned the right appreciation of them, this tablet will serve in two ways as an enduring testimonial; for while, on the one hand, it will bear witness to the magnanimity and love of country of those *qui pro libertate et pro reipublicæ integritate* laid down their lives on the blood-stained field, or languished them away in the unwholesome prison, so, on the other, will it furnish the evidence that one mind animated the mass, and that those who could not themselves share in the sacrifice were prompt to testify their sense of its greatness.

To the faculty and to the students alike it seemed eminently fit that such a memorial should be erected here; that here, as we gather to our daily devotions, we might be reminded of those who only a short time since sat with us on these benches and joined with us in our accustomed hymns of praise; and that here those who in years to come shall fill our places may learn that study is not an end in itself; that liberal culture looks to larger results than are included in mere academic success; that the finest discipline becomes contemptible if not coupled with the manly virtues. Not what we learn, but the use we make of our learning, is what tells the story. Surely, if the instructors in this institution ever grow negligent in inculcating these high lessons the very stone will cry out.

And if any of you, who have been long out of college, are curious about the kind of training that has been furnished of late years, you may study the best proof of it in that inscription, *Abeunt studia in mores*—let the lofty public spirit of these children of our common mother, their fidelty to duty, their valor, their endurance speak for the training she gave them. She carves their names in her holiest place, in recognition of the new lustre they have added to her ancient fame. The evidence here furnished of the intrinsic worth of our established method of academic discipline is the more striking, because it is just here that the common objections to it are urged with the greatest force. That method, you are aware, has been severely criticised as unsuited to the present age. Such exclusive devotion, it has been claimed, to abstract studies but poorly fits the understanding to deal with practical concerns; such prolonged contact with the part is ill adapted to awaken sympathy with the living present. Thus we furnish a puny intellectualism at the price of those manly qualities which are the conditions of all real success. How far these reproaches were well founded, let the experience of this, and kindred institutions, show. When the call of the President revealed the public peril, who sprang to arms? Where all professions, all ranks, all conditions showed such alacrity, it might seem invidious to claim special praise for any single class, but let it never be forgotten that among those who hurried earliest to the strife, in those shameful days when one and another of the men who had been trained at West Point was proving faithless to his trust, was a large proportion of the students of our college; a proportion, in some instances, so large as seriously to interfere with the routine of academic duties. It is safe to affirm that no one class of the American people was represented in so liberal a ratio as the very class whose training has been decried as tending to keep them at a distance from the questions of the day. And in this respect our experience has been the experience of those before us. In that matchless eulogy which Pericles pronounced at the beginning of the Peloponnesian war he proudly claimed that Athens had lost nothing in the cultivation of those arts to which she owed her highest fame; and we, too, on looking back on our record, remembering the readiness with which so many of our educated youth made sacrifice of the hopes of years, recognizing the conspicuous ability so often shown in the novel and arduous positions to which they were summoned, bewailing, alas, what may not even now be mentioned without renewing in the hearts of some here present a grief too sacred and too recent to be disturbed, may repeat with added emphasis the words of the great Athenian orator, "We have not been enfeebled by philosophy."

And never again let it be said, as more than once it was said before the rebellion, that our educated men, as a class, are the most disloyal to our institutions. There is no such antagonism between liberal culture and republican ideas. From a certain narrow national conceit, the offspring of ignorance and prejudice, culture, of course, emancipates the mind; it renders love of country a rational sentiment; it leads us to regard political forms as possessed not of absolute, but only of relative excellence; it warns us against supposing that any contrivances of man are perfect or destined to endure forever; but that an enlargement of the understanding, in the study of philosophy and history, a thoughtful survey of the forces which have shaped society, a just appreciation of the controlling political ideas that underlie the mighty movements of modern times, have any tendency to shake our confidence in the great experiment for which the New World was reserved by Divine Providence for so many years, our recent experience has triumphantly disproved. It is the wiser judgment of one of the profoundest political thinkers of our day, whose views have had no little influence in molding the present generation of American students, that a political system like ours is precisely the one which requires the "greatest maturity of reason, of morality, of civilization, in the society to which it is applied," and if, as Guizot affirms, modern society has penetrated the ways of God, it is because the scope and motive of modern politics are coming to be the more adequate expression of that Divine and Universal Justice which men of genuine culture have been in all ages most swift to recognize, and in advancing which they have come nearest the prize of the mark of their high calling.

The inscription was cut on a block of white marble, which is placed in Manning Hall.

IN. MEMORIAM. FRATRUM. SUORUM
QUI. PRO. LIBERTATE
ET. PRO. REIPUBLICÆ. INTEGRITATE
IN. BELLO. CIVILI. CECIDERUNT
LITERARUM. STUDIOSI
IN. HAC. UNIVERSITATE. COMMORANTES
HANC. TABULAM. POSUERUNT
MDCCCLXVI.

SOCIETIES.

In 1821, in consequence of the revival of 1820, was formed the Religious Society of Brown University. The object of the society will be seen from the preamble:

Impressed with a sense of the numerous temptations to which we are exposed and feeling the continual need and guidance of Almighty God, our Heavenly Father, we unite in this society devotedly to supplicate the throne of grace for the blessing of Heaven on our exertions to promote vital piety and sound morality in this institution.

The regular meeting was held in the university chapel and was a conference meeting. A yearly public meeting was held in the First Baptist Church, and a sermon was preached by some leading clergyman. President Wayland was invited to preach regularly before the society Sunday afternoons, and he continued to do so during the remainder of his presidency, more than twenty years. This society was quite similar in its organization to the Collegiate Young Men's Christian Association.

In May, 1827, a change was made in the name of the society and it was known as the "Society for Missionary Inquiry." The object of the society now was " that the members might possess the means of extending their knowledge respecting the moral and more especially the religious condition of the world." In 1834 the original name was resumed, because a special society for missionary inquiry had been organized. In 1863 the organization of the society was discontinued, but the weekly prayer meetings were held as usual on Wednesday evenings for twenty years.

A notice of the organization of the Young Men's Christian Association of Brown University appeared in the college publication for 1883, and in 1886 the Society for Missionary Inquiry was merged in the Young Men's Christian Association under the name of the Department for Missionary Inquiry. An annual sermon is still preached to the society by some leading divine. The Young Men's Christian Association, which is a branch of the intercollegiate association, has charge of the religious meetings and work of the students. Religious services are held in the chapel every morning, except Saturday and Sunday.

LITERARY SOCIETIES.

Particular attention had been given at Rhode Island College to oratory, and the early presidents had been good public men. The graduates of the early classes had the reputation of being accomplished speakers. A society "for the promotion of social intercourse and for improvement in forensic discussion" was formed in July, 1794. The number was limited to 20, and all the proceedings were secret. The name was the "Misokosmian Society." The literary exercises consisted in the discussion of prepared compositions or extemporaneous speaking on assigned topics.

As this was one of the earliest secret societies at the university, its object, as set forth by the preamble and compact, will be of interest:

Knowledge and virtue are the constituent principles of human happiness, and happiness is the ultimate end of human existence. Individual weakness forbids extensive research in the fields of science. Knowledge, therefore, must forever be exceedingly confined, without that reciprocation of ideas and that ardor of inquiry which alone result from social intercourse. Such are the unalterable laws of our nature that those sentiments of mind and those feelings of heart which make men happy can have no existence out of society. An interchange of wishes and union of interests alone can give birth to benevolence, humanity, friendship, and all the finer emotions of the soul.

The membership was increased to 40. In 1797 the project of forming a library was adopted and the name of the society was changed to that of "Philermenian." The library had a very few volumes, but in 1800 at the anniversary exercises special exertions were made, so that sufficient funds were raised to purchase Dobson's Encyclopedia. This was considered as the "repository of all that is valuable to the scholar." The society had a case for its books in the same room in which was the university library. The society was limited to a membership of 45. In 1806 there were upwards of 100 students residing at the university, and another society was organized, known as the "United Brothers." Its constitution was similar to the "Philermenian." These two societies were of course rivals, but the emulation on the whole was healthy and productive of good. The Philermenians were inclined to the Federal and the Brothers to the Republican party.

A room was given to the Philermenian Society in Hope College on its erection in 1823 and the library was removed to that building.

In 1824 the Franklin Society was established. The reason for this organization was similar to that of the Brothers. That year a large class had entered and, the membership of the other societies being limited, there was a demand for a third society. This society had an existence of ten years and was successful in accumulating a library of several hundred volumes. When the society disbanded an equal proportion of the members were elected to each of the other two. By a provision in the charter the library was transferred to the university library. The two other societies continued to flourish. In 1841 a joint celebration was effected. In 1849 the number of books in the Philermenian library was 3,224 and about the same number in that of the Brothers.

Still another cause at that time contributed very considerably to enhance the practical value of an education at Brown University. There were then in the college two literary societies, composed of undergraduates. These had large and valuable libraries. These volumes were very generally read by the students. But the principal value of these societies was found in their frequent stated meetings for practice in debate, and for reading and criticising compositions. Emulation was then excited in the useful arts of writing and speaking. The students thus accustomed themselves to think upon the great questions of the day and acquired the power of using their knowledge so as most effectually to convince and persuade others. From these debates they went forth to instruct society and to sway popular assemblies by their eloquence. Facts show that those who were then most active in these societies as writers and debaters have since done most for themselves and for the world. Here they trained their youthful faculties and acquired the skill which has since made their power felt. From these societies they looked out upon the theater before them and prepared for the battles to be fought and the work to be done in the great world of living men, where they were expecting to act their part. By these exercises the graduates of Brown University were prepared, when they went forth into the world, very soon to acquire an enviable distinction as popular speakers, ready debaters, men of good sense, and actual power in the conduct of affairs. Hence the opinion, then widely prevalent, that for all practical purposes an education in Brown University was even more desirable than one in most of the other colleges. This result was in no small degree due to the president, who always looked upon these societies as important auxiliaries in his work and warmly cherished them by his counsels and his encouragement. We are sorry that they are now so far abandoned. One of the best methods of practical training is here lost to the students. We do not believe that any equivalent has been found in the secret societies that have taken their place. Beyond all question it is a disgrace to the students, if not to some higher powers, that those libraries are left, as they now are, to be scattered, wasted, and utterly destroyed.

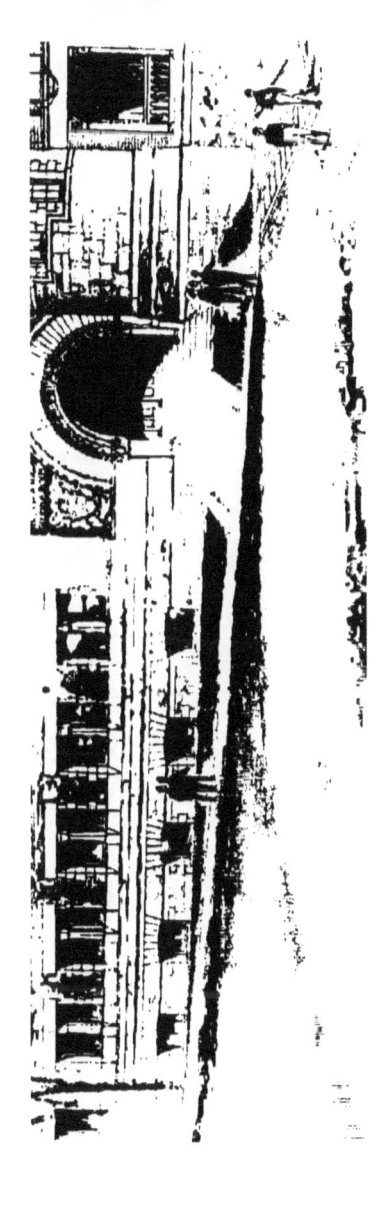

The Alpha of Rhode Island, of the Phi Beta Kappa, was established at Brown in 1830.

The Greek-letter secret societies are representative of all the leading fraternities. They are by reputation formed chiefly for literary purposes, and the leading ones maintain this standard. They have their periods of prosperity and adversity, and the study of any one will present an interesting phase of the society life. In the Liber Brunensis, the annual published by the secret societies, the following fraternities are represented at Brown in the order of their establishment:

Alpha Delta Phi, 1836; Delta Phi, 1838; Psi Upsilon, 1840; Beta Theta Pi, 1847; Delta Kappa Epsilon, 1850; Zeta Psi, 1852; Theta Delta Chi, 1853; Delta Upsilon, 1868; Chi Phi, 1872.

ATHLETICS.

The university has never had a gymnasium, and the want of this has been sadly felt by the various classes. Said the president in one of his last reports:

> We continually suffer great loss in the numbers, the health, the mental power, and the morale of our students from the lack of gymnasium privileges.

The new gymnasium will supply this deficiency. The students have been compelled heretofore to use such privileges as the local gymnasiums of the city have afforded, but these have been at some distance from the college grounds. The middle campus is used for tennis, while Lincoln Field affords good opportunity for baseball and football. Brown has usually taken part in the various intercollegiate sports, but the lack of gymnasium facilities has been a heavy handicap.

With a river near at hand which furnishes a magnificent course for boating, and a good campus for all field sports, and the gymnasium supplementing each, there is no reason why a healthy and a rational interest in athletics should not be developed.

PROFESSOR LINCOLN.

Were no special mention made of Prof. Lincoln, who has been associated with the academic staff of the university longer than any other man, all the graduates of the past fifty years would feel that an essential part of the sketch of Brown had been omitted.

He was the associate of Wayland, Sears, Caswell, Chace, Dunn, Diman, and many others who had the welfare of the university at heart and gave their best efforts to its advancement.

Although he had attained a position where he could rest on his well-won laurels, yet he still continued to guide and instruct the youth of Brown. How many were heard to remark "Prof. Lincoln will never grow old." So it was, and there was no younger man at the college than he. Genial and cordial, of a kindly disposition, he was one to whom the students were drawn by a feeling that here was a man who would sympathize with them and give them kindly advice.

Twice public recognition was made of the esteem and veneration in which he was held by the alumni. The first occasion was the celebration of his fiftieth anniversary of his years of love and labor at his *alma mater.* The exercises were crowned by the presentation to the university of the portrait of the professor.

The second token of regard for Prof. Lincoln was the foundation of the "John Larkin Lincoln Fund." This suggestion was made and carried out by the New York alumni. During his life he received from the income of this fund the sum of $3,000 a year, in lieu of other college salary; the balance of the income during his life, and the whole of it after his death, was to be devoted to the general uses of the university.

Prof. Lincoln is well known as an author of text-books and for public services of an academic nature. But he was best known and best remembered by those who sat under his instruction, and by those who came in contact with him socially. He was ever to all the Christian gentleman.

NOTE.—Since the preparation of the manuscript on Brown University a few additions are necessary to bring it up to date.

In 1891 the university voted that all its examinations should be open to women. In the following year all women holding bachelors' degrees and others who had obtained special permission were allowed to follow any of the courses of instruction that were intended for graduate students. There were also a considerable number of women who presented themselves as candidates for undergraduate examinations; hence classes were formed for them, and the members were instructed by members of the academic staff. These educational facilities for women constitute a department of the university, but as yet it can hardly be called a woman's college, because the university only concerns itself officially with the examinations. The success and increasing attendance of this department indicate that the present quarters are too small. President Andrews asks for a fund of half a million dollars to equip and endow this college. It is his wish that this enlargement shall form no mere "annex," but that women shall have the full university status, and that they may enjoy all the educational advantages now offered to male students of the university.

The Lyman gymnasium affords the best facilities for physical training. A director has charge of the work, and each student is obliged to take four hours per week in physical culture.

University extension is now in charge of a special director, Prof. Wilfred Harold Monroe, who has organized many centers in the surrounding towns and cities.

The death of Prof. Lincoln in October, 1891, was a great blow to the college. For nearly fifty years he had been identified with Brown, and its welfare was very dear to him. A memorial volume published by his son gives a sketch of his life and contains many of his essays.

PART V.

THE RHODE ISLAND COLLEGE OF AGRICULTURE AND MECHANIC ARTS.[1]

HISTORY.

In 1863 the State of Rhode Island received from the United States Government the land-grant scrip which gave to each State a portion of the public lands on condition that the proceeds derived from the sale of these lands be used for the endowment and support of an agricultural and mechanical college. The recipient of the land scrip in Rhode Island was Brown University.

In 1887, through the passage of the Hatch Act, the State received $15,000 for the purpose of establishing an experiment station in connection with its agricultural and mechanical college. When the State accepted the provisions of this act, a committee was appointed by the general assembly to investigate and report as to the best action to be taken by the State toward establishing this station, and at the same time to report on the disposition then being made of the income of the land-grant fund. The report of this committee, after much deliberation and many efforts to ascertain the opinions and wishes of the citizens of the State, was in favor of establishing a new institution, and connecting the experiment station with that, rather than with Brown University, the nominal land-grant college of the State. It was their opinion that the purpose for which the fund was given would be better served if it were given to the new institution, and they were of the belief that the university would willingly turn it over for that purpose. An act was accordingly passed, on March 23, 1888, establishing the Rhode Island Agricultural School, which was located at Kingston and entered its first class in September, 1890.

In August, 1890, the United States Congress passed the "new Morrill bill," appropriating for the further support of the agricultural and mechanical colleges a sum beginning with $15,000 and continuing with a yearly increase of $1,000 until the annual appropriation should reach $25,000. In order that the Rhode Island Agricultural School might receive the benefit of this act, the general assembly of the State amended the chapter of the public statutes establishing the school, and incorporated the institution as the Rhode Island College of Agriculture and Mechanic Arts. The new college, however, did not for a time receive the benefit of this fund, as Brown University filed with

---

[1] By President John H. Washburn.

general treasurer of the State a demand that all moneys received by him under the act of Congress, August 30, 1890, be paid to the treasurer of that institution; and at the same time secured an injunction from the supreme court restraining him from paying the same to the treasurer of the agricultural college. The case was taken before the United States circuit court, and a decision was given in favor of the latter institution. The university, however, appealed to the United States Supreme Court, and the final disposition of the fund would have been greatly delayed had it not been for a new measure taken by the State in April, 1894. This was the passage by the general assembly of a compromise act, by which the state treasurer was authorized to pay to Brown University the sum of $40,000, in consideration of which that institution was to turn over to the State the $50,000 from the land-grant fund, and the accumulated Morrill fund, amounting to $88,000. This has been done, and the college now enjoys the benefit of these funds. Up to that time the institution had no means of support outside of the State appropriations.

COURSES OF STUDY AND FACILITIES FOR INSTRUCTION.

As the State Agricultural School the institution offered a three years' course, comprising two years of high school and one of college work. The course included mathematics, language, science, agriculture, horticulture, and mechanics, the latter consisting then of woodwork only. The first year opened with a class of 30 pupils, and the next year's class was equally large. The institution began its third year as the Rhode Island College of Agriculture and Mechanic Arts, with a new and more advanced course of study. The length of the graduate course, leading now to the degree of bachelor of science, was changed to four years, and it is similar in character to that of the agricultural and mechanical colleges of other States. The graduate course, the same for all students during the freshman year, divides at that time into the agricultural and mechanical courses. They continue the same in many respects, but as the aim in one case is preparation for agricultural pursuits, and in the other for mechanical work, the course taken is modified to suit the end chosen by the student, who must decide at the beginning of his sophomore year which line he wishes to follow. The work in language is similar throughout the course, and the two divisions study botany, physics, the first two terms of chemistry, astronomy, political economy, and pyschology together; but while the agricultural student goes on with chemistry and biology and takes up agriculture and kindred subjects, the mechanical student continues mathematics and takes up practical and theoretical mechanics. The agricultural student receives instruction in woodwork and carpentering, but does not go so far with ironwork, mechanics, and engineering.

Chemical laboratory. College hall. Dining hall.

AGRICULTURAL COLLEGE

THE COLLEGE OF AGRICULTURE AND MECHANIC ARTS. 203

In addition to the graduate courses special courses are given for the benefit of those who can not take the full course in four years, or who wish to give especial attention to a particular line of work. Young women may graduate by substituting work in language, art, or science for the practical agriculture and mechanics required of the young men. The institution gives a short winter course in agriculture and mechanics, as many who would like to avail themselves of the advantages offered by the college can be here only for a limited time during the winter. This course combines practical work in the shops with a certain amount of time spent in the recitation room, the proportion of practical and theoretical work being fixed by the desire and ability of the student, subject to the approval of the faculty. No student, however, is allowed to take shop work alone, but must maintain a fair standing in at least one or two of the subjects presented in the lecture room.

The aims, facilities, and methods of the instruction given by the college may be seen in a brief account of some of the various departments.

THE MECHANICAL DEPARTMENT.

On a new basis and with increased means the work of the college has been extended in many directions. The change from Agricultural School to Agricultural and Mechanical College has made especially important the further development of the mechanical division, which has become a strong department of the institution. A mechanical building has been opened, containing a machine shop, well equipped with lathes, planes, drills, and other machinery and apparatus for iron-work, together with facilities for woodwork and the various branches of mechanical instruction, while a forge shop has been fitted up with forges, anvils, and the other tools necessary for that line of work.

The mechanical instruction begins with graded exercises in the carpenter shop, from which the student goes to the turning lathe and the machine saw, and in the sophomore year takes up constructions, mechanical drawing, and forging. The agricultural juniors continue forging and take up agricultural mechanics, while the mechanical men take lathe work, architectural drawing, strength of materials, and principles of mechanism, followed in the senior year by theoretical and applied mechanics, engineering, and mechanical practice. Many of the young women at the college have taken instruction in woodcarving.

The work in mathematics begins with algebra and geometry in the freshman and trigonometry in the sophomore year. The mechanical juniors take up analytical and descriptive geometry and calculus, with calculus and astronomy in the senior year. The agricultural students also receive instruction in astronomy.

Physics is taught during the sophomore year. The laboratory contains apparatus for the illustration of sound, light, heat, and electricity, which are taken up in the order named. The study of electricity and magnetism is continued during the junior year. The apparatus includes a solar lantern, which is also very useful for illustrated lectures, which are given in connection with many of the subjects taught in the various departments.

THE AGRICULTURAL DEPARTMENT.

The aim of the instruction in this department is to give theoretical and practical agricultural knowledge, and especially to impress upon the student the application of scientific principles to agriculture. The work of the freshman year includes the study of farm buildings, tools and machinery, the arrangement of fields, fencing, and drainage. The sophomore year is given to the study of the breeds of live stock, with lectures on the care of farm crops. Two terms of the junior year are spent on the study of soils, manures, and fertilizers, and the agriculture of the senior year is devoted to the laws of breeding and stock-feeding. This division of the college receives much benefit from the connection with the experiment station, as its farm and work are available for illustration and its library for reference.

The horticultural department maintains a fruit and vegetable garden, including an orchard of 260 trees, a vineyard of 500 vines, and plantations of the smaller fruits, amounting in all to about 350 varieties. This department also has charge of the planting of shade trees about the college grounds, and the care of the walks and lawns. The instruction consists of lecture-room exercises and practical work in the gardens.

Botany and microscopy are taught during the sophomore and junior years. The laboratory is equipped with compound microscopes, micrometers, dissecting instruments, a microphotographing apparatus, etc., with tables for laboratory work and cases for the apparatus and for the library of the department.

BIOLOGY.

The work of this department includes anatomy, physiology, zoology, and veterinary science, with political economy and psychology. The outfit of the division includes a manikin, a large model of the horse, and a number of smaller papier-maché models, various anatomical preparations, dissecting instruments, and other apparatus. The library contains a number of excellent works on biology, political economy, and psychology.

LANGUAGE AND HISTORY.

History is studied only during the freshman year. The first term is devoted to a review of American history and the remainder of the year to general history.

English—comprising rhetoric, composition, and literature—is studied throughout the entire course. In the junior and senior years especial

COLLEGE FARM HOUSE AND BARNS.

THE COLLEGE OF AGRICULTURE AND MECHANIC ARTS. 205

attention is given to English and American literature, the work of the senior year being largely elective. The library is of great advantage to this department, in the line both of history and literature.

French is studied during the sophomore year, and is elective for the juniors and seniors. The work comprises grammar and composition, with the reading of short stories and poems.

German is required during the junior year, and is elected by many of the seniors. The work consists of grammar, composition, conversation, reading, and an outline of German literature. A few standard German works have been added to the library.

ART DEPARTMENT.

The art department has been provided with a large and well-lighted studio, containing a large number of casts, models, drawings, and photographs from the best examples of painting and sculpture, with bric-a-brac, draperies, screens, and other studio properties. The rooms are very conveniently arranged with cases for material and racks for the work of the pupils. A portion of the studio is devoted to an excellent library, which is of the greatest value to the art student. Charcoal drawing, beginning with casts and simple studies, is taken up by the freshman class and carried through the sophomore year, one term of which is given to clay modeling. The seniors are allowed to elect drawing, life work, and painting. One hour each week is given to rapid sketching from life, in which all are at liberty to take part.

COURSE OF STUDY.

Freshman year.

FIRST TERM.

	Hours.
Algebra	5
English	5
Physical geography	3
History	2
Latin (elective)	3

AFTERNOON.

Agriculture[1]	2
Military drill[2]	1
Benchwork in wood	6

SATURDAY.

Military tactics	1
Inspection	1
Military drill[2]	1

Freshman year—Continued.

SECOND TERM.

	Hours.
Algebra	5
English	5
Physiology	3
Latin (elective)	3
History	2

AFTERNOON.

Bookkeeping and business law	5
Woodwork	6
Saturday, same as first term.	

THIRD TERM.

Algebra and logarithms	3
English	4
Geometry	4
Physiology	2
History	2
Latin (elective)	3

---

[1] Farm management, buildings, fences, and tools.
[2] Military instruction will be given on the appointment of an officer by the War Department to the college.

COURSE OF STUDY—Continued.

Freshman year—Continued.

THIRD TERM—Continued.
AFTERNOON.

	Hours.
Free-hand drawing	4
Agriculture [1]	4

Saturday, same as first term.

Agricultural course, sophomore year.

FIRST TERM.

Geometry	5
Agriculture [2]	3
Physics	3
English	2
Modern language [3]	3
Latin (elective)	3

AFTERNOON.

Modeling	2½
Free-hand drawing	2
Practical agriculture [4]	2
Physical laboratory	2
Wood turning	3

Saturday, same as freshman year.

SECOND TERM.

Trigonometry	3
Botany	4
English	2
Physics	3
Modern language	3
Latin (elective)	3

AFTERNOON.

Mechanical drawing	2
Constructions	2½
Wood turning	3
Physical laboratory	2

Saturday, same as first term.

THIRD TERM.

Surveying	1
Physics	3
Botany	5
Modern language	3
Chemistry (inorganic)	3
Latin (elective)	3

AFTERNOON.

Physical laboratory	2
Practical surveying	6
Experimental chemistry	2

Saturday, same as first term.

Mechanical course, sophomore year.

FIRST TERM.

	Hours.
Plane geometry	5
Solid geometry	3
Physics	3
English	2
Modern language [3]	3
Latin (elective)	3

AFTERNOON.

Free-hand drawing	2
Wood turning	6
Physical laboratory	2

Saturday, same as freshman year.

SECOND TERM.

Trigonometry	3
Botany	4
English	2
Physics	3
Modern language	3
Latin (elective)	3

AFTERNOON.

Mechanical drawing	2
Forging	6
Physical laboratory	2

Saturday, same as first term.

THIRD TERM.

Surveying	1
Physics	3
Botany	5
Modern language	3
Chemistry	3
Latin (elective)	3

AFTERNOON.

Experimental chemistry	2
Physical laboratory	2
Mechanical drawing	3
Forging	3

Saturday, same as first term.

Agricultural course, junior year.

FIRST TERM.[5]

Road construction and leveling	3
Zoology and entomology	4
Inorganic chemistry	3
Modern language	3
Horticulture	2
Latin (elective)	

---

[1] Drainage.   [2] Breeds of live stock.
[3] Modern language will be French or German; a course in conversation, composition, and scientific French and German is given.
[4] Farm crops and their cultivation.   [5] Saturdays, same as in freshman year.

A CORNER IN THE MECHANICAL LABORATORY.

WOOD WORK DONE BY STUDENTS.

THE COLLEGE OF AGRICULTURE AND MECHANIC ARTS. 207.

COURSE OF STUDY—Continued.

Agricultural course, junior year—Cont'd.

FIRST TERM—Continued.

AFTERNOON.

	Hours.
Qualitative analysis	4
Practical horticulture	2
Leveling and road surveying	3
French (elective)	3

SECOND TERM.[1]

English	4
Agriculture[2]	3
Organic chemistry	3
Modern language	3
Physiological botany	2
French (elective)	3
Latin (elective)	3

AFTERNOON.

Microscopy	2
Forging	3
Qualitative analysis	6

THIRD TERM.[1]

English	4
Agriculture[2]	4
Agricultural chemistry	4
Modern language	3
French (elective)	3
Latin (elective)	3

AFTERNOON.

Chemical laboratory	6
Elect 1:	
Free-hand drawing	6
Agricultural mechanics[3]	6
Botanical laboratory work	6

Mechanical course, junior year.

FIRST TERM.[1]

Inorganic chemistry	3
Analytical geometry	4
Modern language	3
Electricity and magnetism	3
Descriptive geometry	2
Latin (elective)	3

AFTERNOON.

Qualitative analysis	4
Physical laboratory	2
Lathe work	3

Mechanical course, junior year—Cont'd.

SECOND TERM.[1]

	Hours.
English	4
Analytical geometry	4
Modern language	3
Calculus	3
Latin (elective)	

AFTERNOON.

Qualitative analysis	6
Lathe work	3
Mechanical drawing	3

THIRD TERM.[1]

English	4
Calculus	3
Strength of materials	2
Modern language	3
Principles of mechanism	3
Latin (elective)	

AFTERNOON.

Mechanical laboratory	2
Architectural drawing	2
Elect:	
Chemical laboratory	6
Mechanical drawing	3

Agricultural course, senior year.

FIRST TERM.

Anatomy and physiology of domestic animals, and veterinary science	5
Political economy and science of government	4
Modern language (elective)	3
Agriculture[4]	3

AFTERNOON.

Apiary work	2
Orations	1
Art work (elective)	3

SECOND TERM.

Veterinary science	4
Political economy and science of government	4
Astronomy	4
Market gardening	3
Modern language (elective)	3

AFTERNOON.

Geology	2
Orations	2

---

[1] Saturdays, same as in freshman year.
[2] Soils, manures, and fertilizers.
[3] Wood or iron work.
[4] Stock breeding and feeding.

COURSE OF STUDY—Continued.

Agricultural course, senior year—Cont'd.

THIRD TERM.

	Hours.
Forestry and landscape gardening	2
Geology	2
Mental science	4
Veterinary science	4
Thesis work	3
Modern language (elective)	3

AFTERNOON.

Geology excursions	2
Art work (elective)	3

Mechanical course, senior year.

FIRST TERM.

Calculus	3
Political economy and science of government	4
Theoretical and applied mechanics	5
Elect 1:	
English literature	3
Engineering	3
Modern language	3
Chemistry	3

AFTERNOON.

Orations	2
Practice, mechanical	6
Art work (elective)	3

Mechanical course, senior year—Cont'd.

SECOND TERM.

	Hours.
Astronomy	4
Political economy	4
Theoretical and applied mechanics	4
Elect 1:	
English literature	3
Modern language	3
Engineering	3
Chemistry	3

AFTERNOON.

Orations	2
Practice, mechanical	6

THIRD TERM.

Thesis work	3
Mental science	4
Theoretical and applied mechanics	5
Elect 1:	
English literature	3
Modern language	3
Chemistry	3
Engineering	3

AFTERNOON.

Practice, mechanical	6

www.ingramcontent.com/pod-product-compliance
Lightning Source LLC
Chambersburg PA
CBHW031739230426
43669CB00007B/410